DISPATCHES FROM

THE CAMPUS WAR AGAINST ISRAEL AND JEWS

RICHARD L. CRAVATTS

Published in the United States by the David Horowitz Freedom Center
P.O. Box 55089
Sherman Oaks, CA 91499-1964
http://www.horowitzfreedomcenter.org

Distributed by Publications Management Company
1450 Worcester Road, Suite 8619
Framingham, MA 01702
(617) 755-3199

ISBN-13: 978-0-692-78550-8
ISBN-10: 0-692-78550-7
Manufactured in the United States of America

Cover design by William Karb

First Edition

CONTENTS

Part One   The Ideology of Academic Israel Hatred

1   Introduction: The Ever-Worsening Cognitive
    War Against Israel   3

2   Academic Lies and Distortions to Defame the
    Jewish State   16

3   The Return of the Malevolent Jew:
    The Academic Nazification of Israel   24

4   Moral Psychosis in the Demonization of Israel   32

5   Open Hillel Welcomes the Enemy into
    the Jewish Tent   38

6   The 'Altruistic Evil' of Social Justice for
    the Palestinians   44

7   The Lie of Academic Free Speech   51

8   A Review of *Antisemitism on the Campus: Past and Present* 56

**Part Two   The Malignancy of the Boycott,
               Divestment, and Sanctions (BDS) Movement**

9   Ideological Roots and Tactics of the BDS Movement   67

10 Moral Narcissism and the MLA's Obsession
    with Israel   76

11   The ASA Says Academic Freedom
     for Me, But Not for Thee   82

12   The ASA is 'Shocked, Shocked' that its Invidious
     Academic Boycott Against Israel is Being Criticized   92

13   Women's Studies and the Moral Vacuity of an
     Academic Boycott Against Israel   98

14   Only Israeli Scholars are Complicit in the Actions
     of Their Government?   105

PART THREE   CAMPUS CASE STUDIES

15   For Arizona State BDS Activists, Facts are
     Irrelevant   117

16   Campus Fascists and the Suppression of Academic
     Free Speech   122

17   Blaming the Victim: Who Knew that Identifying
     Palestinian Anti-Semitism is Itself Racist?   127

18   Deconstructing Israel: Academics Meet to Question
     Israel's Right to Exist   135

19   Free Speech on Campus, Depending on Who's
     Speaking   141

20   Ignoring Anti-Semitism in the Name of Palestinian
     Solidarity at UC Davis   147

21   Defining, and Being Able to Condemn,
     Anti-Semitism on California Campuses   153

22   Marching in Support of the Murder of Jews at
     Northeastern University   158

23   Moral Dementia at Stanford and Berkeley   161

24   Pseudo-Scholarship, Intersectionality, and Blood
     Libels Against Israel   164

25   Ideology Parading as Scholarship at Brandeis   169

26   'Speech for me, not for thee' at UC Irvine   174

27   HR 35 and the Boundaries of Academic Free Speech   179

28   Students for Justice in Palestine Seeks Justice for
     All — Except Jews, Of Course   183

29   The Agony of Moral Defeat   188

30   The Eliminationist One-State Solution at the
     Kennedy School of Government   192

31   The Paranoid View of History Infects Oberlin   197

32   The Wesleyan Controversy and a Double Standard
     for Campus Free Speech   203

33   Trying to Give Academic Respectability to the
     Right of Return Fantasy   209

34   Victimology 101 at UC San Diego   215

35   Who May Say What About Whom on
     American Campuses?   221

36   Academic Progressivism Descends into Moral
     Madness   230

Notes   237

Index   241

PART ONE
THE IDEOLOGY OF
ACADEMIC ISRAEL HATRED

1

Introduction:
The Ever-Worsening Cognitive
War Against Israel

The university's war against Israel has been pervasive and inten-
sifying, promulgated by the active participation both of leftist
faculty and radical Muslim student groups on campuses where
the long-suffering Palestinians have replaced South African blacks
as the left's favorite victim group — whose behavior, however violent and politically irrational, is excused as justifiable in a 68 year-old
campaign to demand that Israel grant the Arabs self-determination
and social justice.

The other, and related, trend of anti-Israelism on campuses
— and, indeed, off campuses as well — is that derision of Zionism
and the denunciation of Israel has become a convenient way for
anti-Semites to mask their true prejudice against Jews by claiming
that their problem is only with the policies of Israel, not with Jews
themselves. While classic antisemitism is no longer considered acceptable in most Westernized societies, especially in the aftermath
of the Holocaust, Jew-haters (and some liberal, Israel-hating Jews
themselves) have found a convenient and effective way to mask
their true feelings: they single out the world's only Jewish state for
condemnation and hold it to a standard higher than they do for

any other nation, not coincidentally including those Arab states and the Palestinians themselves, against whom Israel is perpetually and unfairly compared in action, self-defense, and self-determination.

These beliefs permeate the vocabulary of Israel-hatred on campus, and are dangerous and troubling not merely because they vilify the Middle East's only democracy and America's principal ally in that region; they are also of concern because they are based on misrepresentations of history; exaggerate current conditions in Israel, the West Bank, and Gaza; and, most seriously, put forward a complete inversion of truth that enables Israel-haters to load cruel and destructive invective on Zionism without apology, while in reality they are promulgating vile opprobrium that frequently shows its true face as raw anti-Semitism.

THE NEW ACADEMIC FACE OF THE WORLD'S OLDEST HATRED

The unending streams of venom regularly hurled at Israel by academics, of course, are rarely positioned as anything other than simple criticism of a particular nation for a set of particular complaints; there is never any admission or acknowledgement on the part of Israel's many world-wide campus critics that anything other than a concern for the Palestinian cause and a dislike of Israel's current politics are at work in their relentless critiquing of the Middle East's only democracy. In fact, when confronted with the suggestion that their excessive and compulsive demonization of Israel — along with continual attempts to hobble, weaken, or dismantle the Jewish state on behalf of social justice for Palestinians — might sometimes be seen as anti-Semitic in cause or intent, the academic enemies of Israel bristle with indignation and often make wild claims that the dreaded "Israel Lobby" has attempted to silence them and stifle critical discussion about Israeli/Palestinian politics.

But, in fact, it has thankfully become more difficult for actual anti-Semites on campus to inoculate themselves with this defense by merely contending that they are not self-professed anti-Semites, but simply wish to rant against Israel's existence based on a higher moral calling to protect the self-determination of Palestinians. For many actual anti-Semites, as well as those who merely loathe Israel, deranged enmity toward the Jewish state has become a covert, and surrogate, form of anti-Semitism itself, a fact that was addressed in a 2005 "working definition of anti-Semitism" produced by the European Union Monitoring Centre on Racism and Xenophobia (EUMC), which itself had evolved from a comprehensive study of anti-Semitism in the EU it had completed in the previous year. The term "working definition" was significant, not only because it affirmed the importance of guarding against the classic strains of anti-Semitic sentiment, language, and action, but also because it created an explicit equivalence between the hatred and demonization of Israel and Zionism and a yet another stream of Jew-hatred, what is now sometimes called the "new anti-Semitism."

So while the EUMC working definition acknowledged the older manifestations of Jew-hatred such as "Rhetorical and physical manifestations of antisemitism . . . directed toward Jewish or non-Jewish individuals and/or their property, toward Jewish community institutions and religious facilities," it also provided a more comprehensive view of anti-Semitic inclinations, deeply relevant to the current discussion, when it went on to suggest that "such manifestations could also target the state of Israel, conceived as a Jewish collectivity," or "[m]aking . . . allegations about . . . the power of Jews as collective — such as . . . the myth about a world Jewish conspiracy or of Jews controlling the media, economy, government or other societal institutions [as is often brought up in accusations of an Israel Lobby working behind the scenes, for example]."[1]

Even more relevant was the EUMC language, which linked anti-Israel ideology and radicalism with anti-Semitism, including examples of the specific types of speech and behavior that animates the anti-Israel ideology of academia. Specifically, that would include:

- Denying the Jewish people their right to self-determination, e.g., by claiming that the existence of a State of Israel is a racist endeavor.

- Applying double standards by requiring of Israel a behavior not expected or demanded of any other democratic nation.
- Using the symbols and images associated with classic antisemitism (e.g., claims of Jews killing Jesus or blood libel) to characterize Israel or Israelis.
- Drawing comparisons of contemporary Israeli policy to that of the Nazis.
- Holding Jews collectively responsible for actions of the state of Israel.[2]

Why the animus against democratic Israel in academe as the nation defends itself from an unending campaign of aggression from Arab countries? One trend that has permeated the university — and that has had a subsequent influence on the way Israel is perceived — was the coming of two watchwords of higher education: *diversity* and *multiculturalism*. Diversity has seen administrations bending over backward to accommodate the sensitivities of minorities and perceived victims of the majority culture — usually at the expense of fairness and rationality. Multiculturalism has brought with it a type of moral relativism in which every country or victim group is equal, regardless of what vagaries, weaknesses, or fundamental evil may underpin its social structure.

Thus, the decades-old emphasis on bringing multiculturalism to campuses has meant that faculty as well as students have been seeped in an ideology that refuses to demarcate any differences between a democratic state struggling to protect itself (such as Israel) and aggressive, genocidal foes who wish to destroy it with their unending assaults (such as Hamas and Hezbollah). For the multiculturalist left, the moral strengths of the two parties are equivalent, even though the jihadist foes of Israel, for example, have waged an unending struggle with the stated aim of obliterating the Jewish state through the murder of Jews.

Thus, this inclination to worship multiculturalism forces liberals to make excuses for those cultures that have obvious, often irredeemable, moral defects, such as the Islamist foes who currently threaten Israel and the West. "The believer cannot accept the truth about Islamism or much of Islam," observed Jamie Glasov in his recent book, *United in Hate: The Left's Romance with Tyranny and Terror*, "because he would then have to concede that not all cultures are equal, and that some cultures (e.g., America's, with its striving for equality) are superior to others (e.g., Islam's structure of gender apartheid). For the believer to retain his sense of purpose and to avoid the collapse of his identity and community, such thoughts must be suppressed at all cost." One way these truths are "suppressed," says Glasov, is in those instances when liberals make their seemingly irrational judgments about the essential worth of clearly defective cultures — the construction of a curious double standard when looking at cultures other than their own Western models.[3]

The visceral hatred by the left toward their favorite hobgoblins, imperialist America and its codependent oppressor, Israel, finds similar expression from other left-leaning, Israel-loathing professors, such as University of Michigan's Juan Cole, whose regular rants in his blog, *Informed Comment*, take swipes at Israeli and American defense, while simultaneously excusing Arab complicity in violence or terror. In fact, according to Cole, it is the militancy of the West that causes the endemic problems in the Middle East, and marks America guilty for its moral and financial support of Israel.

"When Ariel Sharon sends American-made helicopter gunships and F-16s to fire missiles into civilian residences or crowds in streets," Cole wrote in 2004, "as he has done more than once, then he makes the United States complicit in his war crimes and makes the United States hated among friends of the Palestinians. And this aggression and disregard of Arab life on the part of the proto-fascist Israeli right has gotten more than one American killed, including American soldiers."[4] There is, of course, no mention in Cole's fantasies about why American or Israeli soldiers would be involved in military actions in the first place, affirming the view that it is Western imperialism and oppression that disrupt and embroil the otherwise taciturn political state of the Arab world.

Violence on the part of the oppressed is accepted by liberals because it is deemed to be the fault of the strong nations whose subjugation of those defenseless people is the cause of their violent resistance. In fact, when leftist professors, such as Columbia University's Joseph Massad, apologize for Palestinian terror, they justify it by characterizing the very existence of Israel as being morally defective, based, in their view, on its inherent racist and imperialist nature — one of EUMC's definitions of antisemitism. For Massad in particular, nations that are racist and imperialistic cannot even justify their own self-defense, while the victims of such oppressive regimes are free to "resist," based on the left's notion of universal human rights — but especially for the weak. "What the Palestinians ultimately insist on is that Israel must be taught that it does not have the right to defend its racial supremacy," Massad wrote during the 2009 Israeli defensive incursions into Gaza, "and that the Palestinians have the right to defend their universal humanity against Israel's racist oppression."[5]

Academics' charge of Israel as racist also enables liberals to excuse the moral transgressions of the oppressed, and, as an extension of that thinking, to single out Israel and America for particular and harsh scrutiny owing to their perceived "institutionalized" racism and greater relative power. The self-righteousness the left feels in pointing out Zionism's essential defect of being a racist ideology insulates it from having to also reflect on Arab transgressions, since, as Ruth Wisse has pointed out in *If I Am Not for Myself: The Liberal Betrayal of the Jews*, liberals can excuse their own betrayal of Israel by holding it fully responsible for the very hatreds it inspires. "Ascribing to Israel the blame for its predicament, democratic countries can pursue their self-interest free of any lingering moral scruple," Wisse said. "Israel is examined for its every moral failing to justify policies of disengagement, while the moral failings of Arab countries are considered no one's business but their own, so that their blatant abuses of human rights should not get in the way of realpolitick."[6]

The charge of racism against Israel, of course, has been increasingly uttered by the Jewish state's enemies, particularly after the 1975 United Nations' invidious proclamation that

"Zionism is racism," thereby branding the very ideological existence of Israel as a racist act. "This issue [of Israel] boils down to racism," Julian Perez, a member of Yale University's Students for Justice in Palestine wrote in the *Yale Daily News*, one of many examples of this widely held view of Israel's essential racist ideology. "An entire indigenous population is being denied their human rights by a colonial state that is based on religion and ethnicity," he concluded, promulgating the myth that Palestinian Arabs were indigenous to the region that became Israel, and that the existence of the Jewish state further denies Arabs rights they would otherwise be enjoying had Israel not existed.[7]

Of the many libels from the world community against Israel, perhaps none has gained such traction on campuses as the accusation that the Jewish state now practices apartheid, that the checkpoints, security barrier, Israeli-only roads, barricades, and other remnants of occupation are tantamount to a racist system that victimizes the indigenous Palestinians, just as South African apartheid oppressed and devalued indigenous blacks while stripping them of them civil rights. The same left-leaning activists from universities who carried the banner against the South African regime have now raised that same banner — with the same accusatory language — and superimposed on Israel that it is yet another apartheid regime oppressing Third World victims. Occasionally, the racism libel against Israel is momentarily softened, as happened when the controversial Judge Richard Goldstone (author of the *Goldstone Report on the Gaza War*, which severely rebuked Israel's actions in Operation Cast Lead) announced in a November 2011 op-ed in *The New York Times* that "In Israel, there is no apartheid." But the apartheid charge still resonates effectively on campuses and is used as a theme for continuing to demonize Israel and call into question the Jewish state's moral standing in the community of nations.

Thus, the charge of apartheid is valuable to Israel's detractors, for it both devalues the nation by accusing it of perpetuating what is to the left the greatest crime — racism — in the form of apartheid, which Israel enforces with the complicity of the United States, while simultaneously absolving Arabs of responsibility for the onslaught of terror they continue to inflict on Israel. By pointing to the weakness of the oppressed Palestinians against the superior military and economic might of Israel, the rationale that the wall was built for as a security measure is made to look ridiculous, as if Israel has nothing to fear by being surrounded by a sea of jihadist foes bent on its destruction.

Most curious has been the betrayal of Israel by some liberal Jewish academics, who, poisoned by a pathology that enables them to deflect the hatred of others by absorbing it themselves, have reacted by attacking the Jewish state, the hatred of which is unavoidably tarring them as Jews, in a prejudice they are unwilling to have directed at them. As one example, Professor Jennifer Lowenstein, director of Middle Eastern studies at the University of Wisconsin, glorified Palestinian resistance and the yearning for Arab self-determination while describing Israel as a nation that "speaks with a viper's tongue over the multiple amputee of Palestine whose head shall soon be severed from its body in the name of justice, peace and security."[8]

Then there was the late Tony Judt, of New York University, who claimed that Israel was "an oddity among nations," which no one wanted to have in existence "because it is a Jewish state in which one community — Jews — is set above others, in an age when that sort of state has no place," ultimately meaning that as a Jew, Judt would have to suffer the moral scolding of the world's anti-Semites on behalf of Israel's sin of merely existing — something he was disinclined to do.[9] Echoing one of Israel-haters' current favorite slanders is Richard Falk, professor emeritus of international law and policy at Princeton University and the UN's preposterously titled former "Special *rapporteur* on the situation of human rights in the Palestinian territories occupied since 1967," who wondered if it was "an irresponsible overstatement to associate the treatment of Palestinians with this criminalized Nazi record of collective atrocity?" on the part of Israel, and then quickly answered his own question by saying, "I think not."[10]

SAIDISM AND THE ACADEMIC ROOTS OF 'PALESTINIANISM'

Were it not for Edward W. Said, the Palestinian cause may have echoed through the halls of the United Nations, and influenced diplomacy and statecraft in the Middle East and in the West, but never have captured the imagination of academe. Said, a professor of comparative literature at Columbia University, in 1978 published a provocative and highly influential book, *Orientalism*, that not only had a profound effect on the direction of Middle East studies here and abroad, but eventually provided a foundation for the intellectual aspect of Palestinianism, and inspired reverence from the left and the intellectual elite.

Orientalism gave expression to Said's belief that the West's perception of the Middle East — indeed, the way the East was understood — was the product of cultural imperialism, the tendency, in his view, of Western scholars, artists, writers, sociologists, archeologists, and others to define the East based on its presumed cultural, racial, intellectual, and political inferiority. Not only was this practice endemic in the West's relations with the East, but it represented an insidious aspect in the study and understanding of the Orient by the Occident — that is, Orientalism was, in Said's words, "a Western style for dominating, restructuring, and having authority over the Orient." More pointedly, Said announced that no European was even capable of studying the East without superimposing his or her own cultural biases and "intellectual imperialism," leading Said to the breathtaking thesis that "every European, in what he could say about the Orient, was . . . a racist, an imperialist, and almost totally ethnocentric."[11]

Here, Zionism is the "construct" superimposed on the East (and the hapless Palestinians) by the imperialistic West, another form of aggressive Orientalism. The act of dispossession is itself a violent, racist act, Said asserted, based on the assumption that Western colonial settlers can create a narrative that empowers them and deprives the Eastern "other" of his property and history. Orientialism empowered non-Westerners to believe in the inherent racism and imperialism of Western scholarship and politics, and, according to Martin Kramer in his insightful book, *Ivory Towers on Sand: The Failure of Middle Eastern Studies in America,* is one of Said's lasting contributions to the intellectual climate on campuses when scholars took sides on issues affecting the Middle East. Orientalism, according to Kramer, "also enshrined an acceptable hierarchy of political commitments, with Palestine at the top, followed by the Arab nation and the Islamic world. They were the long-suffering victims of Western racism, American imperialism, and Israeli Zionism — the three legs of the orientalist [*sic*] stool."[12]

Once the Saidian post-colonialists could neutralize the impact of the West in its assessment of the Orient (which for Said and his disciples had come to mean specifically the Middle East), they initiated an entire intellectual enterprise that devalued any scholarship conducted by Westerners, called into question the justice of the imposition of Western culture on non-Western nations, and, in the case of Israel, denounced the creation of this European, colonial settler-state, a cultural "construct" in the midst of the passive, less powerful Muslim world. M. Shahid Alam, for instance, a professor of history at Northeastern University, regularly rants in the virulent online journal *Counterpunch* about the perfidy of Israel, echoing Said's delineation of the hegemonic, racist West imposing its cultural will on the East. "This is the language of racial superiority[,] the doctrine that believes in a hierarchy of races," Alam wrote about Israel, "where the higher races have rights and inferior races are destined for extinction or a marginal existence under the tutelage of higher races. Under the Zionist doctrine, the Jews are a higher race . . . This superiority is also empirically established: the Zionists wanted to take Palestine from the Palestinians and they made it a fact."[13]

Said's charge of Orientalism also stripped Western scholars of their standing in Middle Eastern studies, discrediting them and their potential contribution to scholarly inquiry because of their innate biases and Orientalist orientation. If Western academics were no longer able to conduct scholarship about the Orient that was authentic and valid, who, then, could? The answer, of course, was clear: Middle Easterners and Arab-Americans, who, after the publication of *Orientalism*, began to fill the academic slots in departments of Middle Eastern studies in increasing numbers in a type of faculty affirmative action program.

The language of the "scholarship" of these post-colonial academics is often harsh, and, when involving Israel, sometimes borders on the kind of raw, anti-Semitic ranting that is constant in the state-controlled media of the Arab world. As an example, Hamid Dabashi, Hagop Kevorkian Professor of Iranian Studies and Comparative Literature at Columbia, ensconced in the same department where Said himself once sat, wrote a psychobabble-filled narrative during a visit to Israel. Published in *Al-Ahram Weekly*, it dehumanizes the entire Jewish state in language that drips with repulsive images and hatred:

> What they call "Israel" is no mere military state. A subsumed militarism, a systemic mendacity with an ingrained violence constitutional to the very fusion of its fabric, has penetrated the deepest corners of what these people have to call their "soul" . . . Half a century of systematic maiming and murdering of another people has left its deep marks on the faces of these people . . . There is . . . a vulgarity of character that is bone-deep and structural to the skeletal vertebrae of its culture. No people can perpetrate what these people and their parents and grandparents have perpetrated on Palestinians and remain immune to the cruelty of their own deeds.[14]

This lurid, hateful language used in the critiquing of Israel, given academic respectability by an Ivy League professor, has also begun to show itself in the attitudes and language of students — who themselves regularly engage in half-truths, counter-historical appraisals of Middle Eastern history, and emotional outbursts bordering on what, in a different context, might well be considered anti-Semitic hate speech.

The university's jihad against Israel and Jews is a grim reminder that the world's oldest hatred has not yet vanished; in fact, either because of the widespread negative attitudes toward Israel, or simply due to a lingering, poisonous Jew-hatred in the Arab world and increasingly in the West as well, Jews once again are targets of libels, denunciation, demonization, and slurs against Judaism, against Zionism, and against Israel itself, the Jew of nations.

This hatred metastasized on campus, when it was promulgated by leftist professors with a reverence for Palestinian victimization and by Muslim student groups with a theologically based hatred of the Jewish state. It spread by being enabled by administrators who allowed their campuses to be hijacked by radicals with the purported objective of elevating the Palestinian cause, but whose actual purpose was promoting their own agenda for vilifying and eventually eliminating Israel.

The manifestations of these on-campus hatreds have been obvious and ugly: ripped Israeli flags drizzled with blood; Stars of David juxtaposed with swastikas; charges of apartheid, racism, and genocide leveled against Israelis and also assigned to their proxies, American Jews; accusations of dual loyalties, with American Jews accused of undermining American interests with the covert purpose of assisting Israel; physical threats against Jewish students; and blood libels that transform Israelis into murderous, subhuman monsters who almost gleefully shed Arab blood in their insatiable quest for land — land that, their critics say, they neither deserve nor for which they have any legitimate claim.

The campus war against Israel and Jews is also indicative of the compromised purpose of higher education, where scholarship has been degraded by bias and extremism on the part of a leftist professoriate with a clear political agenda that cites Israel as the new villain in a world yearning for social justice. University leaders and other stakeholders have been noticeably negligent in moderating this radicalism, either because they are unaware of how whole fields of study have been hijacked by academic frauds and morally incoherent scholars, or because they sympathize with the intellectual approach of their faculties and have become complicit in the production of pseudo-scholarship, academic agitprop, and disingenuous "learning experiences" that have a one-sided, biased approach to understanding the Middle East, and particularly the Israeli/Palestinian conflict.

That all this is taking place in the rarified air of college campuses, where civil discourse is the expected norm and scholarly inquiry is the anticipated intellectual product, makes the seething hatreds and bias against Israel and the Jews all the more unexpected and morally dangerous. Only six decades after one of the most horrific crimes against humanity that saw the murder of some six million Jewish souls, the same unsettling tropes against Jews are being restated, this time often targeting the Jewish state that arose, in part, from the ashes of the Holocaust. One would hope this battle would not have to be waged again, that college students, Jews and non-Jews alike, would not have to be confronted with "the longest hatred" once again, this time conflated with the very survival of a democratic Jewish state, precariously coexisting amid a sea of jihadist foes who seek its very elimination.

2

Academic Lies and Distortions to Defame the Jewish State

Jews have been accused of harming and murdering non-Jews since the twelfth century in England, when Jewish convert to Catholicism, Theobald of Cambridge, mendaciously announced that European Jews ritually slaughtered Christian children each year and drank their blood during Passover season.

That medieval blood libel, largely abandoned in the contemporary West, does, however, still appear as part of Arab world's vilification of Jews — now transmogrified into a slander against Israel, the Jew of nations. But in the regular chorus of defamation against Israel by a world infected with Palestinianism, a new, more odious trend has begun to show itself: the blood libel has been revivified; however, to position Israel (and by extension Jews) as demonic agents in the community of nations, the primitive fantasies of the blood libel are now masked with a veneer of academic scholarship and published as politicized scientific study.

In July of 2014, for example, the British medical journal *Lancet* further degraded its academic respectability and credibility by publishing something entitled "An open letter for the people in Gaza," signed by 24 doctors and scientists. In the language of propaganda and politics — as opposed to the reasoned language of science and academically-based inquiry — the signers had as their purpose "denouncing what we witness in the aggression of Gaza by Israel." These doctors and scientists, none of whom has had to live under an unceasing barrage of more than 10,000 rockets and mortars launched from Gaza into Israel, nevertheless denounced what they see as "the perversity of [Israel's] propaganda that justifies the creation of an emergency to masquerade a massacre, a so-called 'defensive aggression.'" Instead, the signers believe there is no basis for Israel's self-defense, that it is actually no more than "a ruthless assault of unlimited duration, extent, and intensity" and an "unacceptable pretext of Israel eradicating political parties and resistance to the occupation and siege they impose."

"The massacre in Gaza spares no one," the letter continued in its hyperbolic, not factual, tones, and, according to the signers, "these attacks aim to terrorise [sic], wound the soul and the body of the people, and make their life impossible in the future, as well as also demolishing their homes and prohibiting the means to rebuild."

Of course, there was no mention of the Palestinians' complicity in their own situation, no reference to the nine years of genocidal aggression by Hamas since Israel's disengagement from Gaza, no examination of the failure of Palestinian leadership to even attempt to start building a civil society and functioning government. Every pathology and failure, including the health and well-being of the entire Gazan society, is the fault of Israel — as a result of its siege, its blockade, its oppression, and its current incursion to suppress Hamas rocket attacks.

"In Gaza," the letter continued, "people suffer from hunger, thirst, pollution, shortage of medicines, electricity, and any means to get an income, not only by being bombed and shelled." And inverting cause and effect, the signers then make the breathtaking claim that Hamas terrorism is a tool for creating a viable Palestinian state, that Hamas rejected a truce not because they are dedicated to extirpating Israel and murdering Jews, but simply because "People in Gaza are resisting this aggression because they want a better and normal life and, even while crying in sorrow, pain, and terror, they reject a temporary truce that does not provide a real chance for a better future."

This is not a scientific report at all, but a politicized, subjective screed designed to demonize Israel and assign total blame for a very complex political and military conflict that is well beyond the expertise of these particular individuals. That it was written by intellectuals in the West in the thralls of Palestinianism is not surprising or particularly unusual, especially in the wake of Israel's Operation Protective Edge to protect its citizens from being murdered. What is troubling, however, is that a formerly-reputable journal such as *Lancet* is now being exploited as vehicle for flabby research and specious science in the pursuit of political ends.

This is not the first time that *Lancet* has strayed in this pseudo-academic manner. The entire so-called "occupation" has also become a target for scientists who attempt to link the general oppression by Israel with a host of pathologies in Palestinian society. Several years ago, feminist scholar Phyllis Chesler critiqued a particularly egregious example of politicized scholarship in a paper published in *Lancet*. Chesler noted that the article, with the biased title of "Association between exposure to political violence and intimate-partner violence in the occupied Palestinian territory: a cross-sectional study," revealed "that Palestinian husbands are more violent towards Palestinian wives as a function of the Israeli 'occupation' — and that the violence increases significantly when the husbands are 'directly' as opposed to 'indirectly' exposed to political violence."

The study, of course, never chose to examine the effect of the conflict on Israeli husbands and wives, who may well share similar emotional stresses to their Palestinian counterparts as a result of the genocidal aggression against them from various jihadist foes, and instead, according to Chesler, attempted "to present Palestinian men as victims even when (or precisely because) those men are battering their wives," defining "Palestinian cultural barbarism, which includes severe child abuse, as also related to the alleged

Israeli occupation." The cultural traditions in the Middle East which enable men to totally dominate family members, treat women as property, and even commit "honor" killings when women shame male family members — all of these, of course, are not included in the emotional equation which might logically lead or contribute to spousal abuse. It is the Israeli occupation, and that alone, that causes such deleterious mental health conditions, "intimate partner violence," in Palestinian marriages. Perhaps a better title for the specious article would have been, "The occupation made me beat my wife."

In 2010, to cite another instance of this trend, the findings of a study conducted by the New Weapons Research Group, a team of scientists based in Italy, were announced on "the use of unconventional weapons and their mid-term effects on the population of after-war areas," in this case Gaza after Israel's "Cast Lead" incursion in 2008-09. "Many Palestinian children still living in precarious situations at ground level in Gaza after Israeli bombing," the study found, "have unusually high concentrations of metals in the hair, indicating environmental contamination, which can cause health and growth damages due to chronic exposure," and these high levels were the direct result of Israeli bombs.

Moreover, suggested Professor Paola Manduca, spokesperson for this study and another principal signer of the Gaza open letter, the presence of metals in children's hair "presents serious problems in the current situation in Gaza, where the construction and removal of damaged structures is difficult or impossible, and," in case anyone does not know who to blame, "certainly represents the major responsibility of those who should remedy the damage to the civilian population under international law."

Environmental contamination of children is certainly a critical issue to address and identify, but questions arise from this particular study due to the shabby way the controls and research were conducted. Was it actually Israeli weaponry that contributed to high metal levels in the hair of the studied group? Are those levels significantly different in Gaza, or do they parallel other high-density cities with refineries, smelters, and other form of pollutants that arise from other, non-military sources? Was the same group of subjects tested prior to Operation Cast Lead to see changes in the incidence of metals in hair after the incursion? Were groups in other towns, which had not been bombed, tested as well, and how do those levels compare with the test group?

Another principal signer of the Gaza letter, and frequent contributor to *Lancet*, is Iain Chalmers, a medical researcher and member of the *Lancet*-Palestinian Health Alliance (LPHA), an initiative between the journal and the group Medical Aid for Palestinians. Not surprisingly, the 2013 *Lancet* edition had a one-sided feature focusing on "the direct and indirect health effects of the Israeli occupation and conflict." Chalmers is a defamer of Israel, who was gleeful about a *Lancet* cover that used the term Palestine, saying, " . . . it's one way in which the Zionists have failed. They have not stopped the use of the word 'Palestine' or 'Palestinian.' They have control in so many different domains. This is one that they cannot suppress."

A third signer of the Gaza open letter was Derek Summerfield, a vitriolic maligner of Israel who has supported efforts to boycott Israeli physicians seeking to attend medical conferences. In a 2008 interview in *Al Ahram* he described the Israeli/ Palestinian conflict as "the most awful crime has been played out down there by a colonial power that considered itself part of Europe. They were grabbing Palestinians' land and torturing them in ways that were reminiscent of South Africa but, as it turns out, far, far worse than South Africa." Summerfield has also suggested, as he did in the *British Medical Journal* in an article entitled "Palestine: The Assault on Health and Other War Crimes," that Israel is a morally malignant regime which capriciously murders Arabs with no justification. Like other haters of the Jewish state, he also has suggested that Israelis exploit the Holocaust as a means of distracting their misdeeds towards the Palestinians, that, as Summerfield sardonically put it, "Israel continues to play the Holocaust story and anti-Semitism as a way of blocking the truth."

The principal signer of the Gaza open letter is Norwegian anesthesiologist and perennial Israel-hater, Mads Gilbert. A political activist and member of the fringe Norwegian Maoist 'Red' party, Gilbert is also a supporter of the Palestinian solidarity movement. While not giving biased medical commentary to the media during the various Gaza incursions, he also has apologized for and gave tacit approval to the 9/11 attacks in New York, saying in an interview that "The attack on New York did not come as a surprise after the policy that the West has led during the last decades . . . The oppressed also have a moral right to attack the USA with any weapon they can come up with," and that while "terror is a bad weapon," he supported a terror attack against the United States "within the context which I [had] mentioned."

Interviewed by Iran's Press TV in 2009, Gilbert announced, without conclusive proof, that, "We have *clear evidence* that the Israelis are using a new type of very high explosive weapons which are called Dense Inert Metal Explosives which is made out of a Tungsten alloy. These weapons have an enormous power to explode." Though he moderated his opinion somewhat in the absence of any proof that his theory about Israel's use of weapons was even valid, he did use *Lancet* to repeat the calumny. "These are scenes out of Dante's Inferno," he said. "Many arrive with extreme amputations, with both legs crushed, [and what] I suspect are wounds inflicted by very powerful explosives called Dime [Dense Inert Metal Explosive]." Once again, a scientific journal published unsubstantiated and highly-biased articles, whose principal purpose seems to be to further malign Israel.

When brutal military assaults and Israel's use of weaponry cannot be blamed for causing health damage to non-Jews, Israel-haters are quick to condemn the general oppression of Zionist occupation and brutality as detriments to Arab health and happiness. In 2005, Psychologists for Social Responsibility (PsySR) took it upon themselves to "condemn the Israeli Army's use of psychological warfare against the Gaza population" through the use of Israeli F-16 jet plane-generated "sonic booms" that, according to PsySR, are a "particularly pernicious form of psychological warfare." While they begrudgingly admit that the reason jet soirees were initiated against the Gazan population in the first place was the hundreds of rockets that had been raining down on Israeli neighborhoods in southern Israel, the psychologists' concern never seemed to extend to Jewish children (75-94 percent of whom, living in Sderot and between the ages of 4-18, as one example, exhibit symptoms of post-traumatic stress disorder), nor did they call for an end to the terrorism that Israeli military operations were attempting to curtail. But the sonic booms, nevertheless, were unacceptable.

Other scholarly publications have been intellectually hijacked with spurious studies that have a fundamental bias to them that discredits the validity of any research. The *Canadian Journal of Psychiatry*, for example, ran an article entitled "The prevalence of psychological morbidity in West Bank Palestinian children," written, oddly enough, by a junior surgical resident and a microbiologist. When members of Scholars for Peace in the Middle East (SPME), an organization of academics seeking balance in discussion of the Israeli/Palestinian conflict, became aware of this bit of defective scholarship, they analyzed the paper themselves and found that it was an example of "weak science, which included the lack of evidence or references, the lack of appropriate scientific design, the choice of nonstandardized test instruments and the inaccurate citing of the psychological literature." What is more, the authors' original thesis, "that 'settlement encroachment' was responsible for the problems of Palestinian children," had relied on the psychiatric "expertise" of linguist Noam Chomsky, whose loathing of Israel is widely known, to help draw the study's conclusions.

Supporters of the Palestinian cause have come to accept the fact that Israel will not be defeated through the use of traditional tools of warfare. Instead, the Jewish state's enemies in the Middle East, abetted by their supporters in the West, have begun to use different, but equally dangerous, tactics to delegitimize and eventually destroy Israel in a cognitive war. By dressing up old hatreds against Jews, combined with a hatred of Israel, and repackaging them as seemingly pure scholarship, Israel's ideological foes have found an effective, but odious, way to insure that the Jew of nations, Israel, is still accused of fostering social chaos and bringing harm to non-Jews — in the bright "lights of perverted science" Winston Churchill feared might well be unleashed by a Nazi victory in the Second World War.

3

The Return of the Malevolent Jew: The Academic Nazification of Israel

"What if the Jews themselves were Nazis?," mused French philosopher, Vladimir Jankélévitch in 1986. "That would be great. We would no longer have to feel sorry for them; they would have deserved what they got."

The recasting of Israelis, and, by extension, Jews as Nazis has, in fact, taken place, just as Jankélévitch envisioned. Israel's 2014 incursion, Operation Protective Edge, provided anti-Semites and loathers of the Jewish state with resurgent justifications for assigning the epithet of Nazi to the Jews yet another time, together with oft-heard accusations of "crimes against humanity, "massacres," genocide," and, according to recent comments by Turkey's prime minister Tayyip Erdoğan, in their treatment of the Palestinians, Israel has demonstrated that ". . . their barbarism has surpassed even Hitler's."

The Nazification of Israelis — and by extension Jews — is both breathtaking in its moral inversion and cruel in the way it makes the actual victims of the Third Reich's horrors a modern-day reincarnation of that same barbarity. It is, in the words of Boston University's Richard Landes, "moral sadism," a salient example of Holocaust inversion that is at once ahistorical, disingenuous, and grotesque in its moral and factual inaccuracy.

In reflecting on the current trend he perceived in the burgeoning of anti-Israelism around the world, Canadian Member of Parliament, Irwin Cotler, once observed that conventional strains of anti-Semitism had been masked, so that those who directed enmity towards Jews were now able to transfer that opprobrium to Israel. How had they effected that? According to Cotler, they did so by redefining Israel as the most glaring example of those human predations, what he called "the embodiment of all evil" of the Twentieth Century: apartheid and Nazism. He defined the process of grafting this opprobrium on Israel as "ideological anti-Semitism," one which "involves the characterization of Israel not only as an apartheid state — and one that must be dismantled as part of the struggle against racism — but as a Nazi one."

Most important for the anti-Israel cause, Cotler contended, once Israel had been tarred with the libels of racism and Nazism, the Jewish state had been made an international outlaw, a pariah, losing its moral right to even exist — exactly, of course, what its foes have consistently sought. "These very labels of Zionism and Israel as 'racist, apartheid and Nazi' supply the criminal indictment," said Cotler. "No further debate is required. The conviction that this triple racism warrants the dismantling of Israel as a moral obligation has been secured. For who would deny that a 'racist, apartheid, Nazi' state should not have any right to exist today?"

Before the creation of the Jewish state, European anti-Semitism was characterized by the deranged fantasies of what Jews represented and what "Jewness" was thought to mean: Jews were imagined to be malicious, unscrupulous, duplicitous, avaricious, disloyal, subhuman, demonic, even, in their complicity in the death of Jesus, deicidal. Islamic anti-Semitism adopted some of these classic tropes, grafting on new ones in the context of the Middle East: that Jews manipulate governments in their rapacity and longing for world domination, and that this insatiable desire for more land is confirmed in their continuing, and widening, "occupation" and "theft" of Muslim lands in Palestine.

What is troubling today is that the characterization of the Israeli as Nazi is a trope now promulgated by Western elites and so-called intellectuals, including a broad contingent of academics who are complicit in, and in fact intellectual enablers of, the campaign to defame Israel by Nazifying its people and accusing Jews again as being the world's moral and existential enemies as demonstrated by their oppression and brutality toward the long-suffering Palestinians. Thus, campus anti-Israel hate-fests sponsored by radical student groups have such odious names as "Holocaust in the Holy Land," "Israel: The Politics of Genocide," or "Israel: The Fourth Reich," creating a clear, though mendacious, linkage between Nazism and Zionism.

One of the early academic voices to have assigned the Nazi epithet to Israel was heard in a November 2000 speech by Francis A. Boyle, a law professor at the University of Illinois and one of the principal promoters of the global Boycott, Divest, and Sanctions (BDS) movement. In that speech, Boyle made the exact linkage to which Cotler alluded, conflating Israel's alleged racism with apartheid-like behavior and suggesting, even more ominously, that the ongoing "genocide" against the Palestinians had parallels with the Nazi's own heinous offenses. "The paradigmatic example of a crime against humanity is what Hitler and the Nazis did to the Jewish People," Boyle said. "This is where the concept of crime against humanity was formulated and came from. And this is what the U.N. Human Rights Commission is now saying that Israel is doing to the Palestinian People. A crime against humanity."

That same trope is repeated and reinforced by other academics, such as Richard Falk, professor emeritus of International Law and Policy at Princeton University, who wondered aloud if it was "an irresponsible overstatement to associate the treatment of Palestinians with this criminalized Nazi record of collective atrocity?" on the part of Israel, and then quickly answered his own question by saying, "I think not."

"The recent developments in Gaza," Falk wrote in 2007 in a vile article entitled "Slouching toward a Palestinian Holocaust," "are especially disturbing because they express so vividly a deliberate intention on the part of Israel and its allies to subject an entire human community to life-endangering conditions of utmost cruelty. The suggestion that this pattern of conduct is a holocaust-in-the-making represents a rather desperate appeal to the governments of the world and to international public opinion to act urgently to prevent these current genocidal tendencies from culminating in a collective tragedy."

In the morally-defective pantheon of the academic defamers of Israel, perhaps no single individual has emerged as the paradigmatic libeler, the most vitriolic and widely-followed character in an inglorious retinue as Norman Finkelstein, late of DePaul University. Finkelstein has loudly and notoriously pronounced his extreme views on the Middle East, not to mention his loathing of what he has called the Holocaust "industry," something he has called an "outright extortion racket;" in fact, he blames Jews themselves for anti-Semitism.

Hamas, designated a terrorist organization by the U.S. State Department, has pure political intentions and passively yearns for truces and safe borders, according to Mr. Finkelstein, while the invidious state of Israel, fearing moderate Arab foes who will force it into peace, is obdurate, conniving, and bellicose. In fact, Finkelstein suggested, Israel is collectively going mad, while everyone else in the rational world yearns for Middle Eastern peace: "I think Israel, as a number of commentators pointed out, is becoming an insane state . . . In the first week of the massacres, there were reports in the Israeli press that Israel did not want to put all its ground forces in Gaza because it was preparing attacks on Iran. Then there were reports it was planning attacks on Lebanon. It is a lunatic state."

In January of 2009, a tenured sociology professor, William I. Robinson, of the University of California, Santa Barbara, sent an odious email to the 80 students in his "Sociology 130SG: The Sociology of Globalization" course with the explicit message that Israelis are the new Nazis. Under the heading "Parallel images of

Nazis and Israelis," the email displayed a photo-collage of 42 side-by-side, grisly photographs meant to suggest an historical equivalence between Israel's treatment of Palestinians in its occupation of Gaza and the Third Reich's subjugation of the Warsaw Ghetto and its treatment of Jews during the Holocaust. Robinson sent the email without supplying any context for it, nor did it seemingly have any specific relevance to or connection with the course's content.

In his email, Robinson wildly claimed that "Gaza is Israel's Warsaw — a vast concentration camp that confined and blockaded Palestinians, subjecting them to the slow death of malnutrition, disease and despair, nearly two years before their subjection to the quick death of Israeli bombs. We are witness to a slow-motion process of genocide . . , a process whose objective is not so much to physically eliminate each and every Palestinian than to eliminate the Palestinians as a people in any meaningful sense of the notion of people-hood."

At Columbia University's Department of Middle Eastern and Asian Languages and Culture (MEALAC), an academic division with a long history of anti-Israel, anti-American bias and politicized scholarship, Joseph Massad, an associate professor of modern Arab politics, regularly espouses his loathing of Israel in fringe, anti-Semitic publications like *Counterpunch* and *The Electronic Intifada*, or in the Arab press, and never misses an opportunity to denigrate the Jewish state as a racist, colonial enterprise, a moral stain on the world without any semblance of legitimacy. In his perfervid imagination, Israelis, as he never tires as mentioning, have become the new Nazis and the Palestinians the Jews. "As Palestinians are murdered and injured in the thousands," he wrote after Operation Cast Lead in January of 2009 when Israel was defending itself against some 6000 rockets attacks from Gaza, "world powers are cheering on . . , and it even happened during World War II as the Nazi genocide was proceeding."

Also on the MEALAC faculty is Columbia's odious professor of Iranian Studies and Comparative Literature, Hamid Dabashi.

To Dabashi, Israel is a form of mechanized, militarized state created, with the support of America, solely to dominate a defenseless people. In an article entitled "Gaza: Poetry after Auschwitz," Dabashi suggested that Israel is actually defined by its Nazi-like nature: "They are Israelis by virtue of what? By a shared and sustained murderous history — from Deir Yassin in 1948 to Gaza in 2014 . . . . After Gaza, not a single living Israeli can utter the word 'Auschwitz' without it sounding like 'Gaza.' Auschwitz as a historical fact is now archival. Auschwitz as a metaphor is now Palestinian. From now on, every time any Israeli, every time any Jew, anywhere in the world, utters the word 'Auschwitz,' or the word 'Holocaust,' the world will hear 'Gaza.'"

In 2002, Mona Baker, professor at Britain's University of Manchester Institute of Science and Technology (UMIST), who had proudly told *The Telegraph* that she "deplore[d] the Israeli state," fired two employees of academic journals she published, Dr. Miriam Shlesinger and Professor Gideon Toury, specifically because they were Israeli Jews. The morally-indignant Ms. Baker could no longer abide Israel's behavior among all the nations of the world. The Jewish state's malefaction knew no limits, she breathlessly exclaimed. "Israel has gone beyond just war crimes," she posited. Moreover, despite the inconvenient facts which show that Palestinians enjoy one of the most robust birth rates in the world, Ms. Baker did not hesitate to suggest the very likely genocide they might face as a result of Israel's apartheid regime. "It is horrific what is going on there. Many of us would like to talk about it as some kind of Holocaust which the world will eventually wake up to, much too late, of course, as they did with the last one."

It is Israel's actions alone — that and the support of the United States — which are the root cause of the Israeli/Palestinian conflict, and the Jewish state's behavior is murderous, unethical, and brutal, according to University of Wisconsin-Madison's Jennifer Lowenstein, Associate Director of the Middle East Studies Program. Israel, she wrote, "speaks with a viper's tongue over the multiple amputee of Palestine whose head shall soon be severed from its body in the name of justice, peace and security." There is no context to Lowenstein's viewpoint, no explanation why Israel has had to defend itself from the unceasing assaults on its citizens by jihadist murderers intent on extirpating Israel itself. Instead, all the suffering is the Palestinians'. "The water and food shortages; the daily electricity blackouts; the open sewage and dangerously inadequate infrastructure; the shortages of food, medicines, and the materials to rebuild the world that is literally crumbling into dust and debris all around them define the average day for Gaza's unpeople . . ," she wrote, and "Israel has made its view known again and again in the strongest possible language, the language of military might, of threats, intimidation, harassment, defamation and degradation."

In the summer of 2014, while the Gaza incursion was raging, Dr. Julio Pino, associate professor of history at Kent State University, published a vitriolic open letter in which he chastised the "academic friends of Israel" who have "chosen to openly work for and brag about academic collaboration with a regime that is the spiritual heir to Nazism . . . I curse you more than the Israelis," he told his academic colleagues, "for while The Chosen drain the blood of innocents without apologies you hide behind the mask of academic objectivity, nobility of research and the reward of teaching to foreign youth . . . ."

Occasionally, when an academic makes public his loathing of the Jewish state, and continues to demonize and libel Israel beyond the bounds of what would be considered acceptable scholarly discourse, there are consequences — though rarely. In the summer of 2015, for instance, Steven Salaita, author of *Israel's Dead Soul* and perennial critic of Zionism, had an employment offer from the University of Illinois withdrawn once the school's president was made aware of some of Salaita's virulent Twitter posts about Israel. During the widely-criticized Gaza incursion, Salaita tweeted that "At this point, if Netanyahu appeared on TV with a necklace made from the teeth of Palestinian children, would anybody be surprised?" He also blamed anti-Semitism on Jews themselves, as many anti-Semites do, by asserting that Israel's behavior causes the hatred of Jews, that "By eagerly conflating Jewishness and Israel, Zionists are partly responsible when people say antisemitic [sic] shit in response to Israeli terror."

As grotesque and distorted as these calumnies against Israel are, as perverse and inaccurate the comparisons drawn between Nazism and Zionism and between Nazis and Israelis are, and as wildly hateful these libels are to the point of being, as defined by the State Department's own working definition, anti-Semitic in nature — the branding of Israel as the Nazi of nations by these academics serves to reinforce, and give credibility to, similar hatreds and biases expressed outside the university walls.

This is a lethal narrative because when it is believed the world naturally asks itself, as Cotler warned: if Israel is a Nazi-like, apartheid regime, standing in opposition to everything for which the civilized community of nations stands, who *cannot* hold Israel accountable and judge it harshly for its transgressions? That against all historical evidence and the force of reason the calumny against Israel that it is a murderous, sadistic, and genocidal regime has been successfully promoted and continues to gain traction indicates that Israel's academic defamers have been successful in inverting history as part of the modern day incarnation of the world's oldest hatred.

4

Moral Psychosis in the Demonization of Israel

O nce Israel launched Operation Protective Edge in July of 2014, the streets of American and European cities were crammed with activists intent on expressing their collective indignation for Israel's perceived crime of defending its citizens from slaughter from the genocidal thugocracy of Hamas.

Rowdy and sometimes violent demonstrations took place in Berlin, Paris, Toronto, London, and Madrid, where blatantly anti-Semitic chants of "Death to Jews!," "Hitler was right!," "Gaza is the real Holocaust," "end Israeli apartheid," and "Jew, Jew, cowardly swine, come out and fight on your own!" could be heard, with similar events taking place in such U.S. cities as Boston, New York, Chicago, Los Angeles, and Seattle.

Joined with Muslim supporters of those wishing to destroy Israel and murder Jews were the usual suspects of peace activists, Israel-haters, social justice advocates, and labor unionists who decried Israel's "genocide" against Gaza as well as the militarism, oppression, imperialism, and brutality imbued in Zionism itself. These radical, Israel-loathing groups include, among others, the corrosive, ubiquitous ANSWER (Act Now to Stop War and End Racism), Code Pink, Jewish Voice for Peace, and Students for Justice in Palestine.

What was particularly revealing, and chilling, about the hate-filled rallies was the virulence of the chants and messages on the placards, much of it seeming to suggest that more sinister hatreds and feelings — over and above concern for the current military operations — were simmering slightly below the surface. Several of the morally self-righteous protesters, for instance, shrieked out, to the accompaniment of drumbeats, "Long live Intifada," a grotesque and murderous reference to the Second Intifada, during which Arab terrorists murdered some 1000 Israelis and wounded more than 14,000 others.

That pro-Palestinian student activists, those who purport to be motivated by a desire to bring "justice" to the Middle East, could publicly call for the renewed slaughter of Jews in the name of Palestinian self-determination demonstrates quite clearly how ideologically debased the human rights movement has become. Activists on and off U.S. campuses, who never have to face a physical threat more serious than getting jostled while waiting in line for a latte at Starbucks, are quick to denounce Israel's very real existential threats and the necessity of the Jewish state to take counter measures to thwart terrorism. And quick to label the killing of Hamas terrorists by the IDF as "genocide," these well-meaning but morally-blind individuals see no contradiction in their calls for the renewed murder of Jews for their own sanctimonious cause.

Other protesters were less overt in their angry chants, carrying signs and shouting out the oft-heard slogan, "Free, Free Palestine," or, as they eventually screamed out, "Palestine will be free, from the river to the sea." That phrase suggests the same situation that a rekindled Intifada would help bring about, namely that if the fictive nation of "Palestine" is "liberated," is free, there will, of course, be no Israel between the Jordan River and Mediterranean — and no Jews.

Another deadly chorus emanated from protesters during the rally: "When people are occupied, resistance is justified." That is an oft-repeated, but disingenuous and false notion that stateless terrorists have some recognized human right to murder civilians whose government has purportedly occupied their territory. That is clearly not any longer the case in Gaza, where every Jew was removed in 2005 and where there is a blockade in effect to prevent the influx of weapons, but clearly no occupation or, as commonly referred to, a "siege." It may be comforting for Israel's ideological foes to rationalize the murder of Jews by claiming some international right to do it with impunity and a sense of righteousness. Unfortunately, however, as legal experts have inconveniently pointed out, the rally participants and their terror-appeasing apologists elsewhere are completely wrong about the legitimacy of murder as part of "resistance" to an occupying force. Article IV of the Third Geneva Convention, the statute which defines combatants and legitimate targets in warfare, is very specific about who may kill and who may be killed, and it does not allow for the murder of either Israeli civilians — or soldiers — by Palestinian suicide bombers who wear no identifying military uniforms and do not follow the accepted rules of wars.

So when pro-Palestinian activists and critics of Israel repeat the claim that Palestinians somehow have an internationally-recognized legal "right" to resist occupation through violent means, they are both legitimizing that terror and helping to insure that its lethal use by Israel's enemies will continue unabated. Those who lend their moral support to terrorism, and who continually see the existence of "grievance-based violence" as a justifiable tool of the oppressed, have helped introduce a sick moral relativism into discussions about radical Islam and Palestinianism, not to mention Israel's right to protect its citizens from being slaughtered. And the notion that Israel cannot, or should not, retaliate against these rocket attacks until a sufficient number of Israelis has been murdered is equally grotesque.

The fact that so many demonstrators felt comfortable with openly supporting a terrorist group with the single purpose of murdering Jews, that they publicly proclaimed that "We are all Hamas now," indicates quite dramatically how prevalent, and acceptable, genocidal Jew-hatred has become, both in the streets and on campuses in America and Europe. This is clearly not, as it is regularly asserted, merely "criticism" of the Israeli government's policies; this is what many define as a new permutation of anti-Semitism — an irrational, seething animus against the Jew of nations, Israel.

These fatuous, morally self-righteous activists, many of whom are from the hard left or the pro-Islamic right, are, without any expertise in military affairs, eager to advise Israeli officials on the rules of war and denounce the lack of "proportionality" in Israel's attempts to defend its population from jihadist murderers. And so eager are they to publicly assert their righteousness as defenders of the Palestinian cause, they embrace and "eroticize" terroristic violence and willingly align themselves with Israel's deadly foes who seek its annihilation, catering, as essayist David Solway lyrically put it, "to the ammoniac hatred of the current brood of crypto-antisemites posing as anti-Zionists."

In fact, the continual pattern of violence in the Arab world against Israel agitates liberals greatly, and makes them condemn Israel, not its foes, for having inspired Arab rage, with the assumption that only peoples with justifiable grievances are moved to violent ends to solve their woes. This explains why the left has regularly glossed over terroristic behavior on the part of Islamists — Hamas, Hezbollah, Fatah, the Al Aqsa Brigades, or others — and has romanticized this violence as "resistance." This rationalization, that violence is an acceptable, if not expected, component of seeking social justice — that is, that the inherent "violence" of imperialism, colonialism, or capitalism will be met by the same violence as the oppressed attempt to throw off their oppressors — is exactly the style of self-defeating rationality that in this age has proven to be an intractable part of the so-called War on Terror.

Abetted by the Arab world, which has also perennially defined Israelis as European interlopers with no legitimate connection to the Levant, Israel-haters are now willing to sacrifice the very survival of the Jewish state because they feel that false charge of racism and apartheid against Israel is more incompatible with their

fervent belief in a perfectible world than the rejectionist and genocidal efforts of the Arab world which, in fact, have necessitated
Israeli security measures — the separation wall, indeed, the occupation itself — all of which, ironically, are pointed to as indica-
tions of exactly how racist Israel's behavior actually is against the
Palestinians.

In fact, observed Harvard's Ruth Wisse, the more hostile the
Arab foes of Israel became, the more difficult it has become for
liberals to absolve Israel for creating the very violent urges that
emerged to eliminate it. "By blaming Israel for Arab complaints,"
she wrote, "liberals anticipate a reasonable, pacific solution to
the conflict . . . The democratic Jewish state is subject to 'rational' persuasion; not so the Arabs. The more determinedly, and
by Western standards, irrationally, Arab governments and their
agents pursue their anti-Israel campaign . . . the more desperately
the liberal imagination tries to blame the Jews for incurring Arab
displeasure."

The language of multiculturalism that animates the hate-Israel
crowd is sprinkled with the code words of oppression, and radicals
in newly-identified victim groups frequently see themselves as deserving of protection and special political, racial, and cultural recognition. Thus, the decades-old emphasis on enshrining multiculturalism has meant that activists have been seeped in an ideology
which refuses to demarcate any differences between a democratic
state struggling to protect itself and aggressive, genocidal foes who
wish to destroy it with their unending assaults. For the multiculturalist left, the moral strengths of the two parties are equivalent,
even though the jihadist foes of Israel, for example, have waged an
unending struggle with the stated aim of obliterating the Jewish
state through the murder of Jews.

There is no other explanation for why educated, well-intentioned and humane individuals, experiencing paroxysms of moral
self-righteousness in which they are compelled to speak out for the
perennial victim, can loudly and publicly advocate for the murder
of Jews — who already have created and live in a viable sovereign

state — on behalf a group of genocidal enemies of Israel whose tragic condition may well be their own doing, and, at any rate, is the not the sole fault of Israel's. That these activists are willing, and ready, to sacrifice the Jewish state, and Jewish lives, in the name of social justice and a specious campaign of self-determination by Palestinian Arabs, shows how morally corrupt and deadly the conversation about human rights has become.

And its lethal nature and intent should frighten us all.

5

Open Hillel Welcomes the Enemy into the Jewish Tent

Winston Churchill could have been observing the sorry state of academic free speech today when he observed that "Everyone is in favor of free speech. Hardly a day passes without its being extolled, but some people's idea of it is that they are free to say what they like, but if anyone else says anything back, that is an outrage." As if to confirm Churchill's prescience, in January of 2016 a cabal of 55 high-minded but morally-incoherent American and Canadian professors formed Open Hillel's Academic Council, a group comprised of well-known Israel-haters who condemned "Hillel International's Standards of Partnership [which] narrowly circumscribe discourse about Israel-Palestine" and which, in its view, "only serve to foster estrangement from the organized Jewish community."

This group of academics and intellectuals, who almost to a person promotes a one-sided, anti-Israel view of the Israeli/Palestinian conflict, and whose teaching and so-called scholarship perpetuates a historically false and factually defective narrative in which Israel is the world's greatest manifestation of malevolence and the Palestinian Arabs are innocent victims of colonial oppression, feel very free to tell Hillel how to achieve its mission: "Hillel's recent aggressive attempts to police discourse about Israel place it in direct conflict with the spirit of the academy," the Council bloviated, adding that "Just as our classrooms must be spaces that embrace diversity of experience and opinion, so must Hillel."

This sentiment is not surprising from these particular academics, given the ideological composition of a group that includes: Peter Beinart, associate professor at the City University of New York, who justifies the BDS campaign because "its recruits are progressives, and that what tips them toward BDS is despair that there seems no other way to end Israel's immoral, undemocratic control of the West Bank and Gaza Strip;" Berkeley's feminist philosopher, Judith Butler, who notoriously and who almost surreally commented that it is important to view "Hamas/Hezbollah as social movements that are progressive, that are on the left, that are part of a global left;" Stanford's Joel Beinin, a self-proclaimed Marxist and rabid anti-Zionist who singles out Israel for criticism of its varied and frequent transgressions, all the while excusing the social and political defects of the neighboring Arab states who surround it and blaming the pathologies of the Middle East on Western imperialism and the continuing colonial impact of the U.S.'s proxy in the Levant, Israel; and UC Irvine's Mark LeVine, associate professor of history, who claims that Israel, like America, essentially receives what it deserves, contending that, "In Israel the violence and terrorism of the latest intifada cannot be understood except as emerging out of decades of occupation, discrimination and dispossession."

Open Hillel, founded in 2013 by "progressive" (read: anti-Zionist) Jewish students at Swarthmore College, was an attempt to challenge Hillel International's guidelines which seek to preserve Hillel's primary desire "to enrich the lives of Jewish students so they may enrich the Jewish people and the world." Part of that enrichment is helping Jewish students to connect and form an enduring relationship with Israel, and so a positive view of the Jewish state is generally fostered and embraced within Hillel chapter walls.

Open Hillel, however, is not satisfied with that approach to forming a Jewish identity; instead, it seeks to invite anti-Jewish, anti-Israel, anti-Zionist voices into Hillel, purportedly to bring a diversity of views into discussions about Israel and the Palestinians, but, as is obvious from the unseemly group behind the movement, to actually bring anti-Israel activism right into the otherwise "safe" space that Hillel provides Jewish students who are forming their own spiritual identities and attitudes about the Jewish state.

And a safe place for Jewish students has obviously become more important as anti-Israel activism has transformed campuses into uncomfortable, antagonistic places for those supporting Israel. A 2015 Brandeis Center for Human Rights Under the Law Anti-Semitism Report, for example, revealed that "more than half of 1,157 self-identified Jewish students at 55 campuses nationwide who took part in an online survey reported having experienced or witnessed anti-Semitism on their campuses during the last academic year."

The idea that Hillel International has very clear guidelines about which type of groups may, and may not, appear at Hillel events was apparently too much for these anti-Israel ideologues, who are not content with flooding the rest of campuses with virulent pro-Palestinian activism that incessantly demonizes, libels, and demeans Israel and its supporters; these activists also want to force this tsunami of anti-Israel hatred, often anti-Semitic in nature, right into Hillel's door — using the disingenuous claim that it is done in the name of academic free speech and diversity of ideas. "Hillel's recent aggressive attempts to police discourse about Israel place it in direct conflict with the spirit of the academy," the Council trumpeted, and, what is more, "Hillel is forcing an unnecessary and destructive choice between academic freedom and membership in the Jewish community."

What are the "aggressive attempts" by Hillel "to police discourse about Israel"? In fact, Hillel's guidelines are designed, not to eliminate any discussion about Israel, but only to prevent self-identified enemies of Israel to participate in Hillel events — those groups such as the virulent Students for Justice in Palestine (SJP) and the Muslim Students Association (MSA), who lead in on-campus agitation against Israel and Jews who support it, and toxic fringe groups like Jewish Voice for Peace and Breaking the

Silence, which use the cover of having Jewish members themselves to openly, and vigorously, seek to weaken and destroy the Jewish state. Hillel's Standards of Partnership state clearly that "Hillel will not partner with . . . organizations, groups, or speakers that . . . Deny the right of Israel to exist as a Jewish and democratic state . . . Delegitimize, demonize, or apply a double standard to Israel . . ; Support boycott of, divestment from, or sanctions against the State of Israel . . ; [or] Exhibit a pattern of disruptive behavior towards campus events or guest speakers or foster an atmosphere of incivility . . . ." — exactly the speech and behavior characteristic of both the activist groups mentioned above and virtually all of the members of the Open Hillel Academic Council.

Students for Justice in Palestine, for example, the campus group currently leading the campaign to delegitimize and demonize Israel, has absolutely no interest in joining Hillel in robust, honest debates about a future Palestinian state or, as the wishful thinking goes, creating two states that will live side by side in peace. SJP has a long history, since its founding in 1993, of bringing vitriolic anti-Israel speakers to their respective campuses, and for sponsoring Israeli Apartheid Weeks, building mock "apartheid walls," and sending mock eviction notices to students in their dorms to help them empathize with Palestinians.

SJP may wish to enter Hillel's tent to spew their venom, and clearly this is the intention of Open Hillel's Academic Council, but not so they can engage in actual dialogue with pro-Israel Jewish students. The whole idea of even legitimizing a pro-Israel view is anathematic to SJP and their fellow-travelers in their never-ending bash-Israel campaign.

In fact, a leaked memorandum from the Binghamton University SJP chapter revealed that its members would be required to *never even engage in dialogue* with pro-Israel groups on their campus, and they would be prohibited from "engaging in any form of official collaboration, cooperation, or event co-sponsorship with [pro-Israel] student organizations and groups, due to their unyielding support for the Apartheid State of Israel." What is more, the memo read, SJP members "shall in no manner engage in any form of official collaboration with any student group which actively opposes the cause of Palestinian liberation nor with groups which have aided and abetted Zionist student organizations in the interest of undermining or denigrating the work of Students for Justice in Palestine," meaning, of course, that the so-called intellectual debate that academics pretend to promote will never take place when SJP is involved.

Why, then, would Hillel ever want to allow SJP, or groups countenancing similar attitudes, to discuss anything about Israel, Zionism, or Judaism inside its walls? Obviously, it would not, which is precisely the reason that Open Hillel wants so badly to force these openly anti-Israel, often anti-Semitic views into a Jewish communal space where an honest discussion of Israel's politics and relationship to its Arab neighbors is productive, but not a negative, one-sided dialogue with Israel as the sole villain and the Palestinians as entirely blameless victims.

And because they cannot win an honest, open ideological debate about the Israeli/Palestinian conflict because they deal solely in untruths, false history, and misrepresentations (the existence of Israeli apartheid, as the central example), SJP has characteristically tried to insure that no pro-Israel voices are heard, either by disrupting or shutting down pro-Israel events and speakers or urging administrators to disinvite speakers they deem to be Islamophobic, too pro-Israel, or critical of their own tactics and activism. Accomplishing that, the memo SJP continued, should include "Political theater to protest the event, engaging in non-violent disruption of the event, or any other tactic deemed appropriate by the attending members not including violence," a clear violation of one of Hillel's Standards of Partnership.

If the august and self-important Open Hillel Academic Council actually wishes to support campus "spaces that embrace diversity of experience and opinion," why is it not demanding that Students for Justice in Palestine, the Muslim Student Association, or other groups central to the Israeli/Palestinian debate embrace the views of pro-Israel students, as they are asking Jews to do with their ideological enemies, and insist that Hillel members and others be invited to participate in pro-Palestinian demonstrations, rallies, conferences, and campaigns to promote "the principle of open discourse" they seem so intent to foist on Hillel alone?

And there is another, more psychologically interesting aspect to a group of academics, most of them Jewish, opposing Hillel policies that attempt to protect Jewish students from the pernicious effects of anti-Israelism and anti-Semitism in campus activism, an aspect that Harvard's insightful Ruth Wisse dealt with in her book, *If I Am Not For Myself: The Liberal Betrayal of the Jews:* the Academic Council targeted Hillel specifically because it provides an intellectually safe place to discuss Israel and how Jews define their relationship with the Jewish state and its surrounding Arab neighbors. Rather than confront the lies and distortions promulgated by the Arab world against Israel over its alleged racism, apartheid, settlements, and lack of a just solution to the occupation, the anti-Israel members of the Academic Council have completely accepted the spurious new narrative of Israel being the sole villain, and in fact often abet it with their own obsessive condemnations of the Jewish state. For Wisse, this behavior could "more accurately be described as the desire to disassociate oneself from a people under attack by advertising one's own goodness," a psychological pattern that has manifested itself conspicuously on campuses and seems to be at play in the current instance with the Open Hillel academics.

The title of Wisse's book, of course, is taken from the well-known quotation from the renowned religious leader Hillel the Elder, for whom Hillel itself was named, in which he asked, "If I am not for myself, who will be for me?" For Hillel International, that means that as Jewish students forge a relationship to Judaism and Israel, they have to act with some self-interest to insure that others, who do not have their best interest at heart, cannot do them harm by defaming, libeling, and assaulting their moral and religious identities — exactly what the poisonous ideology of the Open Hillel Academic Council seems intent on achieving.

6

The 'Altruistic Evil' of Social Justice for the Palestinians

As yet another indication that the university campus has become "an island of repression in a sea of freedom," in March of 2016 a pro-Israel group, Hasbara Fellowships Canada, was barred from participating in a "Social Justice Week" event organized by the Student Association of Durham College and University of Ontario Institute of Technology (UOIT). The stated reason for the exclusion? The student association (which, not coincidentally, had just approved a pro-BDS resolution against Israel) informed the Hasbara group that since the "organization seems closely tied to the state of Israel . . . it would be against the motion to provide any type of resources to your organization."

While the term "social justice" has a seemingly benign and positive connation — and certainly to those who so vigorous fight for it — the reality is that, as columnist Jonah Goldberg observed in his book, *The Tyranny of Clichés: How Liberals Cheat in the War of Ideas*, social justice is actually "an empty vessel to be filled with any and all leftist ideals, and then promptly wielded as a political bludgeon against any and all dissenters . . . ."

That has meant that students, and left-leaning faculty, as well, are urged to advocate for social and economic goals described in decidedly liberal intellectual formulations such as "social and

economic justice," "distributive justice," and "the global interconnections of oppression," this latter view ideal for conflating, at
least in liberal imaginations, the shared complicity of America and
Israel in their long-term oppression of the indigenous people of
the fictive nation of Palestine and the alleged "occupation" of their
land.

So while social justice warriors on campus are quick to welcome a collection of perceived victim groups into their tent —
Muslims, African-Americans, gays, Hispanics, women — they
have been decidedly more hostile when dealing with the Israeli/
Palestinian conflict, the result being that pro-Israel groups (such
as the Hasbara Fellowships in Ontario) are regularly excluded
as being part of the oppressor class responsible for such evils as
imperialism, colonialism, racism, and sexism.

What are the defining characteristics of those well-meaning,
but often misguided individuals who promiscuously proclaim their
commitment to social justice? A number of tactics and behaviors
are common to their efforts:

*Social justice warriors are commonly infatuated with their own vir-
tue, which manifests itself in very public "virtue signaling,"* a way that
self-described activists indicate that they have taken the high moral ground, that they stand for racial equality and the aspirations of
the oppressed, and that they single-mindedly fight for the rights
of, and make excuses for, the oppressed state in which their victims find themselves.

Economist Thorsten Veblen identified an emerging social
phenomenon in which an increasingly more affluent middle class
used spending and material acquisition as a way of signaling their
economic — and social — status. Social justice warriors use
the same psychological device of announcing to others their
self-righteous ideology through what could be called "conspicuous
moral consumption," part and parcel of their virtue signaling.

*The rectitude of students and faculty enthralled by social justice and
pushing for condemnations of Israel manifests itself as what has termed
"moral narcissism,"* the tendency of members of the well-meaning,

(although incompletely) educated elite to align with causes and ideological positions which are based, not on the actual viability or worthiness of a cause, but on how the moral narcissist feels about him- or herself by committing to a particular campaign or movement. Like other members of the academic left, who believe their world view is correct because it seeks to create a world in which social equanimity will be realized by the downtrodden, members of the SJP, Black Lives Matter, LGBT, the Occupy Movement, and other victims' rights grievance groups and movements are content to support such intellectually dishonest campaigns as the BDS movement because it enables them to denounce Israelis as "white," imperialistic, colonial, racist, militaristic oppressors of wholly innocent "brown" Palestinians dispossessed and victimized by the Jewish state's very existence. "Moral narcissists," wrote legal commentator Jay B. Gaskill, "have adopted a camouflage strategy to escape the moral disapproval of others [and] . . . they accomplish this camouflage by cloaking their narcissism in the trappings of 'social justice positioning.'" The moral narcissist's reasoning may be defective, ahistorical, counter-intuitive, or just wrong, but he still feels good about himself.

In debating the Israeli/ Palestinian conflict, social justice activists, of course, demonstrate their hypocrisy by endlessly dwelling on the many evils of Israel without bothering to examine or measure the Palestinians' own central role in contributing to the many pathologies endemic to their civil society and institutions. Like many Western elites do when choosing sides, *social justice warriors infantilize the Palestinian victim and assume he has no agency to ameliorate his own conditions.* In reality, pro-Palestinian activists seem to care very little about the actual self-determination and state building of the hapless Palestinians. As is frequently the case when speaking about the Israeli/Arab conflict, the discussion often glosses over the real problems of Palestinian culture, politics, and society (including its cult of death, terrorism, and martyrdom), and targets all criticism on the perceived defects of Israel, Zionism, and Jewish power. All of the blame for the conflict is placed on the so-called occupation, the "apartheid wall," Jewish racism, the oppression and militarism of the "Zionist regime," and the brutal humiliation, collective punishment, and even "slow-moving" genocide Israel is said to mete out on a daily basis upon the wholly innocent Palestinians. *This is a clear example of another underlying factor in the social justice effort, the soft bigotry of low Palestinian expectations.*

Many academics in the humanities and social sciences, including activists as disparate as Black Lives Matter, Students for Justice in Palestine, and the National Association of Women's Studies, increasingly find a linkage as they seek to affirm the rights of the victimized and name the villains responsible for this oppression. The more that seemingly unrelated instances of oppression can be conflated, it is thought, the greater the ability to confront these oppressors and dilute the negative effect they have on their specific victims and on society at large. This trend has been called "intersectionality," and it has meant that someone who is a gender studies professor, or queer theorist, or American studies expert can, with no actual knowledge or expertise about the Middle East, readily pontificate on the many social pathologies for which he or she accuses Israel, based on its perceived role as a racist, imperialist, colonial oppressor of an innocent indigenous population of Arab victims. For social justice warriors, to know one victim group is to know *any* victim group — with Israel being a tempting and habitual target of their opprobrium. Thus, for instance, supporters of the Black Lives Matter movement have often linked racism and police violence "from Ferguson to Palestine," as their placards have announced, making Israel somehow complicit in American racism and police brutality, and even recently proclaimed in its recent platform that Israel is practicing "apartheid" and is engaged in "genocide" against the Palestinians. "Intersectionality holds that various forms of oppression," said David Bernstein, president and CEO of the Jewish Council for Public Affairs, "constitute an intersecting system of oppression . . , [and] the BDS movement has successfully injected the anti-Israel cause into these intersecting forms of oppression and itself into the interlocking communities of people who hold by them."

Social justice warriors are intent on using "weaponized intolerance," the willingness to abridge speech and human rights of opposing groups in the campaign to seek social justice for the victim. Moreover, so sure are they of their moral uprightness in denouncing white-privilege and conservative thought, that the social justice warriors will not even deign to collaborate, negotiate, or even tolerate the views of those groups and individuals they have decided are essentially unworthy of having their options heard. The New York City Students for Justice in Palestine, for example, announced proudly that, "We reject any and all collaboration, dialogue and coalition work with Zionist organizations through a strict policy of anti-normalization (anti-engagement) and encourage our comrades in other organizations to do the same." That type of behavior violates the concepts of academic freedom and academic free speech — rights that campus radicals prefer to exploit themselves while denying the same freedoms to others and deeming speech with which they disagree "hate speech." Spirited debate between people with opposing views, of course, is acceptable and desirable; shutting down or preventing the speech of one side of the argument, and not permitting those views to be aired in the marketplace of ideas, is not.

Proponents of social justice *apologize for and enable grievance-based violence by abandoning moral precepts and applying a double standard by which they support murder, violence, "resistance," and terror in the name of self-determination — but only that perpetrated by the favored victim.* Anti-Israel campus events regularly include protesters ghoulishly chanting "long live the Intifada" and "'resistance' is justified when people are occupied," in other words, extolling the ongoing homicidal rampage in Israel in which psychopathic terrorists have used knives, guns, stones, and vehicles to randomly murder Jewish civilians. That pro-Palestinian student activists, those who purport to be motivated by a desire to bring "justice" to the Middle East and who, presumably, care about *all* human lives, could publicly call for the renewed slaughter of Jews in the name of Palestinian self-determination demonstrates quite clearly how ideologically debased the human rights movement has become. Activists on university campuses in the United States and Europe, who demand "trigger warnings" from professors to protect their sensibilities prior to reading such innocuous literary works as *Adventures of Huckleberry Finn*, are quick to denounce Israel's very real existential threats and the necessity of the Jewish state to take counter measures to thwart homicidal terrorism against its civilian population.

Those purportedly seeking social justice for the Palestinians regularly exhibit a willful blindness to the quest for social justice for actual *Middle East victims of egregious oppression*, while obsessing, to the exclusion of all other examples, over the perceived perfidy of Israel. For example, this year the National Association of Women's Studies (NWSA) voted to approve an academic boycott against Israeli scholars. It had evidently escaped the notice of the NWSA experts on gender and sexuality issues that if one wanted to punish any Middle Eastern country for its subjugation and abuse of women, Israel would probably not be the first nation to come under reasonable or justifiable scrutiny for a group dedicated "to principles of human rights, justice and freedom for all, including academic freedom." Totalitarian and despotic regimes throughout the region have created an oppressive group of social pathologies that negatively affect women, including genital mutilation, stoning of adulteresses, "honor" killings by fathers and brothers who have been shamed, cultures of gender apartheid in which women are seen as property with no emotional or physical autonomy, ubiquitous sexual assault, and a general subjugation of women, complete with regulations governing behavior, movement, speech, and even requirements that women be covered by burqa or hijab.

This nearly total rejection by those seeking justice for the oppressed of any recognition of goodness on the part of Western countries (and particularly Israel), favoring without hard judgments severely flawed societies of the Third World is, according to British commentator Melanie Phillips, symptomatic of activists' belief in their own moral superiority, a feature which, at least in their own minds, gives them a more genuine, principled, and valuable world view. "In the grip of a group-think that causes them to genuflect to victim-culture and the deconstruction of western morality and the concept of truth," Phillips wrote, "a dismaying number of our supposedly finest minds have been transformed from people who spread enlightenment to those who cast darkness before them."

And we should be careful that, despite their own claims to a moral uprightness, the truth is not being lost in the intellectual darkness created by these self-appointed purveyors of social justice.

7

The Lie of Academic
Free Speech

When GOP presidential candidate Donald Trump's March 11, 2015 rally at the University of Chicago Pavilion was shut down by hundreds of leftist protesters, comprised of activists from Moveon.org, Black Lives Matter, Muslim groups, and even unrepentant domestic terrorist Bill Ayers, the morally indignant activists had one purpose: to disrupt the event, prevent Trump supporters from hearing the candidate's speech, and, most importantly, suppress Trump's ideas and beliefs. Having already decided the Mr. Trump was a veritable racist, Islamophobe, and neo-Nazi, the mob of rioters — inside and outside of the venue — took it upon themselves to decide that Trump, and those who share his vision and ideas, do not even have the right to express their opinions, that their views have been deemed unacceptable by the self-appointed moral arbiters of our day.

The disturbing campaign to suppress speech which is purportedly hurtful, unpleasant, or morally-distasteful — a sample of which was evident at the Chicago rally — is, for anyone following what is happening on campuses, a troubling and recurrent pattern of behavior by some of the same ideologues who shut down Trump: "progressive" leftists and "social justice" advocates from Muslim-led pro-Palestinian groups. Coalescing around the

Israeli/Palestinian conflict, this unholy alliance has been formed in a libelous and vituperative campaign to demonize Israel, attack pro-Israel individuals, and promote a relentless campaign against Israel in the form of the Boycott, Divestment, and Sanctions (BDS) movement. As the ideological assault against Israel and Jews intensified on university campuses, and pro-Israel individuals began answering back to their ideological opponents, the student groups leading the pro-Palestinian charge (including such groups as the radical Students for Justice in Palestine (SJP)) decided that their tactic of unrelenting demonization of Israel was insufficient, and the best way to optimize the propaganda effect of their anti-Israel message was also to suppress or obscure opposing views.

That tactic was a necessary one: in the first place, the message of the anti-Israel crowd is based largely on lies and one-sided arguments presented without context in which the Palestinians are entirely blameless for their fate and Israel is a racist, oppressive, apartheid, colonial regime, with its primary target and victim being the hapless Palestinian Arabs. Israel haters do not wish, of course, to have their arguments inconveniently challenged by facts. Secondly, while they are perfectly content to propel a mendacious campaign of anti-Israel libels, and base their analysis of the Israeli/Palestinian conflict on falsehoods, distortions, and a false reading of history and fact, so certain are they of their moral authority that they will never countenance any views — even facts as opposed to opinions — which contradict their hateful political agenda.

And because they cannot win an honest, open ideological debate about the Israeli/Palestinian conflict because they deal almost exclusively in misrepresentations and untruths (the allegation of Israeli apartheid, as the central example), just as the anti-Trump protesters wished to accomplish, SJP has characteristically tried to insure that no pro-Israel voices are heard, either by disrupting or shutting down pro-Israel events and speakers or urging administrators to disinvite speakers they deem to be Islamophobic, too pro-Israel, or critical of their own tactics and activism.

The thuggish substitution of event disruption and the shutting down of other people's speech for what is supposed to be two-sided academic dialogue and debate occurs with increased regularity, and marks another, more pernicious, aspect of the campus campaign against Israel, Zionism, and Jews.

At University of California, Davis, for example, George Deek, a Jaffa-born Arab Christian, planned to give a 2016 speech entitled "The Art of Middle East Diplomacy," when some 30 pro-Palestinian activists stood up and blocked Deek with banners and took over the event by screaming "From the River to the Sea, Palestine will be free," meaning an Arab state in place of present-day Israel, and chanting such toxic ditties as "long live the Intifada," "Allahu Akbar," and "When Palestine is occupied, resistance is justified," ghoulish calls for the murder of Jews, and "Israel is anti-Black" and "Palestine will be free, fight white supremacy," an intellectually clumsy way of trying to frame Israel as a racist state.

After the cancelled speech, SJP-affiliated individuals proudly took credit for shutting down Deek's speech, claiming that they "recognize that Israel's voice is already over-represented . . . and [they] refuse to provide the State another platform through which to normalize colonial violence. We have no more 'tolerance' for Israeli propaganda." In other words, one side had decided what could, and could not, be uttered on that campus.

In February 2016, Bassam Eid, a Palestinian himself and the founder of the Palestinian Human Rights Monitoring Group, witnessed very startlingly how nothing positive said about Israel is allowed to be heard, even from such a credible, though unusual, source as a Palestinian. During his speech, in which he was critical of Hamas and the Palestinian Authority for their failure to seek peace, Eid was verbally attacked by a student attendee, who said in Arabic, "Dr. Bassam, do not dare talk about us [Palestinians] anymore. You have shamed our God . . . you've shamed us, disgraced us, you are a traitor, you are a traitor, in the name of God you are a traitor . . . You are worse than the Jews and we will hunt you down and find you in every place, be prepared . . . ." When it became obvious that his speech would not be able to continue uninterrupted, Eid cancelled the event and had to be escorted off site by the police.

In November 2015, the University of Minnesota Law School sponsored a lecture by Hebrew University professor Moshe Halbertal, an expert on Israel's military code of ethics, entitled "Protecting Civilians: Moral Challenges of Asymmetric Warfare." The lecture was delayed for 30 minutes by the unruly heckling and chants of some 100 protesters from the Minnesota Anti-War Committee and Students for Justice in Palestine, who indignantly rose from the audience, interrupted, and, not willing to tolerate Israel's legal right to protect its citizens from being murdered by thousands of Hamas-launched rockets that have rained down on southern Israeli towns for years, accused Halbertal of war crimes and complicity in the 2014 Gaza incursion. Chants directed to Halbertal included the customary libels, "These are massacres, not mistakes! These are war crimes! Free, free Palestine!" and "Occupation is a crime, free, free Palestine!," freeing Palestine, of course, meaning: eliminating Israel and replacing it with a new Arab state.

Also in November, as yet another example, the University of Texas at Austin's Institute for Israeli Studies hosted an event with Stanford University's Dr. Gil-Li Vardi, who was to present a study on "The Origin of a Species: The Birth of the Israeli Defense Forces' Military Culture." At the event, twelve members of a so-called "Palestine Solidarity Committee," intent on disrupting the speech, created a human wall in the back of the room with the purpose of not allowing the event to begin. The anti-Israel activists tried, without the benefit of actually knowing what the speaker would say, to prevent her from presenting her viewpoint by shrieking out such taunts as, "You are a former IDF soldier, we do not listen to you."

A pro-Israel student group at Columbia University, Artists 4 Israel, were also denied the opportunity to express views during Israeli Apartheid Week, during which the SJP chapter had erected their version of a mock "apartheid wall," emblazoned with anti-Israel slogans and symbols. To counter the display with a pro-Israel one, Artists 4 Israel had set up a 15-foot inflatable figure, a "pro-Israel Pinocchio," replete with a long nose and a sign that read "'Apartheid' Week Compassion Abuse" as an effective, sardonic swipe at SJP's toxic campaign. The chair and vice chair of Columbia's student government, who not coincidentally are members of Columbia's SJP chapter and pro-BDS activists, ordered the removal of the Pinocchio figure, offering the disingenuous justification that Pinocchio's long nose might be construed as anti-Semitic and that the pump used to inflate the figure was too loud for use on the Columbia grounds.

The university officials and student groups who now try to suppress all thought of which they disapprove; who publicly proclaim their desire for campuses where there will be vigorous discourse, on contentious issues, from many points of view, but allow the expression of only "acceptable" opinions, couched in the language of human rights and social justice; who label speech with which they do not agree as "hateful" or "racist" or "Islamophobic," and demonize or shun the speakers who utter these alternate views; who vilify Israel, Jews, Zionism, and U.S. support for the Jewish state with every sort of invective, but still claim that criticism of Israel is suppressed by a cabal-like "Israel lobby;" and who shout down, heckle, and bully their ideological opponents during on-campus events — all of these individuals have sacrificed one of the core values for which the university exists. In their zeal to be inclusive, and to recognize the needs and aspirations of victim groups, they have pretended to foster inquiry, but they have actually stifled and retarded it. And, as this otherwise noble purpose for the university has devolved, the first victim in the corruption of academic free speech has, unfortunately, been the truth.

8

A Review of *Antisemitism on the Campus: Past and Present*[*]

T he sheltered walls of academe, one would think, might well have been immune from the peculiar disease of antisemitism, given how a dedication to progressive thought and reasoned scholarship is, at least as commonly proclaimed, one of the fundamental virtues of higher education. But just as antisemitism metastasizes randomly in all strata of society in that conspiratorial netherworld where both reason and morality are abandoned, campuses, too, have a history of harboring their own strains of Jew-hatred, and of providing a safe haven for those who either foster or accommodate antisemitic attitudes.

That antisemitism changed in form and intent from the post-World War I era, when prejudice against Jews was principally defined by attempts by the academic mandarins to block access by Jewish students and faculty to slots in elite educational institutions, to the current day, when antipathy toward Jews is more covertly expressed in a new form of antisemitism that targets the Jew of nations, Israel. What both instances have in common, of

*This book review of Eunice G. Pollack's (ed.), *Antisemitism on the Campus: Past and Present*, Academic Studies Press, 2011. 450 pp. $65.00, originally appeared in the *Journal for the Study of Antisemitism*, VOL. 3:785, 2011.

course, is an irrational fear of and obsessive regard for the perceived shortcomings, undue influence, and moral defects of Jews, and the sometimes puzzling lapses in reason that seem to characterize some university administrators, entrenched faculty, and professionals in educational associations.

In eras before the Holocaust, a strain of "polite," somewhat invisible, antisemitism was an integral part of Western societies, and that included the insular, clubby societies that defined elite campuses such as Harvard, for example, where growing numbers of high-achieving, "aggressive" Jewish applicants threatened to displace Yankee scions. A. Lawrence Lowell, Harvard's president in the 1920s, had a peculiar animosity toward Jews and instituted quotas by which to restrict the sheer numbers of Jewish students admitted under his watch. Pressed by an influential Harvard graduate to defend his bias against Jews, Lowell told him that it was because "Jews cheat." When the alum pointed out that students from all faiths and backgrounds cheat, too, Lowell is alleged to have replied, "Don't change the subject. I'm talking about Jews." That obsession with the presumed and projected defects of Jews is eerily similar to the obsessive, even irrational, antipathy expressed toward Israel — and, by extension, to Jews — on campuses in the current day, and the same poisonous stream that tainted campuses in the early twentieth century still flows unabated in the 21st.

That unfortunate historical phenomenon is the subject of a new collection of 21 essays, *Antisemitism on the Campus: Past and Present,* edited by Eunice G. Pollack, professor of history and Jewish studies at the University of North Texas. What becomes clear in the book's broad coverage of several generations of campus antisemitism is that the current form, the "new" antisemitism, is much more slippery, and that while overt Jew-hatred is no longer generally accepted among the Western intelligentsia, the conflation on campus today of the many perceived ills of Zionism and Israel has given actual antisemites a convenient cover for their otherwise unacceptable prejudices.

Organized into six sections, *Antisemitism on Campus* begins with an overview of how campuses have dealt with, and continue to deal with and respond to, the presence of antisemitism on campus and the frequent failure of administrators to adequately ameliorate conditions that would be morally or emotionally oppressive to Jewish students and faculty. Andrew S. Winston writes a troubling piece with the title "Objectionable Traits," examining how Jews from the 1920s to the 1950s were tacitly, though determinedly, thwarted from academic training in psychology due to their perceived inability to enter this profession because they were "covetous, criminal, dishonest . . , ill-mannered, self-defensive . . , and unwilling to assimilate." Moreover, because it was believed "that Jewish interest in education merely reflected acquisitiveness," and that the questionable moral character and foreign ethnic background of Jewish students rendered them unworthy of professional standing, department chairs and faculty exhibited "a shared understanding of the dangers in admitting Jews to the socioculturally homogeneous professoriate." The "polite" campus antisemites of the past here could conveniently justify antisemitism as a logical reaction to the perfidy and unpleasantness of Jews themselves; that is, antisemitism is the fault of Jews for their actions, just as current antisemitism is justified by pointing to the oppressive and unlawful behavior of Israel, and Jews' complicity in it.

The same ethnic and cultural diversity that excluded Jews from certain schools and professions in earlier times, of course, today has elevated other minority groups to special status on campuses. Benjamin Ginsberg of Johns Hopkins University, for instance, describes how university administrators now, in their zeal to make campuses inclusive, diverse, and multicultural, regularly protect the rights and sensibilities of favored campus victim groups (African Americans, gays, Muslim students, and Latinos, for instance), but have been either unwilling or unable to make strong moral stands when Jewish students have been emotionally, verbally, or physically assaulted for their actual or perceived support of Israel or opposition to the Palestinian cause.

Wellesley College's Jerold S. Auerbach writes a more specific tale of his own institution, revealing how Wellesley, like many of the other elite campuses during the early 20th century, maintained an uneasy relationship with its Jewish students, consigning them to dank corners of dorms, screening them for traits of their "Jewishness" during the application process, and treating them as somehow different and inferior to the children from gentile society who comprised the largest part of student bodies at the Ivies and sister schools. Those attitudes, and their dark legacy, persisted at Wellesley until the current day, Auerbach points out, as evidenced by the college's reaction to the incendiary writing and publishing of African-American Tony Martin, an unrepentantly antisemitic Wellesley professor who used *The Secret Relationship between Blacks and Jews,* a spurious bit of scholarship purporting that Jews were key players in the slave trade, in his teaching, and who, after many Jews reacted to his outrageous theories, wrote his own screed, *The Jewish Onslaught,* in which he castigated a malevolent "Jewish lobby" for trying to suppress the "truths" he had attempted to reveal to his students. As regularly occurs on other campuses where Jews, Zionists, or Israel are the target of demonization, at Wellesley the administration circled its wagons around Martin under the protective shield of academic free speech and ignored the inconvenient details of whether what he taught was true, scholarly, or even morally appropriate.

The thorny American topic of racism has inserted itself into discussions about Jews on campuses, particularly in relation to Israel and the promiscuous way it is referred to as an "apartheid" state by its campus defamers. Professor Pollack, in fact, includes an essay of her own, "African Americans and the Legitimization of Antisemitism on Campus," which explores the troubling friction between blacks and Jews since the civil rights era; a second essay in the book also investigates the promotion of antisemitism through the music of rap artists, although the incidence of African-American antisemitism on campus, while part of the larger attack on Israel and Zionism, has not in itself been a significant issue.

But the charge of racism also enables leftist faculty, administrators, and students to excuse the moral transgressions of the oppressed Palestinians, and, as an extension of that thinking, to single out Israel and America for particular and harsh scrutiny owing to their perceived "institutionalized" racism and greater relative power. The self-righteousness the left feels in pointing out Zionism's essential defect of being a racist ideology insulates it from having to also reflect on Arab transgressions, since, as suggested by earlier anti-Semites — who blame Jews themselves for the fact they are disliked — liberals (many of them Jews themselves) can excuse their own betrayal of Israel by holding it fully responsible for the very hatreds it inspires.

This "unholy alliance" between the Arab world and leftists, which might seem initially incompatible, serves both sides well: Arab nations, who wish to deflect the pathologies of their own societies, savor being able to assign the West's worst appellation of "racist" to Israel, and campus liberals at the same time fulfill their Marxist dreams of trying to envision and help create what Harvard's Ruth Wisse has called the "ideal of the egalitarian state."

That ideology has meant that the current occurrences of antisemitism on campus, as discussed in a series of essays at the end of this book, have to be examined through a prism that includes the Israeli/Palestinian conflict, since on most campuses the accusation against Israel is that it is essentially a "racist" regime. As the wry Professor Edward Alexander observes in one of his two essays here, "Because [liberals] usually pride themselves on the rejection of anything smacking of racism and prejudice, they must cast the Israelis themselves as the new Nazis in order to make antisemitism, which had (so to speak) been given a bad name by the Holocaust, again 'respectable,' but under the new name of anti-Zionism."

The present-day campus is rife with anti-Zionists, of course, all of whom are quick to deny they harbor any anti-Semitic sentiment but who leap to their collective feet to virulently denounce what they perceive to be Israel's apartheid, racism, occupation, oppression, militarism, and Nazi-like behavior. But those collective libels and slurs against the Jewish state are precisely what have come to define the "new" campus antisemitism, observes Kenneth L. Marcus in his contribution in this book, "Hostile Environment: Campus Antisemitism as a Civil Rights Violation." "As the State Department observed in 2008," Marcus writes, "a distinguishing feature of the new antisemitism is 'criticism of Zionism or Israeli policy that — whether intentionally or unintentionally — has the effect of promoting prejudice against all Jews by demonizing Israel and Israelis and attributing Israel's perceived faults to its Jewish character.'" Marcus should know well whereof he speaks, since he and the four other contributors to the final section of this book, "Combatting Antisemitism" — Tammi Rossman-Benjamin, Evelyn Avery, Rachel Fish, and Alvin Rosenfeld — have all been in the trenches in the battle against campus extremism aimed at Israel and Jews.

Marcus, President of the Louis D. Brandeis Center for Human Rights Under the Law and former director of the U.S. Commission on Civil Rights, also accuses universities of using what he calls "First Amendment opportunism" when they provide moral cover for extremist speech on campus with which they seemingly agree, but seek to criminalize other speech on the same campus when it is deemed hate speech by those who disagree with its point of view — its content. UC Santa Cruz's Rossman-Benjamin, whose essay surveys the "academic delegitimization of anti-Zionism," filed a 2009 civil rights action with the U.S. Department of Education's Office for Civil Rights, arguing that UCSC had created a "hostile environment" for Jewish students. On her campus, Rossman-Benjamin had observed an odious pattern of bias and radicalism against Israel and Jews, under the guise of a scholarly critique of Israeli policies, a process in which, she said, "Professors, academic departments and residential colleges at UCSC promote and encourage anti-Israel, anti-Zionist and anti-Jewish views and behavior, much of which is based on either misleading information or outright falsehoods." More to the point, it was not only the presence of this virulently anti-Israel, anti-Semitic speech and action that was of significance, but the fact that it was singularly directed, unceasingly, at one group of students: Jews. And what was more, Rossman-Benjamin added, "no other . . . group on campus has been subjected . . . to such hostile and demonizing criticism."

Campus antisemitism, as chronicled in *Antisemitism on the Campus* — both in the classic, earlier forms as a logical outgrowth of European and Christian strains, and now in its new, more covert form as purported criticism of Israel and Zionism — is a grim reminder that the world's oldest hatred has not yet vanished; in fact, either because of the widespread negative attitudes toward Israel, or simply due to a lingering, poisonous Jew-hatred in the Arab world and increasingly in the West as well, Jews once again are witness to libels, denunciation, demonization, and slurs against Judaism, against Zionism, and against Israel itself, the Jew of nations. The campus war against Israel, which is the most salient form of contemporary antisemitism, is also indicative of the devolution of higher education, where scholarship has been degraded by bias and extremism on the part of a leftist professoriate with a clear political agenda that enlists Israel as the new villain in a world yearning for social justice. University leaders and other stakeholders have been noticeably feckless in moderating this radicalism, either because they are unaware of how whole fields of study have been hijacked by academic frauds and morally incoherent scholars, or because they sympathize with the intellectual approach of their faculties and have become complicit with the production of pseudo-scholarship, academic agitprop, and disingenuous "learning experiences" that have a one-sided, biased approach to understanding the Middle East, and particularly the Israeli/Palestinian conflict.

That a collection of twenty-one essays was necessary to write in order to examine campus antisemitism would be unfortunate, especially if those articles revealed only a troubling era in academia's cloudy past. But, as suggested by the title of one of the book's other essays, "New Wine in Old Bottles," the way in which Jews are marginalized, demonized, libeled, intimidated, and slandered on campus may have changed and been dressed in new clothing to obscure actual intent, but the world's longest hatred, unfortunately, shows no sign of disappearing, along with other human pathologies, into the dustbin of history.

PART TWO

THE MALIGNANCY OF THE BOYCOTT, DIVESTMENT, AND SANCTIONS (BDS) MOVEMENT

9

Ideological Roots and Tactics
of the BDS Movement

In reflecting on the current trend he perceived in the burgeoning of anti-Israelism around the world, former Canadian Member of Parliament, Irwin Cotler, observed that conventional strains of anti-Semitism had been masked, so that those who directed enmity towards Jews were now able to transfer that opprobrium to the Jew of nations, Israel. How had they effected that? According to Cotler, by redefining Israel as the most glaring example of those paramount evils, what he called "the embodiment of all evil" of the Twentieth Century: apartheid and Nazism. He defined this process as "ideological anti-Semitism," one which "involves the characterization of Israel not only as an apartheid state — and one that must be dismantled as part of the struggle against racism — but as a Nazi one." For Israel's mortal foes, these designations served to coalesce disparate negative feelings about Israel, and helped energize a broad movement to continually assault the many moral and legal injustices Zionism was said to have caused.

If critics were able to point to Israel as the most salient example of lingering racism and Nazi-like subjugation, they could subject Israel to unrelenting criticism and denunciation. The UN Human Rights Council could, year after year, promiscuously single out Israel for condemnation and censure. The Palestinians could be transformed in the mind of human rights activists into the new South Africans, with Zionism as the new regime that enforced apartheid-like laws of discrimination on helpless "colored" Arabs. And Western apologists for Arab terror could also comfort themselves with the notion that criminal racism deserved — and even demanded — assault by those oppressed by its use.

Most important for the anti-Israel cause, according to Cotler, once Israel had been tarred with the libels of racism and Nazism, the Jewish state was made an international outlaw, a pariah, losing its moral right to even exist — exactly, of course, what its foes have consistently sought. "These very labels of Zionism and Israel as 'racist, apartheid and Nazi' supply the criminal indictment," said Cotler. "No further debate is required. The conviction that this triple racism warrants the dismantling of Israel as a moral obligation has been secured. For who would deny that a 'racist, apartheid, Nazi' state should not have any right to exist today?"[1]

For campus activists against Israel, the defamatory essence of the racism charge found a perfect use when, in 2000, it formed the basis of a BDS campaign designed to bully universities into ending their financial ties with companies doing business with Israel. Basing its efforts on the South African divestment campaign of 1980s, the anti-Israel model was grafted onto the now-familiar charge and solution: since Israel, like South Africa, was perceived to be a nation practicing racism in an apartheid society, at the expense of an oppressed minority, university investments would be curtailed until Israel amended its racist ways and met the demands of those calling for divestment.

That Israel's society is multi-racial, ethnically diverse, and one in which Arabs, as twenty percent of the population, enjoy more civil and human rights than they would as citizens in surrounding countries was, for the purposes of the BDS movement, of course, overlooked. So, too, was the baselessness of the charge of apartheid, which, as even critics finally admit, did not exactly pertain to Israel and its relationship to the Palestinians. But the racism charge had already gained considerable traction in the hate-Israel circles, thanks in no small part to the UN's invidious 1975 General Assembly Resolution 3379, which had "determine[d] that Zionism is a form of racism and racial discrimination." And when the International Court of Justice deemed Israel's security barrier illegal in 2004, the divestment proponents had yet another way to condemn Israel — thus the favorite name for the barrier of Israel's enemies became the "Apartheid Wall." The now-frequent references to Israeli behavior towards and treatment of the Palestinians in Gaza and West bank as Nazi-like also helped solidify the very characterization that Cotler spoke of a Zionism predicated on racism, fascism, and assumed supremacy.

Positioned as a morally upright effort to assert and protect the rights of the long-suffering Palestinians, these efforts at demonizing Israel are in fact not benign gestures of peace activists and well-meaning academics in pursuit of social justice for the Palestinians. There is a far more sinister and deadly agenda which aims to create a new Palestinian state, not, as is frequently though disingenuously described as one that will exist side by side with Israel in peace, but actually as a new entity that will either economically or demographically subsume Israel — a war of propaganda, falsehoods, slanders, and distortions of history by which Israel's enemies vanquish the Jewish state with ideas rather than arms.

In fact, Gil Troy, professor of history at McGill University, observed that the BDS movement is a more about diminishing the stature of Israel world-wide and less about actually ameliorating some of the root problems that define the Israeli/Palestinian conflict. "The BDS debate is not about 'occupation' or borders or the peace process," Troy wrote in the *Jerusalem Post*. "The BDS campaign assails Israel's legitimacy, declaring it so odious that no one should drink any Israeli wine, no one should enjoy an Israeli film, no one should collaborate with any Israeli academic. The BDS movement is an obscene campaign of blacklisting, demonizing and slandering," which, in his view, requires that Israel's supporters "must name, shame, and reframe" in order to counteract the odious effects of the movement.[2]

Thus, on campuses today where boycott and divestment initiatives spring up in the rarified air of moral relativism, Israel is regularly, though falsely, condemned for being created "illegally" — through the "theft" of Palestinian lands and property — and thus has no "right to exist." The government is accused of a "brutal," illegal "occupation" of Palestinian lands, especially Gaza and the West Bank, of being a "colonial settler state," a Zionist "regime," a land-hungry nation building an "apartheid wall" as a further land grab, a usurper of property that was lived on and owned by a Palestinian "people" "from time immemorial." Zionism is regularly equated with Nazism, and the perceived offenses of Israel's government and military are likened to Nazi crimes against humanity; the notion is that Israel is creating a "Holocaust on the Holy Land" through "ethnic cleansing," ongoing "genocide" of Arabs, and the elimination of the rights of an innocent, "indigenous people" who merely seek self-determination and the peaceful creation of a Palestinian homeland.

Even worse, the struggle between "white" European colonial Jewish settlers in Israel and "brown" Third World Palestinians has been framed as a second coming of apartheid — Israel's occupation of the West Bank and its treatment of its own Arab citizens likened to the racist, separatist behavior that defined apartheid South Africa. That is why calls for divestment and boycotts against Israel are so appealing to the moral defectives and Western elite who wish to superimpose the South African model of oppression — even though it is not at all honest or accurate to do so — on Israel's own society. South African archbishop and Nobel Prize winner Desmond Tutu, in congratulating the UC Berkeley community for its assault against Israel, told them that "[Your predecessors] changed the moral climate in the United States and the consequence was the anti-Apartheid legislation, which helped to dismantle apartheid non-violently. Today it is your turn."[3] In fact, he added, it was a "principled stand" against "the injustice of the Israeli occupation of Palestinian land and violation of Palestinian human rights."[4]

In a campus environment where racism is the twentieth century's greatest ideological sin, the ability to brand Israel as an illegitimate and racist state was an irresistible way for BDS supporters to find a new cause célèbre by which to nourish their own moral righteousness.

Of the many libels from the world community against Israel, perhaps none has gained such traction on campuses as the accusation that the Jewish state now practices apartheid, that the checkpoints, security barrier, Israeli-only roads, barricades, and other apparatus of occupation are tantamount to a racist system which victimizes the indigenous Palestinians, just as South African apartheid oppressed and devalued indigenous blacks while stripping them of them civil rights.

These notions help reinforce BDSer's notion that the imperialism of Western nations is once again responsible for setting up racist, oppressive caste systems in developing countries, systems that have to be dismantled through protest, resistance, and divestment campaigns. It has also formed the basis of divestment petitions which become "working documents" in the strategic vilification of Israel. A January 2003 document created by New Jersey Solidarity and the Rutgers University Campaign for Divestment from Israeli Apartheid, "Acting for Human Rights, Taking a Stand for Justice," for instance, proclaimed that "The world, and specifically the United States, can no longer be silent about the criminal Israeli regime. Conceived by colonial powers without the consent of the indigenous Palestinian people, the State of Israel has continued to pursue its institutionalized policies of racism, discrimination and oppression."[5]

And the apartheid comparison is a simple and powerful way for Israel's campus enemies to heap yet another moral condemnation on the Jewish state, particularly because it reenergizes the campus liberals who made South African apartheid their cause of the moment during the 1990s. Even though Arab citizens of Israel (one-fifth of the population) enjoy more human and civil rights than their brethren in any other Arab nation, the apartheid accusation is effective because it once again points to the social disparity between Israelis and Third-world Arabs, Israeli citizens or not. Israel's need for self-defense, in the mind of its detractors, does not even justify the "apartheid wall," since as a strong Western democracy it presumably should not have established its illegitimate state on Arab lands in the first place, nor should it be surprised when those indigenous inhabitants try to reclaim their stolen property by using terrorism as their only available tactic against an oppressive, militarily-strong regime.

The rallying cry on campus to gather behind the divestment movement seems to have arisen as the result of a November 2000 speech by Francis A. Boyle, a law professor at the University of Illinois. In that speech, Boyle carelessly conflated Israel's alleged racism with apartheid-like behavior and suggesting, even more ominously, that the ongoing "genocide" against the Palestinians had parallels with the Nazi's own heinous offenses. "The paradigmatic example of a crime against humanity is what Hitler and the Nazis did to the Jewish People," Boyle said. "This is where the concept of crime against humanity was formulated and came from. And this is what the U.N. Human Rights Commission is now saying that Israel is doing to the Palestinian People. A crime against humanity."[6]

Boyle's idea, to introduce a divestment campaign, was a result of his fear of potential Israeli malignancy, because, he cautioned, "if something is not done quite soon by the American People and the United States Government to stop Israeli war crimes and crimes against humanity against the Palestinian People, *it could very well degenerate into genocide, if it is not there already,*"[7] an odd fear, given the fact that some 600,000 Palestinian refugees created at the birth of Israel in the 1940s were now estimated to be some five million. So in order to prevent a *new* Holocaust, this time perpetrated against Palestinians by Jews, Boyle exhorted campus groups to take up the banner of divestment against Israel and the compliant forces in Washington that enabled it:

> You students can go out, research what the anti-apartheid movement did in this country, and your predecessors starting twenty years ago, and do the exact same thing here.

You have to. If you want to see peace in the Middle East, you're going to have to go out and do something because so far the United States Government is not an honest broker. They never have been. I have been at these negotiations. I can tell you that the United States fully supports whatever Israel wants.[8]

It turns out that Professor Doyle did not serendipitously come to the divestment movement in a moment of moral indignation during which he was suddenly struck by the suffering of the Palestinians. In fact, as Accuracy in Academia discovered in a report they compiled on Boyle, the professor, whose other intellectual oddities include a belief that the U.S. government was involved in a conspiracy behind 9-11 and that we also invaded and conquered Hawaii, not only sympathized with the Palestinian cause from afar, but was one of its key strategists. As a freshly-minted graduate student, the report revealed, "Boyle went to work for the Palestinian Liberation Organization (PLO) from 1987-1989 while they were still a U.S.-designated terrorist group. Once that tenure ran out, Boyle served as the legal advisor to the Yasser Arafat-led Palestinian Delegation from 1991-1993." The report further noted that Boyle "continued to advise Palestinian leadership during his formulation of the student BDS movement in the Fall of 2000."[9]

As the tactical sophistication of the BDS movement has developed, methods were put into place by divestment proponents which helped solidify the movement, and enabled campaigns on different campuses around the country to speak in a unified, consistent voice. One of these were detailed manuals, or guidebooks, written by individual BSD groups, but shared with others so that tactical approaches could be compared, built upon, and disseminated widely among those intent on weakening the Jewish state.

To accomplish that, anti-Israel activists relentlessly seek to libel and defame the Jewish state through a campaign of lies, distortions of history and fact, and accusations that the "facts on the ground" are exactly opposite of what the radicals claim: namely, that Israel alone bears all responsibility for the absence of peace and the innocent Palestinians have been continually oppressed by a racist, brutal military regime intent on ethnic cleansing. Realistic political debate, and the actual facts on the ground, are regularly ignored and glossed over, with the only discussion focusing on the malefactions of Israel, and Israel alone.

This approach was apparently successful for Israel's enemies, since every time Israel was vilified or demonized, and its reputation tarnished in the court of world opinion, a concurrent event took place; namely, the elevation of the Palestinian cause as one deserving support from those with an interest in social justice. "Divestment campaigns and requests for institutional divestment," a guidebook entitled "Fighting the New Apartheid: A Guide to Campus Divestment From Israel" suggested, "provide debate material that places Palestine solidarity groups in the most favorable position to present their case. No other form of activism has generated as much debate and attention towards the plight of the Palestinians as does divestment. No other approach has presented the Palestinian struggle in a more positive light than does divestment."[10]

Repeatedly focusing the world's attention on the defects of Israel's fundamental being would be the most effective strategy, and, the guide instructed, divestment activists should insure that "the argument is more directed towards questioning the nature of the exclusively-Jewish nature of Israel and the racist policies that allow the existence of such a project. This argument is far more effective and winnable than that of debating specific events and facts."[11] In other words, the core purpose of the BDS movement is to weaken and sully Israel's standing in the community of nations through a campaign of false vilification, libel, and distortion of truth and history.

The charges of racism and oppression also enable BDS supporters to excuse the moral transgressions of the victim, and, as an extension of that thinking, to single out Israel and America for particular and harsh scrutiny owing to their perceived "institutionalized" racism and greater relative power. The self-righteousness BDS supporters feel in pointing out Zionism's essential defect of being a racist ideology insulates it from having to also reflect on the social and cultural pathologies of Arab states, since, as Harvard's Ruth Wisse has pointed out in *If I Am Not For Myself: The Liberal*

Betrayal of the Jews, liberals, and others seeking so-called "social jus-tice" for the Palestinians, can excuse their own betrayal of Israel by holding it fully responsible for the very hatreds it inspires. "In the case of the Arab war against the Jewish state," Wisse wrote, "obscuring Arab intentions requires identifying Jews as the cause of the conflict. The notion of Jewish responsibility for Arab re-jectionism is almost irresistibly attractive to liberals, because the truth otherwise seems so bleak."[12]

Of course, BDS supporters are silent on all of these obstacles to education and the free exchange of ideas, both in Israel, the West Bank and Gaza, and the wider world of Israel's neighbors. It is easy to demonize Israel, and certainly it requires no bravery in academia, where moral narcissists console each other in an echo chamber of good intentions, willing to sacrifice academic integrity, true scholarship, and vigorous, honest debate in the process.

10

Moral Narcissism and the MLA's Obsession with Israel

Characterized by the same paroxysms of self-righteousness as were evident in the much-maligned and tendentious academic boycott by the American Studies Association (ASA), members of the Modern Language Association (MLA) headed to Chicago during the first week of January 2014 for the organization's 129th convention. The annual meeting, which is generally attended by a third of the MLA's 30,000 members, has, as *New Criterion* editor, Roger Kimball, wryly noted, customarily "provided observers of the academic scene with a spectacle as appalling as it is rich in unintended comedy," complete with a "full range of barbarous jargon, intellectual posturing, and aggressive politicization that has infected the academic study of the humanities in this country . . . ."

But that year's conference promised even more intellectual acting out, given that the MLA's Radical Caucus proposed a resolution that called on the U.S. State Department "to contest Israel's arbitrary denials of entry to Gaza and the West Bank by U.S. academics who have been invited to teach, confer, or do research at Palestinian universities." Why the focus on Israel by these scholars of the English language and humanities? Because, as presiding officer Samer M. Ali smugly put it, as far as the MLA is concerned,

Israel deserves to be demonized for its perceived transgressions, and the "question that [attendees] will be debating is not whether Israel is violating the rights of Palestinians, but what to do about it."

The lure of Palestinianism has proven to be positivity irresistible to left-leaning humanists and literary scholars who burrow into Western thought to uncover the dark underpinnings of imperialism, militarism, colonialism, oppression, racism, and, as a result of one of the MLA's notorious past presidents, Edward Said, the theory of "Orientalism," a mode of thought which claimed to reveal the inherent racism and imperialism imbedded in Western scholarship and politics. The fascination with Third-world victimism, identity politics, and multiculturalism, coupled with harsh critiques of both the U.S. and its proxy in the Middle East, Israel, have all led academics like those in the ASA and the MLA — whose fields are, in a normal world, unrelated to these issues — to involve themselves aggressively in answering calls for boycotts, divestment, and sanctions solely against the Jewish state.

As a result of this obsessive reverence for the purported victims of Israeli policies, one panel planned for the MLA meeting had drawn considerable attention, "Academic Boycotts: A Conversation about Israel and Palestine," which, as the MLA website put it, "addresses the political movement Boycott, Divestment, and Sanctions against Israel, seen by its defenders as a viable means to end the Palestinian occupation." Besides its seeming irrelevancy at a conference for scholars of language and humanities, this odious panel had been condemned for its blatant one-sidedness: each of the four panelists is a vocal and avowed ideological enemy of, and proponent of boycotts against, Israel.

One of them, Omar Barghouti, ironically also a doctoral student at Tel Aviv University, is the co-founder of the Palestinian Campaign for the Academic and Cultural Boycott of Israel (PAC-BI), which has been relentlessly urging academic associations to institute boycotts against Israel. Barghouti apologizes for and condones the murder of Jews by Arab terrorists, having mistakenly asserted that "International law does give people under occupation the right to resist in any way, including armed resistance." He also, as is characteristic of those in the BDS movement, accuses Israel of being a racist entity, suggesting that apartheid is "alive and well inside Israel . . ; it is legalized and institutionalized racism and that's what makes it apartheid."

Another panelist, University of California's David Lloyd, is one of BDS's original supporters, whose belief it is that "If there has been anywhere a systematic denial of academic freedom to a whole population, rather than to specific individuals or to institutions, it is surely in Palestine under Israeli occupation." Moreover, Lloyd has proclaimed, Israel is committing something he calls "scholasticide" on the hapless Palestinians, since, as he wrote, "Palestinian education, like Palestinian culture and civil society, has been systematically and maliciously targeted for destruction, and "in the time-honored manner of settler colonialism, a powerful and well-armed state seeks to extinguish the cultural life and identity of an indigenous people."

The fulminations against Israel expected from this panel were not surprising given the MLA's ideological history, nor was the fact that its members had collectively already determined that this panel would be a monologue of vitriol aimed at the Jewish state, not an academic debate, and that there was one oppressor, Israel, and one victim, the Palestinians. When it comes to Israel, even academics, people who have chosen as their life's work scholarly discussion and open inquiry, are perfectly willing to vitiate what the academy is supposed to represent and abandon even the pretense of honest debate. The PACBI's own language not only confirms its disdain for Israel's side of the conversation, it specifically calls for suppressing opposing views, since Israel, in its view, is illegitimate for being a racist oppressor in the first place — exactly what is taking place on the MLA panel. "Events and projects," PACBI guidelines read, "involving Palestinians and/or Arabs and Israelis that promote 'balance' between the 'two sides' in presenting their respective narratives or 'traumas,' as if on par, or are otherwise based on the false premise that the colonizers and the colonized, the oppressors and the oppressed, are equally responsible for the 'conflict,' are intentionally deceptive, intellectually dishonest and morally reprehensible." In other words, the default position is that Israel is to blame, and that the Palestinians are blameless victims.

The charges of racism and oppression also enable the left-leaning members of the MLA to excuse the moral transgressions of the victim, and, as an extension of that thinking, to single out Israel and America for particular and harsh scrutiny owing to their perceived "institutionalized" racism and greater relative power.

One wonders why, in asking the U.S. State Department to monitor and report on instances in which U.S. scholars are denied access to Palestinian schools in the West Bank and Gaza by Israel, the MLA's resolution limited the request only to instances in which students and faculty are denied access to educational institutions as a result of Israeli policy? Would not the self-anointed guardians of academic freedom and unrestrained academic debate be concerned with similar injustices plaguing other nations surrounding the one country, Israel, where they have now focused their moral opprobrium?

The MLA was silent, for example, about the situation in Egypt where universities in November reversed their policy of preventing police from entering campuses to suppress student protests. A Cairo University student was shot in the head and killed by police one week later; at Al-Azhar University twelve students were sentenced to 17-year terms for a campus takeover, thirty-eight students were sentenced to year and a half sentences for protests, and another student was killed in his dorm by police.

No MLA resolutions were forthcoming when bomb blasts decimated the campus of Aleppo University in Syria during exam week, killing 82 and wounding 192 in the explosions. The MLA resolution also apparently did not request that the State Department monitor other instances where students are denied access to their schools, such as the September 2013 incident when security forces of the genocidal thugocracy of Hamas beat up and dispersed some 200 Palestinian students attempting to enter Egypt and travel to their universities through the Rafah crossing. Hamas has also been actively recruiting students from West Bank Palestinian universities and sending them through its dawa, or indoctrination, centers to recruit them into Islamist ideology and jihad.

The MLA scholars whose entire professional lives are defined by a love of books and learning were also curiously silent when two-thirds of over 80,000 historic books in the Greek Orthodox Al-Saeh Library in Tripoli were destroyed by arson this month, the fire set by Muslims enraged after a pamphlet insulting Mohammed was allegedly found in one of the library's books.

One might expect that the MLA would also be concerned with women's rights in the Middle East, given members like Berkeley's feminist philosopher, Judith Butler, who notoriously delivered a paper at a past MLA conference entitled, "The Lesbian Phallus: Or, Does Heterosexuality Exist?," and who more recently, and almost surreally, commented that it is important to view "Hamas/Hezbollah as social movements that are progressive, that are on the left, that are part of a global left." Perhaps MLA resolutions should be passed to help offer Muslim women greater educational opportunities, since statistics indicate that while only 22 percent of men in the Middle East and North Africa are illiterate, that rate soars to 42 percent for Muslim women. Hamas also imposes dress codes on girls, and a UN report noted that in Egypt, over 99 percent of women and girls had experienced sexual harassment in some form.

And, finally, if MLA members were so concerned with education and Israel, and the side effects of social strife, perhaps they should also have asked for State Department reports on the unrelenting rocket fire from Hamas-controlled Gaza into southern Israeli towns, such as Sderot, where over 43 percent of middle school students suffer from post-traumatic stress disorder as a result of prolonged shelling of civilian neighborhoods and schools since the 2005 disengagement.

Of course, the MLA's Radical Caucus was silent on all of these obstacles to education and the free exchange of ideas, both in Israel, the West Bank and Gaza, and the wider world of Israel's neighbors. It is easy to demonize Israel, and certainly it requires no bravery in academia, where moral narcissists console each other in an echo chamber of good intentions, willing to sacrifice academic integrity, true scholarship, and vigorous, honest debate in the process.

11

The ASA Says Academic Freedom for Me, But Not for Thee

As yet more evidence that well-meaning but clueless academics are willing to violate the central values of the academy in their collective quest for social justice for the world's oppressed, the fatuous members of the American Studies Association (ASA) passed a December 2013 resolution to institute an academic boycott against Israeli universities. Admitting that the organization consciously made the decision to ignore the academic transgressions of universities in any number of other totalitarian, oppressive countries which stifle dissent and imprison errant professors, and which might actually deserve to be censured, ASA president Curtis Marez, a University of California at San Diego associate professor of ethnic studies, said "that many nations, including many of Israel's neighbors, are generally judged to have human-rights records that are worse than Israel's, or comparable." Nevertheless, he contended, his tendentious organization would focus solely on Israeli institutions, since, as he stated quite tellingly and disingenuously, "One has to start somewhere."

It was a comment that has garnered universal obloquy, primarily because to accept that the ASA was starting with Israel and would then subsequently call for boycotts elsewhere one would have to believe that this left-leaning group, academics who

Professor Bruce Thornton of California State Fresno has characterized as a "motley crew of Marxists, squishy leftists, radical feminists, deconstructionists, social constructionists, multiculturalists, and other postmodern warriors against patriarchal corporate hegemony," would of course call for boycotts against other errant university systems in other countries. But Professor Marez hinted that was unlikely, that Israel would be the sole target for boycott, since while "the current resolution answers the call of Palestinian civil society, to my knowledge there has never been a similar call for boycott from the civil society in another country."

That may well be true, but one has to wonder exactly what was so compelling about Palestinian "civil" society that motivated an academic association to call for an academic boycott — something which such reputable groups as the American Association of University Professors (AAUP), for example, have pointedly and historically denounced as anathematic to higher education.

Those Palestinian students who the ASA pretends to care for so deeply, together with "the Israeli system of occupation, colonization and apartheid that daily violates Palestinian academic and other freedoms," something ASA members evidently believe to be solely the fault of Israel's, what circumstances of those students' current conditions are the direct result of the culture and ideology of the Palestinian Arabs themselves? Is any part of the Palestinians' lives their own responsibility, or is all of their existence defined by Jewish occupation, dispossession, and brutality, that banality of evil ASA apparently can see in no other state on earth than in Israel?

The ASA has obviously overlooked the pathologies of Palestinian society, crystallized and made more malevolent by the rule of Hamas itself, in which Palestinian children are inculcated, nearly from birth, with seething, blind, unrelenting, and obsessive hatred of Jews, so that kindergartners graduate with blood-soaked hands while toting plastic AK-47s and dedicate their lives to jihad, and older children and college students are recruited to hide explosives on their bodies to transform themselves into *shahids* — a new generation of kindling for radical Islam's cult of death.

Parents of these children the ASA cares so much about, in fact, glorify death and martyrdom and seek the death of their children if they distinguish themselves by murdering Jewish civilians. Hamas also broadcasts children's TV shows with animal characters who repeat hateful propaganda about Israel, and who encourage children to attack and kill Jews, behaviour the ASA, of course, never mentions and fails to condemn.

All of these alleged transgressions on the part of Israel are often further conflated with the ASA's view that the "brutal occupation" of Zionism has unleashed these "crimes against humanity" through U.S. complicity, that as its proxy in the Middle East, Israel tarnishes America through its misdeeds and mirrors the U.S.'s own imperialistic, militant, and anti-Muslim impulses. Thus, those ASA members who shared their ideology on the association's web site in support of the boycott were very clear in their contempt for what they characterize as an "occupation, dispossession and discrimination from which Palestinians daily suffer." "This is what the ASA is about," said University of Florida's Malini Johar Schueller. "The ASA has been interested in work on imperialism, settler colonialism, and it just seems logical that they supported this."

The language used by these ASA members is part of the cognitive war against Israel on campuses worldwide, through which Israel is regularly, though falsely, condemned for being created "illegally" — through the "theft" of Palestinian lands and property — and thus has no right to exist. The government is accused of a "brutal," illegal "occupation" of Palestinian territory, especially Gaza and the West Bank, of being a "colonial settler state," a Zionist "regime," a land-hungry nation building an "apartheid wall" as a further land grab, a usurper of property that was lived on and owned by a Palestinian "people" "from time immemorial."

In fact, many of the American studies professors who populate the ASA have made very specific analogies, not only comparing

Israel and the apartheid of South Africa, but also comparing the dispossession of the indigenous native Americans to the hapless Palestinians, who have now become the left's victim group of the moment. And many of these American studies experts harbor the same disdain for the United States as they seem to exhibit when speaking of Israel — another explanation for why an academic association whose core focus is American studies would mount such a misguided assault on a country — and area of scholarship — completely outside of their intellectual orbits.

One of those morally-incoherent scholars is Eric Cheyfitz, professor of American Studies and Humane Letters at Cornell University and, not coincidentally, one of the defenders of discredited academic fraud, Ward Churchill. In his essay, "Why I Support the Academic Boycott of Israel," Cheyfitz articulated very clearly the prevailing ideology of the ASA — that is, that America and Israel are imperialistic, militaristic powers who have and continue to exploit the "wretched of the earth," and that these countries' self-pride is misguided and undeserved. "It is worth noting in this respect that just as the myth of American exceptionalism seeks to erase the genocide and ongoing settler colonialism of Indigenous peoples here in the United States," Cheyfitz pontificated, "so the myth of Israeli exceptionalism seeks to erase Israeli colonialism in Palestine and claim original rights to Palestinian lands."

"As a professor of Native American and Indigenous studies," he continued, "I am acutely aware of how the agendas of settler colonialism — land grab being the primary one as it is in Palestine — actively decimated the Indigenous population of the United States." This kind of language in academia helps reinforce the left's notion that the imperialism of Western nations is responsible for setting up racist, oppressive caste systems in developing countries, systems that have to be dismantled through protest, resistance, and divestment campaigns. It has also formed the basis of divestment and boycott petitions that become the ideological blueprints for a virulent campaign to demonize Israel as a racist, "colonial settler" state that lost its moral legitimacy upon its founding by stealing the land of and dispossessing the indigenous Arab Palestinians.

What is more, according to the ASA's collective thinking, the United States, in providing continuous financial support for Israel, is directly responsible for the social injustices taking place in the occupied territories, and, therefore, a response from an American studies association is justified. "As an organization that represents a leading voice in the humanities and cultural studies, and indeed on contemporary issues nationwide," a statement on the ASA web site crowed, "the ASA is in a unique position to articulate its commitment to social justice and its opposition to extant projects of settler colonialism and racial exclusion, and to help lead the way nationally for other institutions to take part in this worldwide solidarity movement."

Coupled with academia's fervent desire to make campuses socially ideal settings where racial and cultural strife cease to exist is the other newly-popular impulse: to inculcate students with a longing for what is called "social justice," a nebulous term, lifted from Marxist thought, that empowers left-leaning administrators and faculty with the false ethical security derived from feeling that they are bringing positive moral and ethical precepts to campuses.

For the left, those seeking social justice, therefore, do so with the intention of leveling the economic, cultural, and political playing fields; they seek to reconstruct society in a way that disadvantages the powerful and the elites, and overthrows them if necessary — in order that the weak and dispossessed can acquire equal standing. In other words, the left yearns for a utopian society that does not yet exist, and is willing to reconstruct and overturn the existing status quo — often at a terrible human cost — in the pursuit of seeking so-called "justice" for those who, in their view, have been passed over or abused by history. For this reason those organizations and individuals calling for boycotts, divestment, or sanctions against Israel rarely, if ever, note the grave existential threats Israel faces on a daily basis, that the so-called "siege" of Gaza is necessitated by the fact that, since the disengagement in 2005,

Hamas has cavalierly lobbed some 12,000 missiles into southern Israeli towns with the specific intention of killing Jews, and that the dreaded occupation itself is the result, not of an Israeli "land grab," but a response to Arab aggression.

This rationalization, that violence is an acceptable, if not welcome, component of seeking social justice — that is, that the inherent "violence" of imperialism, colonialism, or capitalism will be met by the same violence as the oppressed attempt to throw off their oppressors — is exactly the style of self-defeating rationality that has proven to be an intractable part of our age's war on terror and part of the reason that campus antagonists of Israel are so quick to apologize for or totally ignore terrorism on the part of Arabs wishing to murder Jews as part of their "resistance" to occupation.

"American scholars now understand the physical violence that's part of the Israeli occupation; they understand the massive restrictions on academic freedom for Palestinian scholars that is part of living under an illegal occupation," said Bill Mullen, a professor of English and American studies at Purdue University and a member of the ASA's Caucus on Academic and Community Activism, which first put forward the boycott resolution. "These facts are now irrefutable to so many people," professor Mullen contended, absent any evidence that would support such an outrageous claim, based only on the opinions of like-minded ideologues speaking to each other in an echo chamber, "that the vote indicates a kind of coming to consensus around the illegitimacy of Israel's occupation of Palestine."

Overlooking the fact that Israel has clear legal rights and historic claims to Judea and Samaria, or whatever other part of the Levant Professor Mullen defines as comprising Palestine, his use of the term "occupation of Palestine" is also profoundly revealing because it confirms that either he is manifestly confused about history and thinks there was some factitious state called Palestine comprised of the West Bank and Gaza that he believes Israel now illegally occupies, or, more likely, as many in the BDS movement do, he believes that a country of Palestine existed on all of what is now present-day Israel and even *that* territory is illegally occupied by Israel — in other words, Israel itself has no legal standing and no legitimacy as a sovereign nation.

Mullen continued that he thinks "what the vote indicates is that people recognize the illegal occupation of Palestine as one of the major civil rights issues of our time globally," presumably unimpressed by the other, one would think, more compelling situations one could find in the slaughter of hundreds of thousands of Syrian civilians in the past years, the murder and mass rape of hundreds of thousands of black Christians and Animists in Sudan, gender apartheid in Saudi Arabia, stoning and honor killings throughout the Arab world, and the suppression of human and civil rights of gays, dissidents, and scholars in any number of Middle East nations. But the Palestinians, who have rejected the opportunity for statehood on at least a half dozen occasions since 1937, define for Professor Mullen and his fellow travelers in the ASA "one of the major civil rights issues of our time."

Of course, no acknowledgement is ever forthcoming from the ASA boycott proponents as to the reasons why "the illegal occupation of Palestine" exists in the first place as part of daily life for Israeli citizens as well as Arab ones; that is, that Israel's so-called "brutal occupation" and its military incursions were necessitated by Arab aggression and terrorism, and the use of defensive force has not been a random occurrence based on the whims of a bellicose, sadistic Israeli military. According to its own statement about the boycott, the ASA, in part, called for an academic boycott because the organization's members could not abide by Israeli universities conducting research to support Israel's military. "This complicity has been extensively documented," the ASA web site reads, "and manifests through direct research and production of military technologies," including the "development of weapon systems used by the occupation army in committing grave violations of human rights." In fact, by targeting institutions which help develop military technology for Israel, the ASA boycotters are not taking the high moral ground they purport to seek; they are actually helping to achieve what Israel's Arab foes have long wanted: a militarily-weak Israel whose defenseless citizens can be massacred and, in the favorite exhortation of its jihadist foes, "driven into the sea."

While they would never accept an attempt to boycott themselves — in which individual academics are tarred, not only by the institutional behavior of their respective universities, but also for the actions and policies of their governments — that is precisely what the ASA boycott does to Israeli academics and why it is so intellectually grotesque. Because they heeded the call from Palestinian "civil society" to implement a boycott against Israel, the ASA has become an association of academics boycotting fellow academics, even though, in the same way Whoopi Goldberg defended Roman Polanski by claiming he had not committed "rape" rape, ASA members are shameless in their assertion that this is not actually an academic boycott, that it targets institutions not individuals, and that, at any rate, it is critical because the Palestinian cause is so profoundly important to the world that it is reason enough to abandon fundamental academic values. "People who truly believe in academic freedom," wrote Stanford professor David Palumbo Liu with breathtaking audacity on the ASA web site, "would realize protesting the blatant and systemic denial of academic freedom to Palestinians, which is coupled with material deprivation of a staggering scale, far outweighs concerns we in the West might have about our own rather privileged academic freedoms."

In other words, Israeli scholars are too privileged to enjoy the same academic freedoms as anyone else, and especially the perennially suffering Palestinians, whose fate is clearly the responsibility of Israel. Statehood, academic freedom, national sovereignty, the rule of the law — all these are brushed aside by the ideology of the left in their pursuit for social justice for the ever-present victim, a way of thinking critiqued by James Burnham in his insightful book, *Suicide of the West: An Essay on the Meaning and Destiny of Liberalism*. The academic virtues, the "exceptionalism" of the U.S. and

Israel that ASA members dismiss and demean, are, according to Burnham, "precisely [the] ideals and institutions that liberalism has criticized, attacked and in part overthrown as superstitious, archaic, reactionary and irrational. In their place liberalism proposes a set of pale and bloodless abstractions — pale and bloodless for the very reason that they have no roots in the past, in deep feeling and in suffering."

There is another, far darker and more pernicious, aspect to the call for a boycott of Israeli universities. Because what such a boycott does is to effectively silence the scholars of an entire country — a group comprised of what the ASA seemingly defines as racists, imperialists, and colonial interlopers on stolen Arab land — Israeli academics have been suppressed and robbed of the ability to speak. For many on the left who were students and faculty members during the 1960s, and who are now populating the ASA, it was the influence of the Marxist philosopher Herbert Marcuse and his notion of "repressive tolerance" that changed the way intellectuals understood who should, and should not, have the right to free speech — in short, whose views should prevail in the marketplace of ideas. Marcuse realized that liberal progressivism could not achieve radical social and cultural change if its views had to compete on an equal plane with the conservative ideology of the Right. Why? Because in his view, the repressive force of the existing establishment could not be weakened unless its ability to control speech — and ideas — was diluted. That would only be accomplished, according to Marcuse, by favoring "partisan" speech to promote "progressive" or revolutionary change, and that speech would, by necessity, be "intolerant towards the protagonists of the repressive status quo."

The ASA's boycott accomplishes precisely what Marcuse advocated: "the withdrawal of toleration of speech and assembly from groups and movements which promote aggressive policies, armament, chauvinism, discrimination on the grounds of race and religion . . . ," but in being very selectively targeted at Israel, and Jews, this boycott parallels the actions of radical student groups such as Students for Justice in Palestine, who regularly shout down or prevent pro-Israel speakers (such as Ambassador Michael Oren at UC Irvine) from even expressing their side of the story about the Israeli/Palestinian conflict.

There is no surprise that an academic association like the ASA would call for a boycott against only one country — Israel — precisely because a large number of its ranks are steeped in a world view defined by post-colonial, anti-American, anti-Israel thinking, and dedicated to the elevation of identity politics and a cult of victimhood. That they profess to hold high-minded, well-intentioned motives, and speak with such rectitude, does not excuse the fact that their efforts are in the end a betrayal of what the university has, and should, stand for — the free exchange of ideas, even bad ones.

"People we used to think of as harmless drudges pursuing mouldy futilities," observed Edward Alexander, professor emeritus at the University of Washington, in speaking about a professoriate that has lost its intellectual compass, "are now revealing to us the explosive power of boredom, a power that may well frighten us."

12

The ASA is 'Shocked, Shocked' that its Invidious Academic Boycott Against Israel is Being Criticized

Six days after its membership voted to implement an academic boycott against Israeli universities, the American Studies Association's Caucus on Academic and Community Activism on December 21, 2013 hurriedly issued a defensive appeal for support, bemoaning, in the wake of a tsunami of backlash and censure against the boycott, what it defined as a "campaign of intimidation against the ASA."

Instead of taking responsibility for the significant and profoundly damaging action it collectively took by approving the boycott in the first place, the ASA saw the wide-ranging negative response from the academic community to their action, not as justifiable criticism of an intellectually-defective boycott, but as an attack on the organization's integrity, its stated solidarity with the Palestinians, and its overall credibility as an academic organization. The ASA also struck back with a well-worn, fatuous tactic used by those individuals and groups who have participated in the demonization and delegitimization of Israel before as part of the boycott, divestment, and sanctions (BDS) campaign: instead of acknowledging that any of the criticism was justified from the many individuals and groups who immediately denounced the boycott, the ASA reflexively, and disingenuously, accused "powerful and well-funded academic and non-academic organizations" of "mount[ing] a public campaign aimed at destroying the Association."

The paranoid notion that "powerful and well-funded" interests had any desire to even notice, let alone seek to destroy, the ASA, is ridiculous. More troubling is that this statement reveals that ASA members naively believed that they could institute a broad academic boycott against Israel, call for Jewish academics to be shunned from the community of world scholars while simultaneously singling out and attacking the Jewish state as an illegal, colonial occupier on stolen Palestinian land, and tar the reputation of Israeli scholars by making them complicit in, and responsible for, the actions of their government in perpetrating what the ASA defines as an "illegal occupation" without anyone with opposing views answering back these slanders with counter-arguments.

The ASA claimed that the wide condemnation came after the boycott vote, not because the boycott's concept was intellectually defective and ran counter to academia's values, but "because it dared to express criticism of Israel." In other words, for the ASA, the issue is not that the boycott itself was based on historical distortions, post-colonial guilt, half-truths, and a misreading of law, politics, and facts; instead, asserted the ASA, presidents and faculty members from many of the world's finest universities, other academic associations, Jewish organizations, and other clear-thinking people from around the world who loudly denounced the decision to call for an academic boycott did so, not because they actually thought an academic boycott was morally and intellectually wrong, but because they were all only interested in deflecting criticism of what the ASA sees as Israel's many and chronic transgressions.

More significant is that, in singling out Israel, and Jewish academics, to be boycotted, many, including former Harvard president Lawrence Summers, observed that the ASA boycott was possibly anti-Semitic, "if not in intent, then in effect." "These organizations falsely accuse the ASA membership of being anti-semitic [sic]," the ASA message said, "bent on the destruction of Israel. But the goal of the boycott is to show solidarity with the beleaguered Palestinians, who have been subject to decades of occupation in the West Bank and Gaza Strip."

The motivation of the boycott may well have been to "show solidarity with the beleaguered Palestinians," but several working definitions of anti-Semitism, including those by the U.S. State Department and the European Union Agency for Fundamental Rights, suggest that such actions, in targeting Israel and holding it to a different standard of behavior than all other nations — something which this boycott clearly does — is one criteria by which speech and actions *can* be considered anti-Semitic, which of course the ASA vigorously denies.

Whether or not the ASA feels it is being anti-Semitic is not relevant; anti-Semites rarely admit to their behavior, or to the consequences of their actions and speech. And the ASA's accusation that outsiders attacked its boycott, not on its own merits, but in a furtive attempt to stifle criticism of Israel, was also consistent with a pattern that David Hirsh of Engage in Britain has termed the "Livingstone Formulation," part of which is "the counteraccusation that the raisers of the issue of antisemitism do so with dishonest intent, in order to de-legitimize criticism of Israel. The allegation is that the accuser chooses to 'play the antisemitism card' rather than to relate seriously to, or to refute, the criticisms of Israel." So not only did the ASA reject some of the claims of underlying anti-Semitism in the boycott itself, it also decided that those organizations and individuals who made efforts to expose that anti-Semitism were not authentic, but merely attempts to promote their own, pro-Israel agenda. "Intimidation and frivolous legal arguments against boycott," the ASA appeal claimed, "are part of a long-standing history of repression of Palestinian human rights activism in the United States."

In its eagerness to deflect any further accusations of anti-Semitism, the ASA also deployed another favorite tactic of those wishing to act in an anti-Semitic way while disavowing any involvement with such behavior, namely, trotting out Jewish fellow travelers, generally exhibiting paroxysms of self-loathing, who support their mission — in this case, the boycott of Israeli universities.

"Many Jewish members of ASA support the resolution," the appeal proudly announced. "These include Eric Cheyfitz, who posted this comment to the ASA website: 'I am a Jew with a daughter and three grandchildren who are citizens of Israel.'" Cheyfitz, who seemingly is repulsed by both Israel and the U.S. for their imperialism and genocidal impulses towards indigenous populations, is a professor of American Studies at Cornell University. In his essay, "Why I Support the Academic Boycott of Israel," Cheyfitz articulated very clearly the prevailing ideology of the ASA — that is, that America and Israel are imperialistic, militaristic powers who have and continue to exploit Third-world victims, and that these countries' self-pride is misguided and undeserved. "It is worth noting in this respect that just as the myth of American exceptionalism seeks to erase the genocide and ongoing settler colonialism of Indigenous peoples here in the United States," Cheyfitz pontificated, "so the myth of Israeli exceptionalism seeks to erase Israeli colonialism in Palestine and claim original rights to Palestinian lands."

Another Jewish supporter of the ASA boycott was the virulent Richard Falk, whose view was that "The ASA outcome is part of a campaign to construct a new subjectivity surrounding the Israel/Palestine conflict." Falk, former Princeton professor, has claimed that "to divest from companies profiting from business with Israel . . . is to express solidarity with victims of massive crimes against humanity and to call upon Israel to respect U.N. authority and the elemental rules of international law by withdrawing from occupied Palestinian territory." Morally-incoherent views are business-as-usual for Falk, whose repeated comparisons of Israelis to Nazis have made it quite clear that he was clearly ideologically ill-equipped in his UN role as an impartial observer. "The recent developments in Gaza," Falk wrote in 2007, "are especially disturbing because they express so vividly a deliberate intention on the part of Israel and its allies to subject an entire human community to life-endangering conditions of utmost cruelty. The suggestion that this pattern of conduct is a holocaust-in-the-making represents a rather desperate appeal to the governments of the world and to international public opinion to act urgently to prevent these current genocidal tendencies from culminating in a collective tragedy."

Professor Falk, who commentator Ron Radosh has characterized as a "conspiracy mongering flake" for his wild assertions that, among other things, neoconservatives in the Bush administration may have been complicit in the 9/11 attacks, is constantly looking for ways to condemn Israel and accuse it of perpetrating genocide, and is similar to professor Cheyfitz in one important way: both have "in published word and action opposed settler colonialism wherever it exists, including of course the Palestinian West Bank, Gaza, and East Jerusalem."

Protestations and defenses aside, the issue is far more obvious than the members of ASA care to realize, and much less insidious. Those who speak back to ideologues do so not to suppress criticism of Israel; academic freedom grants the professors the right to spew forth any academic meanderings they wish, but it clearly does not make them free from being challenged for their thoughts.

The collateral notion that, in siding with "Palestinian solidarity," the ASA can inoculate itself from any accusations of anti-Semitism or even ill-advised academic behavior is another example of the defective reasoning frequently used by those engaged in the cognitive war against Israel. Feeling empowered by the moral self-righteousness they claim in pursuit of Palestinian self-determination, in assisting the victim, they feel free to malign Israel and accuse it of being the world's primary purveyor of evil.

The core issue is that just as the pro-Palestinian activists within the ASA have the right under the umbrella of academic free speech to express their views — no matter how factually inaccurate, vitriolic, or repellent they may be — those within and outside academia with opposing views also have the right, under the same precepts of free expression, to question the ASA's views, and to call them anti-Semitic, or racist, or genocidal, or merely historically inaccurate or incorrect if, in fact, that is the case. It is naïve and unrealistic, at best, for ASA leadership to think it could call for such a potentially damaging boycott, which seriously violates fundamental academic principles, without any response from a great many people with opposing views about the wisdom of such an action.

That the academics of the ASA do not understand, or choose to ignore, such a fundamental concept is troubling.

13

Women's Studies and the Moral Vacuity of an Academic Boycott Against Israel

Yet another academic association — this time the National Women's Studies Association (NWSA) — in December, 2015 followed the lead of the American Studies Association, the American Anthropological Association, the Asian Studies Association, and several others by ignobly voting to approve another academic boycott of Israel.

With the characteristic pseudo-intellectual babble that currently dilutes the scholarly relevance of the social sciences and humanities, the NWSA's recommendation to approve a boycott announced that, "As feminist scholars, activists, teachers, and public intellectuals we recognize the interconnectedness of systemic forms of oppression," that "interconnectedness," no doubt, justifying the singling out of Israeli academics for their particularly odious role in the oppression of women in the Middle East. "In the spirit of this intersectional perspective," these moral termagants continued, "we cannot overlook the injustice and violence, including sexual and gender-based violence, perpetrated against Palestinians and other Arabs in the West Bank, Gaza Strip, within Israel and in the Golan Heights, as well as the colonial displacement of hundreds of thousands of Palestinians during the 1948 Nakba."

Apparently, this rarified "intersectional perspective" has not enabled NWSA members to notice the injustice and violence currently being meted out *against* Israelis, either as a result of the shower of some 12,000 Hamas rockets launched from Gaza since 2005 with the intention of murdering Jewish civilians, or as part of the 2015 "knife Intifada" which claimed the lives of over 20 Israelis who were murdered by psychopathic Palestinians wielding knives, guns, rocks, and automobiles used as weapons.

But facts and history are not the concern of the morally-elevated professoriate. Based on this politically-charged, biased language, the boycotters expose that they have, with the breathtaking certainty that only the very sanctimonious and intellectually-elite can do, framed the Israeli/Palestinian conflict in such a way that they have determined precisely which side is worthy of opprobrium and which, by virtue of its perennial victimhood, is worthy of complete moral support. Revealingly, the language conjuring up "the colonial displacement of hundreds of thousands of Palestinians during the 1948 Nakba" reveals the victim-centric, oppression-laden world view of the NWSA, in which the legal creation of the Jewish state is framed as an unjust colonial enterprise during which innocent, indigenous Arabs in a factitious country called Palestine experience a "Nakba," a catastrophe, in which they were either ethnically cleansed from their lands or remained and now live in the oppressive, apartheid, racist state of Israel.

That historically inaccurate view is not at all surprising, given the ideologues within the NWSA who both crafted the language of the recommendation and pushed through the boycott resolution within the organization. One of these virulent anti-Israel activists, Simona Sharoni, is one of the co-founders of Feminists for Justice in Palestine, the ad-hoc group that sponsored NWSA's pro-boycott campaign. Sharoni, a professor of gender and women's studies at the State University of New York at Plattsburgh, is also, not coincidentally, one of the founders of the anti-Israel International Solidarity Movement (ISM)-linked group, Women in Black, an organization that is an apologist for the terrorist group

Hamas and works diligently to interfere with Israel's self-defense. In fact, Rachel Corrie, the notorious ISM activist who was killed in 2003 while throwing herself in front of an armored bulldozer to interfere with the IDF as it attempted to destroy a terrorist's home in Rafah, was Sharoni's protégé, making it quite clear where Sharoni stands, ideologically, when it comes to the Israeli/Palestinian conflict and how she influenced the NWSA vote.

Another toxic anti-Israel activist who promoted the NWSA boycott vote was Rabab Abdulhadi, ethnic studies professor and Director of the Arab and Muslim Ethnicities and Diasporas Initiative (AMED) at San Francisco State University. Abdulhadi welcomed the shift in NWSA's ideology to an anti-Israel position, observing that the organization previously "went hand in hand with Zionist influence in the women's movement and women's and feminist scholarship." Her enmity toward Israel is so extreme that she not only denounces Zionism and the colonial oppression she believes Israel represents, but extols the virtue of terrorism against Israelis.

In 2013, for example, AMED sponsored an event where students could make posters that said, "My Heroes Have Always Killed Colonizers," meaning Jews, along with images of the convicted hijacker and member of the Popular Front for the Liberation of Palestine, Leila Khaled, holding a gun. Abdulhadi has referred to Khaled as "an icon for women's liberation," and has lauded Sheikh Raed Salah, the leader of the northern branch of the Islamic Movement in Israel who has been convicted of funding Hamas. Abdulhadi and a SFSU delegation met with these two vile individuals on a recent trip.

Also in 2013, the American Studies Association voted to approve a boycott of Israeli universities, at that time the largest academic group to do so. When asked why, of all the nations on earth, many with abysmal records on human and civil rights and educational opportunities, Israel had been singled out for condemnation, Curtis Marez, ASA's then-president and an associate professor of ethnic studies at the University of California, San Diego, disingenuously answered that "one has to start somewhere." Just as it was very clear what the darker motivations of the ASA were in targeting Israel alone for derision, it is equally clear that the moral narcissists of the NWSA are so blinded by their obsession with the perceived oppression, gender violence, and racism of Israel that the organization could make such a breathtakingly obtuse statement as the allegation that Israel is guilty of "sexual and gender-based violence, perpetrated against Palestinians and other Arabs in the West Bank, Gaza Strip, within Israel and in the Golan Heights."

Perhaps it has escaped the notice of the NWSA experts on gender and sexuality issues that if one wanted to punish any Middle Eastern country for its subjugation and abuse of women, Israel would probably not be the first nation to come under reasonable or justifiable scrutiny for a group dedicated "to principles of human rights, justice and freedom for all, including academic freedom." Totalitarian and despotic regimes throughout the region have created an oppressive group of social pathologies that negatively affect women, including genital mutilation, stoning of adulteresses, "honor" killings by fathers and brothers who have been shamed, cultures of gender apartheid in which women are seen as property with no emotional or physical autonomy, ubiquitous sexual assault, and a general subjugation of women, complete with regulations governing behavior, movement, speech, and even requirements that women be covered by burqa or hijab.

The society of the Palestinian territories, most appropriately, might provide some examples of relevance for feminists trying to identify misogyny and suppression of the human and civil rights women, even though the NWSA saw fit to answer "the 2005 call by Palestinian civil society for Boycott, Divestment, and Sanctions (BDS) of economic, military and cultural entities and projects sponsored by the state of Israel," and have not a single negative word to say about the Palestinians and the conditions of Arab women. In fact, according to Palestinian Authority (PA) Minister of Women's Affairs, Haifa Al-Agha, women in this culture are singularly "unique," but not in the way someone with Western values might think; she was quoted in the official PA daily *Al-Hayat Al-Jadida* as observing "the Palestinian woman's uniqueness, which differentiates her from the women of the world, as [only] she receives the news of her son's martyrdom with cries of joy."

Perhaps mothers embrace this cult of death for their children because of the oppression they experience in their own lives. Zainab Al-Ghneimi, head of the Women's Legal Counseling Center, commented that a Palestinian man "believes he has bought the woman and paid for her, and therefore she has become his property and must obey his orders . . . [Palestinian] laws give him the right of ownership, based on the man being the guardian, and he is the one who commands and prohibits." This gloomy situation for women was supported by a study discussed in a November 2014 *Al-Hayat Al-Jadida* story which reported that "53% of Palestinian women have been exposed to violence — 63.3% of them once — and that 18% of non-married young women have been exposed to physical, psychological and sexual violence." Even more depressing, the newspaper reported in a 2015 article, Palestinian women feel that violence and abuse towards them is justified. The story reported that "41% of the women agreed that violence was justified if the woman leaves home without notifying her husband, while 74% agreed that violence was justified if she neglected her children."

Nor would NWSA members have difficulty looking for the oppression of women in some of Israel's neighboring countries, nations with dreadful records of protecting the rights, lives, and bodies of women. A 2015 Thomson Reuters Foundation poll, for example, "assessed 22 Arab states on violence against women, reproductive rights, treatment of women within the family, their integration into society and attitudes towards a woman's role in politics and the economy," and raised serious concerns about the status of women in those countries — all of which seemed to slipped off the moral radar screens of the NWSA.

Egypt, which was the worst offender for providing a safe haven for women, was rampant with "sexual violence, harassment and trafficking combined with a breakdown of security, high rates of female genital mutilation and a rollback of freedoms since the 2011 revolution." The country's anarchy and political instability have meant that women have also become sexual prey, with 99.3 percent of women and girls likely to be sexually harassed and "27.2 million women and girls — or 91 percent of the female population" becoming victims of female genital mutilation.

Iraq appears second in the rankings, many of the problems affecting women the result of "a dramatic deterioration in conditions for women since the 2003 U.S.-led invasion," as well as "mass displacement [that] has made women vulnerable to trafficking and sexual violence." "The Iraqi penal code," the study found, also "allows men who kill their wives to serve a maximum of three years in prison rather than a life sentence."

In Saudi Arabia, as yet another example, women are considered to be the virtual property of men, cannot go out in public unaccompanied, and "are banned from driving and need a guardian's permission to travel, enroll in education, marry or undergo healthcare procedures." The male-dominated culture means that "marital rape is not recognized and rape victims risk being charged with adultery."

Syria, which has imploded from internecine warfare and murderous carnage, resulting in the death of more than 250,000 Syrians, has become even more dangerous for women, the Thomson report found, so that in the fog of civil war "Girls as young as 12 have been married in refugee camps," and "more than 4,000 cases of rape and sexual mutilation have been reported to the Syrian Network for Human Rights," with "reports of government forces and armed militias sexually abusing women and girls during home raids and in detention centres [sic]."

Stoning to death of women, who are most likely to be victims of this form of torture, is still widely practiced throughout the Middle East — for example, in Iran where stoning is a legal punishment and which, according to the Thomson report, "has the world's highest rate of execution by stoning;" in Nigeria where stoning is a punishment for adultery in the country's 12 northern states; in Somalia where "stonings happen more regularly . . . than many other Muslim-majority countries, primarily in areas under the control of Islamist groups like al Shabaab and Hizbul Islam;" and Sudan where "stoning is a legal form of punishment for adultery under the 1991 penal code." Tellingly, Israel is not on the list of countries which have legalized or tolerate stonings, but the NWSA's high-minded and self-righteous activists still chose to focus on the perceived political and social defects of Israel and wore blinders when faced with the pathologies and cultural misogyny of the repressive nations surrounding the Jewish state.

Like other members of the academic left, who believe their world view is correct and virtuous because it seeks to create a world in which social equanimity will be realized by the downtrodden, members of the NWSA, similar to their fellow travelers in other academic associations, are content to support such intellectually dishonest campaigns as academic boycotts because doing so enables them to denounce Israel as an imperialistic, racist, militaristic oppressor.

The moral narcissist's reasoning may be defective, ahistorical, counter-intuitive, or just wrong, but he still feels good about himself. But in this world view there can be only one enemy of justice, and Israel is that enemy.

14

Only Israeli Scholars are Complicit in the Actions of Their Government?

As one shocking example of how ideologically detached the professoriate of U.S. universities has become from the thought and beliefs of normal citizens, at a 2003 "peace rally" at Columbia University held to denounce America's initiation of the liberation of Iraq from Saddam Hussein's treachery, many were stunned and mortified when Columbia anthropology professor Nicholas De Genova asserted the insidious, perverse notion that "The only true heroes are those who find ways that help defeat the U.S. military. I personally would like to see a million Mogadishus," alluding to the 1993 ambush and slaughter of American forces in Somalia.

Opposition to the government, its military policies, the War on Terror, the Patriot Act, extra-judicial assassinations by unmanned drones — all of these, at various times and during different presidential administrations, have drawn the condemnation of great swathes of academia, precisely because, like Professor De Genova, the academy has become ideologically imbalanced. In fact, a 2003 study, "How Politically Diverse Are the Social Sciences and Humanities?," identified the existence of highly-biased campuses where self-identified Democrats (liberals) outnumber Republicans (conservatives) at alarming rates, with "results [that] support the view that the social science and humanities faculty are pretty much a one-party system." The study found that the ratios between Democrats and Republicans in the different academic departments ranged from a low of 3-to-1 in Economics to a shocking 30.2-to-1 imbalance of Democrats to Republicans among Anthropology faculty, the average of the ratios being 15.1-to-1.

As the recent calls for boycotts and sanctions against Israeli universities by the American Studies Association (ASA) and the Modern Language Association (MLA) clearly indicate, an ideological imbalance in the professoriate has resulted in a collective antipathy toward Israel as the latest villain in the academic left's panoply of oppressors — this time the victim of the moment the Palestinians. These alleged transgressions on the part of Israel are often further conflated with the view that the "brutal occupation" of Zionism has unleashed "crimes against humanity" through U.S. complicity, that as its proxy in the Middle East, Israel tarnishes America through its misdeeds and mirrors the U.S.'s own imperialistic, militant, and anti-Muslim impulses.

This view of the colonial oppression by the occupier, Israel, against a guiltless indigenous people, the Palestinians, is, of course, nothing new on campus. What was unique about the MLA's and the ASA's approach was the breathtakingly Orwellian notion that not only was the Jewish state itself guilty of the many alleged transgressions assigned to it by its libelers, but a boycott against Israeli academics was warranted because the academic establishment itself is complicit in Zionism's excesses and a central element of the bemoaned occupation, oppression, and denial of Palestinian self-determination.

This fatuous notion, in fact, is one of the core principles of the Palestinian Campaign for the Academic and Cultural Boycott of Israel (PACBI), articulated in its "Academic Freedom or Academic Privilege: In defense of the Academic Boycott of Israel," which suggests that "Israeli universities . . . are part and parcel of the prevailing ideology that accepts and treats the political regime in all its aspects — the military, the intelligence agencies, the

government — as a benign feature of the social-political land-
scape." Moreover, in the post-colonial gibberish that characterizes the language of victimhood, it is *academics themselves* who facili-
tate and perpetuate the unjust occupation, since, in the PACBI's
view, "academia is, by and large, Israel's *most* effective propaganda
tool to colonize people's minds and falsely project the state as a
normal country on the world stage despite its violations of international law, and its occupation, apartheid and colonialism."

At the 2014 MLA annual conference in Chicago, delegates
considered a resolution to call on the U.S. State Department "to
contest Israel's arbitrary denials of entry to Gaza and the West
Bank by U.S. academics who have been invited to teach, confer,
or do research at Palestinian universities." The panel discussion
which addressed that issue was called, "Academic Boycotts: A
Conversation about Israel and Palestine," and included, as one of
its panelists, Omar Barghouti, the co-founder of the PACBI. His
view is that Israeli academia not only has a moral obligation to
right the wrongs in Israel, but it is a co-enabler, if not co-conspir-
ator, in the continued occupation and oppression of Palestinians.

"For decades," Barghouti has written, "Israeli academic institutions have been complicit in Israel's colonial and racist policies.
Funded by the government, they have consistently and organically
contributed to the military-security establishment, and, therefore,
to perpetuating its crimes, its abuse of Palestinian human rights
and its distinct system of apartheid." Ignoring the highly-visible
contingent of Israeli academics on the far left who ferociously denounce the same Zionism, occupation, and oppression that are
Barghouti's regular targets of attack, he nonetheless contends that
academics do not merely accept Israeli policies affecting the Palestinians, their research and scholarship helps perpetuate the status
quo. "Not only do most Israeli academics defend or justify their
state's colonial narrative," Barghouti suggests, "they play a more
active role in the process of oppression."

Why an academic boycott? Because, Barghouti says, a boycott "directly targets the academy itself as one of the pillars of this

oppressive order." And the language of the ASA resolution that led to a vote to boycott Israeli academic institutions contained the nearly identical sentiment; namely, the ASA's decision was based on a recognition of "the extent to which Israeli institutions of higher education are a party to state policies that violate human rights."

Making academics responsible for — even complicit in — the machinations of the current government, and justifying a boycott as a result — as if Israeli academics, in this instance, even have the collective power to influence and change the status of the occupation and other aspects of the Israeli/Palestinian conflict — is normally an anathematic proposition for professors, just as it would have been for the invidious Professor De Genova if Columbia University had been boycotted for the perceived excesses of the Bush White House during the invasion of Iraq.

And besides applying a perverse double standard to Israeli academics by making them liable for the actions of their government, and punishing them for this perceived liability, the idea that universities in Israel are any more influential in shaping government policy, administering the nation's laws, or overseeing its defense is itself a radical departure from what is ever blamed on the university and the people who comprise it. The ASA also made central to its academic boycott the idea that Israeli universities conduct research to support Israel's military, and that this research contributes to the continuing plight of the Palestinians. "This complicity has been extensively documented," the ASA web site reads, "and manifests through direct research and production of military technologies," including the "development of weapon systems used by the occupation army in committing grave violations of human rights."

As the academic boycotters might have noticed, and should know had they not been experiencing paroxysms of self-righteous indignation towards Israel, like Israel's universities, U.S. universities rely on, and frequently accept, billions of dollars of defense-applied contracts from the Department of Defense; specifically, between 2000 and 2006 the total number of contracts to universities rose from 5,887 to 52,667, with $46.7 billion granted to universities in 2006 alone.

In fact, many of the universities where some of the foremost defamers of Israel teach have benefitted from the largesse of the Department of Defense, and could, by the same logic being applied to Israeli universities, be condemned for facilitating and contributing to the creation of the military/industrial complex that many on the left decry as emblematic of U.S. imperialism, colonialism, and militarism, similar to how Israel is maligned for the same offenses. Those anti-Israel American scholars, then, would find themselves boycotted, even though they obviously do not share the ideology of an imperialistic, hegemonic United States.

David Lloyd, another anti-Israel, pro-boycott speaker who spoke on the MLA panel, is a professor at UC Riverside, part of the California university system that, in 2009, received $766,179,039 in defense-related research funding. That embarrassing detail about his own university system aside, Lloyd is still content with denouncing any connection with Israeli universities and the country's military. "By endorsing the boycott," he wrote, "we withhold our consent from collaboration with academic institutions that are part and parcel of Israel's ongoing occupation, furnishing its technical infrastructure and expanding onto stolen lands." Israeli academics' silence, for Lloyd, is consent — and complicity. "We continue to wait for Israel's own institutions to condemn forthrightly both the occupation and the denial of academic freedom to Palestinians."

Stanford University, as another example, which in 2011 received nearly $72 million from the Department of Defense, is home to Joel Beinin, professor of history and Middle East history. Beinin, a self-proclaimed Marxist, is a rabid anti-Zionist who singles out Israel for criticism of its varied and frequent transgressions, all the while excusing the social and political defects of the neighboring Arab states who surround it and blaming the pathologies of the Middle East on Western imperialism and the continuing colonial impact of the U.S.'s proxy in the Levant, Israel. In fact, in those rare instances when Beinin is even willing to admit to the existence of Islamic terrorism, he is quick to find its root cause with its victims, not its perpetrators. Terrorism, Beinin has wildly suggested, is a "product of post-colonial anxieties about U.S. global supremacy, and the regional dominance of the U.S. alliance [with Israel] in the Middle East," not, of course, the product of a jihadist impulse of barbaric madmen seeking to impose their own form of Islamic imperialism in the Middle East and into the West, as well.

Beinin's intent, as it is for Israel-haters worldwide, is to make any defensive actions on the part of Israel seem an overreaction, regardless of how many of its citizens have been murdered or how many threats against its very existence have been proclaimed. "According to both Ehud Barak and Ariel Sharon," Beinin wrote, dismissively, "Israel is engaged in a war *despite the spectacularly unequal military balance in the conflict* [emphasis added]," as if a nation reacting to unprovoked attacks on its citizens is compelled to insure that its enemy is equally armed and that the fight will be "fair" — something only a college professor, from the comfort and safety of his Stanford office, could possibly consider.

Another Israel-loathing, anti-American academic who shares Beinin's world view is Massachusetts Institute of Technology's unctuous Noam Chomsky. MIT, like Stanford, has also been very successful in attracting Department of Defense funding, $876,792,510 in 2009 alone, which has seemingly not impeded Chomsky from making his views widely known about how atrocious his country and its military are.

Chomsky, who Harvard's Alan Dershowitz has called the "godfather" of anti-Israel thought, when he is not lecturing on the evils of American capitalism and its ruthless lust for "empire," busies himself by blaming Israel for every problem of the Middle East's highly dysfunctional, authoritarian regimes. If Chomsky's vituperation against America has been a defining theme in his intellectual jihad, an obsessive, apoplectic hatred for Israel has more completely dominated his screeds and spurious scholarship. Like other anti-Zionists in the West and in the Arab world, Chomsky does not even recognize the legitimacy of Israel, believing that its very existence was, and is, a moral transgression against an indigenous people, and that the creation of Israel was "wrong and disastrous . . . There is not now and never will be democracy in Israel." And Israeli Jews are not solely responsible for the crimes of the Jewish state; American Jews, too, in Chomsky's opinion, share culpability. "In the American Jewish community," he scolded, "there is little willingness to face the fact that the Palestinian Arabs have suffered a monstrous historical injustice, whatever one may think of the competing claims. Until this is recognized, discussion of the Middle East crisis cannot even begin."

Chomsky draws the perverse parallel between Israelis and Nazis so frequently in his writings that, to paraphrase the wry Professor Edward Alexander, he would be rendered nearly speechless if he was unable to use the epithet of Nazi against Israel in every sentence he utters. The rogue state of "Israel has tried killing, beating, gassing, mass arrests, deportation, destruction of houses, curfews and other forms of harsh collective punishment," Chomsky wrote, and yet, even in the face of this hideous, Nazi-like behavior by Israel, "nothing has succeeded in enforcing obedience or eliciting a violent response."

In 2011, the University of Michigan was awarded almost $15 million in defense contracts, which ought to have been upsetting to the school's conspiracy-frenzied Juan Cole, whose regular rants in his blog, *Informed Comment*, take swipes at Israeli and American defense, while simultaneously excusing Arab complicity for violence or terror. In fact, according to Cole, it is the militancy of the West that causes the endemic problems in the Middle East, and makes America guilty for its moral and financial support of Israel. "When Ariel Sharon sends American-made helicopter gunships and F-16s to fire missiles into civilian residences or crowds in streets," Cole wrote in 2004, "as he has done more than once, then he makes the United States complicit in his war crimes and makes the United States hated among friends of the Palestinians.

And this aggression and disregard of Arab life on the part of the proto-fascist Israeli Right has gotten more than one American killed, including American soldiers." There is, of course, no mention in Cole's fantasies about why American or Israeli soldiers would be involved in military actions in the first place, affirming the view that it is Western imperialism and oppression that disrupt and embroil the otherwise taciturn political state of the Arab world.

The run-up to the Iraq war, Cole suggested, was simply another example of the manipulation of U.S. foreign policy under the influence of the nefarious Likud, operating in a behind-the-scenes cabal within the American government. "It is an echo of the one-two punch secretly planned by the pro-Likud faction in the Department of Defense," Cole revealed. "First, Iraq would be taken out by the United States, and then Iran . . . These pro-Likud intellectuals concluded that 9-11 would give them carte blanche to use the Pentagon as Israel's Gurkha regiment, fighting elective wars on behalf of Tel Aviv (not wars that really needed to be fought, but wars that the Likud coalition thought it would be nice to see fought so as to increase Israel's ability to annex land and act aggressively, especially if someone else's boys did the dying)."

At Harvard, which annually receives some $44 million of DoD funding, Sara Roy, a researcher at the University's Center for Middle East Studies (CMES), has been an apologist for Hamas, intent on absolving Hamas from any wrongdoing. She and Boston University professor Augustus Richard Norton co-authored an article for the *Christian Science Monitor* in which they conjured up the fantasy of a "New Hamas," a now-benign political group the authors felt were deserving of recognition by Western diplomats. And in her own op-ed in the *Monitor*, she only started counting rockets lobbed into Israel from Gaza after, she said, Israel violated some illusory cease fire of which apparently only she and the "new" Hamas were aware. In her view, it seemingly was only Israel's defensive reaction to the attempted murder of its citizens that prompted Hamas rocket attacks from Gaza, nothing else.

"Since Nov. 4," Roy wrote, "when Israel effectively broke the truce with Hamas by attacking Gaza on a scale then unprecedented — a fact now buried with Gaza's dead — the violence has escalated as Hamas responded by sending hundreds of rockets into Israel to kill Israeli civilians."

Those who have criticized the decisions by the ASA and the MLA to call for academic boycotts against Israeli universities, did so, first, because academic boycotts are antithetical to the core principles upon which the university was founded. That is, suppressing the academic freedom of one country's scholars, making it impossible for them to express their views or disseminate their scholarship, and banishing them from contact with other scholars defies what the university is supposed to stand for — among other things, an open and free exchange of ideas in an international "marketplace of ideas." That alone is reason to reject calls for academic boycotts.

But the current accusation made against Israeli scholars — which are not, tellingly, made against any other academics from any other country — that imputes a moral responsibility on Israeli academics for the political behavior of their government is particularly baleful. In this perverse assault on academic integrity, and even good sense, a whole nation of scholars is tarred with same brush of virulent anti-Israel activism, so, as commentator Howard Jacobson put it, "All are guilty by association with the heinous ideology of their country, that is to say, guilty by simple virtue of being Israelis."

PART THREE
CAMPUS CASE STUDIES

15

For Arizona State BDS Activists, Facts are Irrelevant

The eleventh-hour June 5, 2012 vote by Arizona State University's student government to divest holdings in targeted companies that supply military equipment to Israel is part of a troubling trend that exposes dangerous radicalism on campuses by BDS proponents, disguised as an effort to achieve social justice for the Palestinians. In that May, for instance, the student government at University of Massachusetts, Boston voted on a similar resolution to demand "that the UMass Foundation, Inc. divest its funds from Boeing Company and other entities that perpetuate and profit from war crimes and/or human rights violations," those illegal acts, naturally, being perpetrated by Israel.

In November of 2011, the New York University chapter of Students for Justice in Palestine, in the same ideological vein, submitted an "Open Letter to TIAA-CREF CEO and President Roger W. Ferguson from NYU Faculty and Staff," signed by over 70 members of the NYU community, which had as its purpose "to pressure TIAA-CREF into divesting its holdings in 5 key companies which profit from the illegal Israeli occupation and oppression of the Palestinians." The effort signaled a shift in the tactics of the BDS movement away from simply boycotting academics, theater groups, or hummus, and instead attempting to strip Israel of its ability to defend itself, militarily, from those foes who are clearly more concerned with the extirpation of the Jewish state than they are with Palestinian human rights and nationhood.

Of course, no acknowledgement is ever forthcoming from divestment proponents as to the reasons why "illegal Israeli occupation and oppression of the Palestinians" exists in the first place as part of daily life for Israeli citizens as well as Arab ones. There is no mention of the fact that Israel's so-called "brutal occupation" and its military incursions were necessitated by Arab aggression and terrorism, and that the use of defensive force has not been a random occurrence based on the whims of a bellicose, sadistic Israeli military.

In fact, by targeting firms that supply arms to Israel — a divestment ploy begun in a similar 2002 campaign at Columbia University — supporters are not taking the high moral ground they purport to seek; they are actually helping to achieve what Israel's Arab foes have long wanted: a militarily weak Israel whose defenseless citizens can be massacred and, in the favorite exhortation of its jihadist foes, "driven into the sea." More ironically, the divestment proponents who wish to hobble Israel's military strength fall into the morally convenient trap of ascribing the root cause of terrorism not where it belongs — with the homicidal madmen who perpetrate it in the name of jihad — but once again to Israel, due to its very presence in the Levant and its perceived racist, territory-hungry, brutal, and oppressive character.

The ASU divestment call included an additional, rather odious, element that the earlier efforts had not included: Not only did students in this case demand "that ASU divest from and blacklist companies that continue to provide the Israel Defense Forces with weapons and militarized equipment," but, they added, they would also target companies for divestment that "are complicit with the genocidal regime in Darfur."

The conflation of the Israeli/Palestinian conflict and the genocide being perpetrated against black Christians and animists in Sudan is morally incoherent, a grotesque inversion of the facts, and yet another disingenuous and repellent tactic in the BDS movement to demonize and delegitimize Israel. The killing fields of Darfur are the work of Arab Janjaweed, who, on behalf of the Bashir government, have been responsible, since only 2003, for the slaughter of some 400,000 innocents, the displacement of over 2,500,000 people, gang rapes of thousands of women and young girls, the decimation of entire villages, and a death toll that still reaches 5,000 monthly. Israel's use of weaponry and military equipment to defend itself over its 68 years of existence has nothing in common with the Bashir government's campaign to suppress and extinguish portions of Sudan's own populace, based on internecine tribal and religious conflict.

But facts are not important in the BDS campaign. What is important, and effective, is being able to utter the words "Israel" and "genocide" in the same breath, just as the BDS movement, and other enemies of Israel on campus, regularly conflate the words "racism" and "apartheid" with Israel, and for the same reason: to position Israel as an immoral state, the cause of instability in the Middle East, an impediment to peace in the region, and the source of the radical Islamism that threatens the West. And while the campus demonizers of Israel are ordinarily silent when Muslims murder co-religionists or non-Muslims, the Darfur genocide represents such a barbaric excess that it has obviously proven to be irresistible for the divestment ideologues to equate Israel's self-defense against external foes with Sudan's internal, genocidal ethnic cleansing.

More significantly, the morally-obtuse ASU students and other BDS supporters who have called for stripping Israel of its military protection — if they are truly interested in ending warfare — might well direct their concern about arms proliferation and military clashes at other of the region's states and terrorist organizations, and not the only democratic nation and reliable American ally.

Syria, for example, where Syrian President Bashar Assad's regime has slaughtered over 250,000 of the country's citizens, has also been instrumental in funneling weaponry to terrorist groups intent on murdering Israelis. A 2008 U.S. State Department report pointed out "that Syria provided political and material support to Hezbollah and allowed Iran to use Syrian territory as a transit point for assistance to Hezbollah, Hamas, [and] Palestine Islamic Jihad . . . among others, based their external leadership within Syria's borders." Syria's internal problems have not prevented the transfer of weapons and intelligence; in fact, the rate has increased since the revolt. The IDF has claimed that Syria regularly trains Hezbollah on using advanced anti-aircraft weapon systems against Israeli targets.

Iran, of course, also has a long history of funding terrorism and fueling jihad in the Middle East, and particularly for any group or state interested in murdering Jews. The State Department report noted that "in 2008, Iran provided more than $200 million in funding to Lebanese Hezbollah and trained over 3,000 Hezbollah fighters at camps in Iran," and that "since the end of the 2006 Israeli-Hezbollah conflict, Iran has assisted Hezbollah in rearming, in violation of UN Security Council Resolution 1701.1."

Speaking at a 2011 rally, Hassan Nasrallah, Hezbollah's secretary-general, boasted about the size of his group's deadly arsenal, some 40,000 rockets and missiles aimed at Israel and one of the world's largest stockpile of weapons. "We are growing in numbers," Nasrallah crowed, and "our training is getting better and our weapons are increasing. And for those who are betting that our weapons are rusting, we say that our weapons are being renewed."

Iran's fingerprints are on the weapons and armaments flowing into Gaza to Hamas, as well. A 2011 U.S. State Department report from the Office of the Coordinator for Counter terrorism observed that "Iran increased the provision of medium-range rockets" and the unrelenting barrage of rockets and mortars from Gaza into southern Israeli towns "demonstrated technological advancements, and "the rockets could also be launched from greater distances and with larger warheads.

"In addition," the report continued, "Israeli experts assessed that Hamas successfully smuggled Fajr-5 rockets from the Sinai Peninsula through tunnels into Gaza, and subsequently began producing these rockets in Gaza, which were capable of striking Tel Aviv suburbs."

If misguided divestment proponents insist on promoting a campaign to strip Israel of its ability to protect its citizens from being murdered while ignoring the lethal arms buildup in the hands of terrorist organizations and rogue states, they will expose themselves, and their motives, as being disingenuous at best, and anti-Semitic and genocidal at worst.

16

Campus Fascists and the Suppression of Academic Free Speech

Of the many intellectual perversions currently taking root on college campuses, perhaps none is more contradictory to what should be one of higher education's core values than the suppression of free speech. With alarming regularity, speakers are shouted down, booed, jeered, and barraged with vitriol, all at the hands of groups who give lip service to the notion of academic free speech, and who demand it when their speech is at issue, but have no interest in listening to, or letting others listen to, ideas that contradict their own world view.

This is the tragic and inevitable result of a decades of grievance-based victimism by self-designated groups who frame their rights and demands on identity politics. Those who see themselves as perennial victims also feel very comfortable, when they express their feelings of being oppressed, in projecting that same victimization outward on their oppressors.

Of course, the issue that most regularly energizes the moral narcissism of campus ideologues is the Israeli/Palestinian debate, and recent events have confirmed that, if anything, activists have been emboldened by the fact that their misbehavior is rarely addressed by administrations in the same way, for instance, that university officials are so quick to do when minority students feel "unsafe" on the University of Minnesota campus in a drive-by racist rant by an anonymous sociopath.

On November 3, 2015, for example, the University of Minnesota Law School sponsored a lecture by Hebrew University professor Moshe Halbertal, an expert on Israel's military code of ethics, entitled "Protecting Civilians: Moral Challenges of Asymmetric Warfare." The lecture was delayed for 30 minutes by the unruly heckling and chants of some 100 protesters from the Minnesota Anti-War Committee and Students for Justice in Palestine (SJP), who indignantly rose from the audience, interrupted, and accused Halbertal of war crimes and complicity in the previous summer's Gaza incursion. Chants directed to Halbertal included the customary libels, "These are massacres, not mistakes! These are war crimes! Free, free Palestine!" and "Occupation is a crime, free, free Palestine!," freeing Palestine, of course, meaning eliminating Israel and replacing it with a new Arab state.

On November 13th, as yet another example, the University of Texas at Austin's Institute for Israeli Studies hosted an event with Stanford University's Dr. Gil-Li Vardi, who was to present a study on "The Origin of a Species: The Birth of the Israeli Defense Forces' Military Culture." At the event, twelve members of a so-called "Palestine Solidarity Committee," intent on disrupting the speech, created a human wall in the back of the room with the purpose of not allowing the event to begin. When the vocal protesters were asked to remain quiet and listen to the presentation, they made it patently obvious that they would never even engage in dialogue with the presenter, saying, "You are a former IDF soldier, we do not listen to you."

Anti-Israel campus activists, and particularly the virulent Students for Justice in Palestine, use the victim mantle to shield their actions from self-examination, feeling that, as representatives of the dispossessed and perennially-oppressed Palestinians, they can adopt any tactic to campaign against Israel, Zionism, occupation, and purported Israeli apartheid. That has meant that at several campuses in the CUNY system, for example, SJP used the

November 16, 2015 Million Student March, a nationwide student demonstration for free public college tuition, to also slander Israel and Jews. The protest, advertised on Facebook by "NYC Students for Justice in Palestine" and other affiliate groups, ascribed, using the tropes of classic anti-Semitism, the financial situation at CUNY to its "Zionist administration [that] invests in Israeli companies, companies that support the Israeli occupation, hosts birthright programs and study abroad programs in occupied Palestine, and reproduces settler-colonial ideology . . . through Zionist content of education . . . [aiming] to produce the next generation of professional Zionists."

Giving lie to the oft-repeated, but false claim that their invective is merely "criticism" of Israel and not full-fledged Jew-hatred, witnesses and a videotape revealed a more virulent sentiment from the SJP Hunter radicals involved in the demonstration with such chants as:

"Zionists go home!"
"Zionists out of CUNY!"
"Jews out of CUNY!"
"Jews are racist sons of bitches!"
"I hope someone gets y'all!"
"When we take control of CUNY, we are gonna kick you out and make sure you don't graduate!"
"Go home!"
"Get out of the Middle East!"
"Get out of America!"
"From the river to the sea, Palestine will be free"

So when, with not a bit of self-awareness or embarrassment, these moral narcissists at CUNY accuse the administration of being a sinister cabal of Zionist reprobates intent on promulgating racist policies for the good of Israel and to the detriment of good people like themselves (people who deserve, among other benefits, education without cost); and when they ghoulishly and malignantly shriek, "Intifada, Intifada, long live Intifada," an unambiguous call for the murder of Jews at the hands of psychopathic terrorists, they should not be indignant, as they generally are, when others — both on and off their respective campuses — use their own freedom of expression to point out how lethal this ideology is, that, despite the fact that its rhetoric is draped in the language of so-called "social justice," it exposes a malignant double standard in its rage, lethality, and accusatory rhetoric against Israel.

These sanctimonious activists may well feel that they have access to all the truth and facts, but even if this were true — which it demonstrably and regularly is not — it does not empower them with the right to have the *only* voice to trumpet their ideology and to disrupt, shout down, or totally eliminate competing opinions in political or academic debates. No one individual or group has the moral authority or intellectual might to decide what may and may not be discussed, and especially young, sanctimonious students — whose expertise and knowledge about the Middle East, in particular, is frequently characterized by distortions, lies, lack of context, corrosive bias against Israel, and errors in history and fact.

College administrators regularly give lip service to the enshrined value of academic free speech and robust debate about controversial issues, and that is an admirable goal and an intellectual environment in which scholarship and learning can thrive. But university communities also thrive when they operate with civility and decorum, meaning that when it comes to academic free speech, students and faculty have the right to express their ideas, no matter how controversial, but, importantly, they must also insure that this speech takes place in what the courts in First Amendment cases have referred to as an appropriate "time, place, and manner."

Most universities, as a matter of course, have codes of conduct which proscribe inappropriate speech and behavior, and it was never the purpose of academic free speech, from either a legal or moral standpoint, to allow whiny intellectual thugs to determine which ideas could be aired and which could not — a fascistic tactic that has no place in the academy where at least the pretense of scholarly inquiry and debate still remains.

And the other, oft-expressed accusation that counter-speech to this activism is merely a disingenuous effort on the part of Israel's defenders to suppress Palestinian solidarity and "chill" the free speech of these arrogant, malignant activists is yet another attempt to neutralize and eliminate an opposing view, deeming it malicious in its intent and therefore undeserving of attention. Because they most likely know that their arguments and ideology are defective and cannot stand up to the scrutiny that an actual vigorous debate will bring, these champions of free speech in reality wish for that privilege and right to be enjoyed only by them.

"The peculiar evil of silencing the expression of an opinion is," observed John Stuart Mill in *On Liberty*, "that . . . [i]f the opinion is right, [individuals] are deprived of the opportunity of exchanging error for truth: if wrong, they lose, what is almost as great a benefit, the clearer perception and livelier impression of truth, produced by its collision with error."

True intellectual diversity — the ideal that is often bandied about but rarely achieved — must be dedicated to the protection of unfettered speech, representing opposing viewpoints, where the best ideas become clear through the utterance of weaker ones. Universities, if they truly believe that academic free speech helps achieve "the clearer perception and livelier impression of truth," must insure that rights to expression are not trampled on by those whose ideology is so virulent that they are unable, and unwilling, to, as Mill put it, "exchange error for truth."

17

Blaming the Victim: Who Knew that Identifying Palestinian Anti-Semitism is Itself Racist?

In August 2010, the Yale Initiative for the Interdisciplinary Study of Antisemitism (YIISA) brought together some 110 scholars to present papers and share ideas relevant to the theme of "Global Antisemitism: A Crisis of Modernity." The conference had as its seemingly straightforward, and productive, objective to further the initiative's primary role of identifying and seeking to explain current manifestations of the world's oldest hatred.

The need for such a conference, though distressing, seemed to be justified based on both anecdotal and statistic studies, including a 2009 report by the Stephen Roth Institute for the Study of Contemporary Anti-Semitism and Racism at Tel Aviv University which noted a doubling of anti-Semitic incidents from the prior year, 1,129 in 2009 compared to 559 in 2008.

Equally troubling were the 2008 findings of the European Commissioner for Justice, Freedom, and Security, Franco Frattini, which revealed that of the documented anti-Semitic incidents on the European continent, Muslims were responsible for fully half, a statistic made more alarming by the fact that European Muslims, based on being only 3-4% of the population, committed 24 to

32.3 times the number of anti-Semitic incidents as European non-Muslims.

None of this seemed to matter to the critics of the Yale conference, who were incensed that many of the scholars who participated were "right-wing extremists" articulating "odious views," including anti-Muslim, anti-Palestinian attitudes, about the perpetrators of anti-Semitism, according to Maen Rashid Areikat, the U.S. representative of the Palestine Liberation Organization. "As Palestinians, we strongly support principles of academic freedom and free speech," Mr. Areikat wrote, without a hint of irony, in an indignant open letter to Yale's president Richard Levin, "however racist propaganda masquerading as scholarship does not fall into this category."

Mr. Areikat's assertion that academic freedom and free speech are cardinal principles in Palestinian culture is a novel, if not delusional, way of assessing what passes for scholarly, hate-free inquiry in the territories, particularly when it comes to discussing Jews and Israel. The higher educational system which he alludes to has not been free of the perverse indoctrination and teaching of terror, either. When Hamas formed its cabinet after being voted into office, for example, 13 of its ministers had been teachers at either at the Islamic University in Gaza or at the Al-Najah National University in Nablus.

In fact, wrote Matthew Levitt, director of The Washington Institute's Stein Program on Terrorism, Intelligence, and Policy, with some 11,000 students, Al-Najah is the largest university in the territories and "the terrorist recruitment, indoctrination and radicalization of students for which Al-Najah is known typically take place via various student groups," among them the Hamas-affiliated Islamic Bloc. "Of the thirteen members of Al-Najah's 2004 student council, eight," he observed " — including the chairperson — belong to Hamas's Islamic Bloc."

Sometimes students take their ideological lead from college administrators who are not hesitant to make their political feelings know. In fact, Sari Nusseibeh, president of Al-Quds University, took the opportunity during a 2002 appearance on Al-Jazeera to congratulate the mother of a suicide bomber with whom he appeared by rhapsodizing, "When I hear the words of Umm Nidal, I recall the verse [from the Koran] stating that 'Paradise lies under the feet of mothers.' All respect is due to this mother; it is due to every Palestinian mother and every female Palestinian who is a Jihad fighter on this land."

Perhaps Mr. Areikat also forgot the efforts of other students at Al-Najah University who fondly remembered the outbreak of the Second Intifada by constructing a macabre attraction called "The Sbarro Cafe Exhibition," named for the location of a 2001 suicide bombing of a Jerusalem pizza parlor where fifteen Jews were murdered and dozens more wounded. Created not as a memorial but as an inspiration for further terror-laden savagery, the diorama included scattered pizza slices amid Israeli body parts, splattered blood, and calls to martyrdom with Koran and Kalashnikovs close by.

Nor are Palestinian students unimaginative in demonstrating their newly-found hatreds and their desire to slaughter Jews when they actively participate in student government activities. "During student elections at Bir Zeit University in 2003," Matthew Levitt recounted, "Hamas candidates reenacted suicide bombings by blowing up models of Israeli buses. In one Bir Zeit campus debate, a Hamas candidate taunted his Fatah challenger by boasting, 'Hamas activists in this University killed 135 Zionists. How many did Fatah activists from Bir Zeit kill?'"

Student school spirit aside, Mr. Areikat's principal objection to the Yale conference proceedings was "the clear political agenda behind a number of the conference's presentations and the attempt to conflate Palestinian identity and criticism of Israel with anti-Semitism," this specific accusation aimed at one of the conference's papers, presented by Itamar Marcus of Palestinian Media Watch, "The Central Role of Palestinian Antisemitism in Creating the Palestinian Identity." Yale Law School student Yaman Salahi also complained in the *Yale Daily News* about Marcus' topic, a viewpoint, he contended, that "reduces an entire people and its history to irrationality and hatred."

Mr. Salahi was also seemingly indignant that some of the conference "speakers at times seemed to conflate anti-Israel sentiment with anti-Semitism," as if the repugnant, vicious, and unrelenting world-wide assault on the Jewish state does not regularly morph into evident, and at times blatant, strains of raw anti-Semitism. This vilification of Zionism, Israel, and Jews has found particular and visible virulence in the Arab world, and certainly among the Palestinians and their supporters, in a process that Bassam Tibi, professor at the University of Goettingen and Islamic scholar, has termed "The Islamist Islamization of Antisemitism" — that is, the morphing of classical European anti-Semitism into a strain of Jew-hatred linked to Koranic texts and jihadist rage against non-Muslim infidels, and particularly the Jews.

In fact, Palestinian society, politics, and culture, despite Mr. Areikat's assertions, are demonstrably defined not only by casual anti-Semitism, but by a genocidally-inspired Jew-hatred aimed at demonizing, dehumanizing, and, finally, extirpating the Jewish state. These attitudes are endemic to Palestinian society and culture, not incidental to it because the hatreds are limited to a few individuals, and not masked or obscured because the perpetrators are embarrassed to express these attitudes publicly — as they usually are in the West. In fact, protestations from critics of the Yale conference aside, the identification of deeply-rooted political and theological Palestinian anti-Semitism is not only obvious to even the most casual observer, but an important aspect to an understanding of global contemporary anti-Semitism, precisely why the paper was presented at the Yale event.

A 2007 report on terrorist attacks by the Pew Research Center, for example, noted that while terrorism was declining that year world-wide, "70% of Palestinians believe[d] that suicide bombings against [Jewish] civilians can be often or sometimes justified, a position starkly at odds with Muslims in other Middle Eastern, Asian, and African nations." Similarly, a 2008 poll conducted by

the Palestinian Center for Policy and Survey Research shortly after a brutal massacre at the Mercaz Harav seminary in Jerusalem
in which 8 people, mainly teenagers, were murdered and some 40
wounded revealed that a troubling 83.5% of Palestinians approved
of the terrorist attack against civilians; the same poll indicated that
63.6% supported rocket attacks on Israeli towns designed to murder Jews.

Those who kill Jews in Israel are not only excused for their
homicidal impulses by Palestinian officials and society at large,
they are glorified for having achieved martyrdom by murdering
the eternal enemies of Islam. In March of 2010, for instance, with
the tacit approval of Mahmoud Abbas, the so-called "moderate"
Palestinian president, West Bank Palestinian students from Fatah's youth division helped dedicate a public square to the memory
of Dalal Mughrabi, who in 1978 hijacked a bus and immolated
herself and 37 civilians, injuring some 70 others in Israel's worst
terrorist attack. In 2008, *Al-Hayat Al-Jadida*, an official daily newspaper of the Palestinian National Authority, noted that a summer
camp had been named in "honor and admiration" of Mughrabi, as
well.

Speaking at a memorial service on the fourth anniversary of
Yasser Arafat's death, Mahmoud Abbas also celebrated the legacy
of other murderers of Jews. "The path of the shahids," he said,
"Arafat, George Habash and Sheikh Ahmed Yassin — is the path
that we cherish," that path presumably being one on which the
spilled blood of Jews helps to insure martyr status for the icons of
the Palestinian thugocracy.

This process of inspiring Jew-hatred begins early, so Palestinian children are inculcated, nearly from birth, with seething, blind,
unrelenting, and obsessive hatred of Jews and the 'Zionist regime'; kindergartners have performed at graduation exercises with
blood-soaked hands while toting plastic AK-47s and dedicating
their lives to jihad, and older children have been recruited to hide
explosives on their bodies to transform themselves into *shahids* —
a new generation of kindling for radical Islam's cult of death.

Palestinian schoolbooks dehumanize and vilify Jews, accuse them of theft, rapacity, bloodthirstiness, and duplicity, replace Palestine for Israel in geography books, and contort history and fact to such an extent that when she reviewed samples of them, then-senator Hillary Clinton suggested that the use of these texts "profoundly poisons the minds of these children" against Jews. Even children's shows on Palestinian TV are not immune to this vile propaganda and incitement, with perverse characters like Farfur, Mickey Mouse's demonic twin, who playfully regurgitated hateful propaganda about Israel on the Hamas-affiliated al-Aqsa TV to encourage children to become martyrs and attack and kill Jews, and uttered such pleasantries to the audience of children as "You and I are laying the foundation for a world led by Islamists" and the suggestion that children "resist" Israel, "the oppressive invading Zionist occupation," resistance, of course, being a Palestinian euphemism for terrorism against Jews.

Apparently, the indoctrination of children to despise Israel and Jews has been successful in creating a new generation of young people willing to embrace genocide in pursuit of martyrdom. In August 2007, for instance, as IDF forces attempted to suppress Qassam rocket attacks into southern Israeli towns from Hamas-controlled Gaza, a 15 year-old Palestinian boy, a would-be suicide bomber intent on immolating both himself and Israeli soldiers, was intercepted with two explosive devices strapped to his body. The attempt suicide mission was not even an isolated example of child abuse in Palestinian culture, and, fact, had been occurring since the Al-Aqsa Intifada that began in 2000: a 2004 study, the "Global Report on the Use of Child Soldiers," revealed that between October 2000 and March 2004 alone, Palestinian children were involved in at least nine documented suicide attacks, blindly embracing death in their zeal to conform to a culture of genocidal Jew-hatred.

Jews have been the mortal enemies of Islam ever since they rebuffed the entreaties of Mohammed when he requested that they abandon Judaism and accept Islam, a request they politely declined. As a result of that enmity, of course, the Koran and hadith literature are replete with descriptions of the essential vileness, cruelty, wickedness, and moral defects of Jews, attitudes of which punctuate contemporary thought in the Arab world. One well-worn hadith, which not coincidently appears in Article 7 of the Hamas charter, justifies the killing of Jews to help redeem mankind. "As is it written: the hour [of Judgment Day] shall not arrive until the Muslims fight and kill the Jews. Who are hiding behind stones and trees; and [then] the stones are trees will say: 'Oh Muslim, be the servant of Allah, there is a Jews hiding [behind me]. Come and kill him.'"

The Jews as enemy of Islam is a core precept that finds voice in sermons and religious teachings, and also helps dehumanize Jews as a subspecies of human worthy of extermination. In a 2009 broadcast on al-Aqsa TV of Friday prayers and sermons, as one example, the common theme of the threat of the Jews to mosques and the House of Islam in general was exhorted by the speaker that particular day. "Today we look at Al-Aqsa as it sighs beneath the yoke of the Jews," he said, "beneath the yoke of the sons of monkeys and pigs, brothers of monkeys and pigs. Destroy the Jews and their helpers."

Non-Muslim Palestinians have also exploited theology to demonize Jews, such as the curious Sabeel Ecumenical Liberation Theology Center, founded by Anglican Priest Rev. Dr. Naim Ateek, which positions the long-oppressed Palestinians as Marxist victims who must be "liberated" from the evil-doings of their Zionist oppressors. Sabeel's attacks on Israel and Zionism are virulent and unrelenting, even as the organization and its founder profess to be seeking justice for the Palestinians while assigning all blame for the lack of peace on Israel. Even more insidious is Ateek's own casting of Jews once more as the murderers of Christ, leveling the grotesque, long-abandoned deicide charge against Jews, as he did in his Easter 2001 message when he suggested that "It seems to many of us that Jesus is on the cross again with thousands of crucified Palestinians around him . . . Palestinian men, women, and children being crucified. Palestine has become one huge Golgotha. The Israeli government crucifixion system is operating daily. Palestine has become the place of the skull."

Like many of those who express anti-Semitic thought and action but nevertheless profess to harbor no enmity against Jews, only disapproval of Israeli behavior, Mr. Areikat and other critics of the Yale conference bristle when they are identified and made accountable for their hatreds. So convinced are they that they are immune from the charge of anti-Semitism because they seek a self-righteous "social justice" for the suffering, weak Palestinians, they feel no need to restrain themselves for every kind of inventive hurled against the evil they perceive in the very existence of the Jewish state. But that obsessive hatred and desire to weaken and eventually destroy Israel, even through the murder of Jews, cannot be separated from one essential truth: they despise and want to dismantle Israel not because its policies or actions are so beyond acceptable standards of nationhood, but precisely because Israel is, and always will be, the Jew among nations.

18

Deconstructing Israel: Academics Meet to Question Israel's Right to Exist

In April of 2015, faculty at the University of Southampton in England planned a three-day conference, "International Law and the State of Israel: Legitimacy, Responsibility and Exceptionalism," conceived of to "explore the relatedness of the suffering and injustice in Palestine to the foundation and protection of a state of such nature and asks what role International Law should play in the situation."

Not content with the way history and law have worked out independent of their intellectual meddling, the conference sponsors claimed that the event would have great scholarly value and " . . . is unique because it concerns the legitimacy in International Law of the Jewish state of Israel" and "will focus on exploring themes of Legitimacy, Responsibility and Exceptionalism; all of which are posed by Israel's very nature."

What does that elevated and academically-inane doublespeak actually mean? Obviously, it is clear, both by the questions posited as the themes of inquiry of the conference, not to mention the list of toxic intellectuals who were scheduled to present papers at the event, that the purpose and end product of the conference was yet another formalized indictment of Israel — nicely disguised as a bit of academic inquiry and brave new scholarship.

The problem, of course, is that each of published list of speakers had impeccable anti-Israel, anti-Western, anti-American credentials and ideological track records which essentially guaranteed that the conference would devolve into a hate-Israel rally, with each presenter echoing and building on a bucket of collective calumnies. There was, first, Richard Falk, professor emeritus of International Law and Policy at Princeton University, who once wondered aloud if it was "an irresponsible overstatement to associate the treatment of Palestinians with this criminalized Nazi record of collective atrocity?" on the part of Israel, and then quickly answered his own question by saying, "I think not."

Then there was the conference's organizer, Professor Oren Ben-Dor of Southampton's Law School, whose bias against Israel is blatantly clear in such expressive phrases as the one in which he characterized the Jewish state as "the arrogant and self-righteous Zionist entity." Another key speaker was George Bisharat, professor of law at Hastings College of the Law in San Francisco, who has promoted boycotts against what he perceived as Israeli apartheid and has linked the Holocaust with the treatment by Israel of the Palestinians. "In the West we are amply reminded of the suffering of Jewish people in World War II," he wrote, " . . . But we seldom confront the impact of Israel's policies on Palestinians."

Another on this grisly list of academics wishing to shred the existence of Israel was the fatuous Ilan Pappé, for 23 years a professor at Haifa University, whose anti-Israel, anti-Zionism views are widely embraced for their stridency, as is his "revisionist" style of history which casts Israel as the perennial villain of the Middle East. He has called Zionism "a very clear ideology of exclusion, racism and expulsion," and was forced to resign from Haifa and decamp to Exeter University in England because he sided with a 2007 British-led boycott of Israeli campuses, including his own.

What is notable, and frightening, was the primary objective of this conference; it was not, as is more customary in inquisitions of Israel's place in the community of nations, to discuss the legality of settlements, the dreaded occupation, the "siege" of Gaza, the status of Jerusalem, or the so-called legal "right of return" of Palestinian refugees. Instead, the conference sessions were designed to outline a tactical approach for questioning the fundamental legitimacy of Israel itself, to judge it as being illegal under international law and moral codes, and to investigate and recommend steps by which legal action could be instigated by the international community to deconstruct a sovereign nation, reverse history, and rebuild a new version of Israel based on the utopian fantasies of academics in the thralls of Palestinianism and a desire to achieve social justice for the perennially suffering Arabs of "historic Palestine" — a territory that these activist scholars apparently believe should never have been under Jewish sovereignty in the first place.

In short, the goal of this conference was to help achieve what Arab foes of the Jewish state have been trying to accomplish themselves since 1948; namely, extirpating Israel, although this time in a cognitive, cool war instead of through a conventional war with Katyusha rockets, suicide vests, and AK-47s. This objective, as the participants seemed not to have grasped, is not only breathtakingly presumptuous, but hallucinatory, as well, since the idea of breaking apart of thriving, sovereign democracy with the hope of creating an even better nation by blending in millions of Jew-hating new citizens is so perverse and unworkable as to expose its meretriciousness from the start.

Even when the entire world had been morally mobilized to pressure the South African regime to dismantle apartheid — a movement that animated many campuses in the 1980s — there was no effort, even then, to destroy South Africa as a nation. There were no questions asked about its right to exist, either morally or legally. The world stood up to pressure the Afrikaner government to radically change its apartheid policies and extend civil rights to its black population, but no one suggested, even though they abhorred what the white government stood for, that there should have never been a South Africa, that it was so antithetical to human rights and Western values that it had no right to have been created in the first place, or that destroying the state as it existed and transforming it into something else to suit the ideology of groups seeking social justice for the oppressed blacks was equitable, reasonable, or just.

When Israel is in the dock, however, apparently any question about its existence seems reasonable to those speaking. If states can in fact be judged by the "community of nations," or even a conclave of intellectual mandarins in the academy, and deemed unworthy of being able to continue to exist because they have violated the perceive standards of political, moral, or civil behavior, there are certainly other states besides Israel these eager intellectuals might gauge with their moral compasses.

What kind of a country has Syria become, as one obvious example, having devolved into a barbaric, hellish killing field, with over 250,000 of its citizens exterminated in an internecine conflict marked by torture, gassing, and public executions, including the deaths of some 15,000 children, one million suffering refuges created, and the social, cultural, and physical infrastructure of the entire nation decimated in the deadly embrace of civil war. Five times as many people have been killed in the past two years of Syrian unrest as were killed — on both sides — in the 68-year Israel-Arab conflict, yet Western powers have been loath to even intervene to stop the bloodshed in Syria, let alone call for the dismantling of the country and the starting up anew based on the apparent unworthiness of the nation as a result of what it has become and what it has done, and continues to do, to its own citizens.

The Southampton conference also intended to review the circumstances of the creation of Israel and how that process was essentially unjust in both affecting Palestinian Arabs who fled or were displaced from what became the Jewish state, and for allegedly denying civil and human rights to those Arabs who remained in Israel after statehood was achieved. "For its initial existence," the tendentious conference materials read, "the State of Israel has depended on a unilateral declaration of statehood in addition to both the expulsion (or, as some would say, the ethnic cleansing) of large numbers of non-Jewish Palestinian Arabs in 1947-49 and the prevention of their return. Furthermore, the Jewish nature of the state has profoundly affected the economic, constitutional, political and social life of those non-Jewish Arabs who were allowed to stay."

The transfer of populations and a change in demographics involving minority groups has occurred during the creation of other modern states, of course, often with unintended negative consequences. When British India was partitioned in 1947, for example, shortly before Israel was created, Hindus comprised some 20 percent of the population of what became Pakistan. Hindus currently comprise a mere one percent of Pakistan's population, the result of catastrophic ethnic cleansing during which millions of Hindus were forcibly expelled from their homeland and hundreds of thousands killed.

And when Bengal was partitioned in 1950, between India and E. Pakistan (Western and Eastern Bengal), as many as 500,000 Hindus were also massacred by Muslims and up to 4.5 million Hindu refugees were created from Bengal alone.

Given that the Palestinian refugee issue appeared shortly after the partition of India, and that Palestinians and their academic supporters in the West continue to assert an "enshrined" and "sacred" right of return to what is considered to be their country — including much of what now comprises Israel itself — could not a similar right of return be asserted, and demanded, by millions of Hindus who lost property, civil and human rights, and historic and cultural connections to their ancestral homes as a result of the desire to create the exclusively Islamic state of Pakistan?

The right of return for Hindus would also incorporate a right to reclaim cultural and social aspects of their identity. There are also nearly 360 sacred Hindu sites are located in Pakistan, for example, but neither is the government ready to ensure the upkeep of these sites, nor is it willing to hand them back to the Hindu community. And cultural, religious, and social traits Hindus are continually purged and marginalized as a way of insuring that Hindu identity is permanently erased and the likelihood of a return of

Hindus into the fabric of Pakistani life is minimal.

What can be done to protect the right of return for Hindus to Pakistan, based on the same moral and legal claims likely to be discussed with great passion and commitment by the Southampton conference participants when they are busy vilifying Israel?

What should not be lost on observers is that in the decision to obsessively focus on the perfidiousness of Israel, and Israel alone, the Southampton conference participants have thereby affirmed the perceived ideological superiority of the Palestinian Arab movement for self-affirmation. They have embraced 'Palestinianism' completely as their choice of a cause to defend — with the genocidal terrorism, rabid anti-Semitism, political truculence, internecine violence, and general cultural self-destruction that has defined the Palestinian cause since it was minted in the 1960s as a political tool against Israel.

This conference would not only be defined by an obsessive, pathological inclination to demonize Israel; it would also reveal a breathtaking double standard by applying a moral yardstick to Israel not used to measure the political or social behavior of any other country — including those with far more dismal records of human rights abuses, racism, genocide, terrorism, totalitarianism, and gender apartheid, among many other national pathologies.

And in making a moral exception when Israel is the target of this collective moral opprobrium, those calling for an intense critique of Israel's very right to exist — while engaging in biased, pseudo-scholarship — are not only violating some of the fundamental tenets of scholarship, but are repeating the impulses that have historically served to marginalize, demonize, and expel Jews from society — what many justifiably believe to be a new permutation of anti-Semitism, now aimed at the Jew of nations, Israel.

19

Free Speech on Campus, Depending on Who's Speaking

In what is yet more evidence that universities have become, at least where campus free speech is concerned, as Harvard's wise Abigail Thernstrom has described them, "islands of repression in a sea of freedom," the University of California, San Diego had been undergoing collective apoplexy over some incendiary racial slurs made by students involved in an off-campus fraternity party and in a subsequent broadcast from the school's radio station. The discovery of a noose and a roughly-fashioned Ku Klux Klan hood on campus only helped stoke tensions and inflame rage at the perceived racism.

Coinciding with celebrations for Black History Month, the February 15, 2010 ghetto-themed party was advertised on Facebook as the "Compton Cookout," with the suggested dress involving over-sized T-shirts, gold chains, and other stereotypical wear of "thuggish" black men; women were advised to dress like "ghetto chicks" and be ostentatious, boorish, and combative. More outrage was added to the evolving controversy when days later Kris Gregorian, editor of satirical student publication the *Koala*, with a long history of insulting minority groups, impoliticly suggested on the school's TV station that members of UCSD's Black Student Union who loudly protested the party's theme were "ungrateful niggers."

Though black, Hispanic, Muslim and many white students and administrators immediately leveled blame at white fraternity members, *Koala* writers, and other purported racists lurking on campus, it turns out that a comedian with the improbable (not to mention derogatory) stage name of Jiggaboo Jones, an African-American himself, had actually orchestrated the party for some 250 people as part of a promotional event, something he had done at other West Coast locations. But the damage had been done, and self-righteous members of the UCSD campus stampeded on one another to profess their outrage, indignation, and shock at the loutish behavior of and "state of emergency" created by a small group of students involved at a private party held off-campus.

Members of the Black Student Union wasted no time in drafting a 6-page memo for school officials (who eagerly embraced them), in which they itemized a veritable encyclopedia of demands by which, it was felt, the racist climate could be modified, with the "aim to move the university past *hurtful* incidents and improve the campus climate by enhancing diversity on the campus, in the curriculum and throughout the UC San Diego community." Cries of "institutionalized racism" and a "toxic environment" at UCSD were heard. Because the BSU felt that African-Americans were being "racially demoralized," those demands included, among others, establishing ethnic studies programs, a "rewrite [of] the Student Code of Conduct," presumably meaning a speech code that would proscribe certain speech deemed inappropriate by the code's creators, and, ominously, a mandatory "diversity sensitivity requirement for every undergraduate student."

While calling for further investigation into the specific incidents that had sparked the outrage, and promising to identify and punish the perpetrators, embarrassed school officials also met with angry minority students, promised to increase efforts at diversity, pledged more minority faculty hiring and student enrollment, set up psychological counseling facilities, met with community leaders and state officials, and even flew in Berkeley's law school dean,

Christopher Edley, to help arbitrate the situation. The president of the University's Associated Students also took the breathtakingly audacious step, with the apparent approval of school officials, of not only closing down the student TV station but freezing funding for *all* 33 on-campus student publications, not just the offensive *Koala*. The danger of racist expression meant that all expression would be curtailed — at least until a way could be found to defund the offending publication and TV station.

For Tara Sweeney, senior program officer at the Foundation for Individual Rights in Education (FIRE), a Pennsylvania-based advocacy group that defends campus speech controversies and has contacted the UCSD administration in the past and in relation to these events, the constitutional issue is very clear: publishing or otherwise expressing "a parody, no matter how objectionable to some, is in no way tantamount to 'harassment.'"

The hypocrisy of campus speech control is also evident at UC San Diego, since the extent to which officials will tolerate errant speech apparently depends on which group is uttering it. When white frat boys, with an evident dearth of social tact, make fun of black people — a clearly protected, "under-represented," campus victim group — no one on campus seems to have had the slightest difficulty in denouncing the vile expressions as blatant racism — indeed, as essential hate speech that might well be criminally punishable. School administrators have not come to the defense of the *Koala* or its editor with the argument that the views expressed, though vile, were protected, not unlawful, speech; they also have not publicly announced, as they did in 1995 regarding another student publication, that university officials should not and cannot be in the business of censoring student-run publications.

Voz Fronteriza, a UCSD Chicano-oriented student publication published by MEChA, self-described as "shamelessly leftist" and intended "to advance anti-imperialist movements and/or any struggle for the self-determination of oppressed/exploited people throughout the world," in 1995 grotesquely cheered after the death of a Latino Immigration and Naturalization Service officer;

even worse, the publication urged the murder of other Latino officials, deemed by the thoughtful editors to be "race traitors." Inter-
estingly, when those outrageous sentiments came to light, UCSD's
Vice Chancellor Joseph W. Watson was adamant that *Voz Fronteriza*, despite the odious nature of its content and the potentially
"hurtful" language, had the "right to publish their views without
adverse administrative action," since, he correctly pointed out,
"student newspapers are protected by the first amendment of the
U.S. constitution." Watson was even more emphatic and direct,
issuing a statement that UCSD, in fact, was "legally prohibited
from censuring the content of student publications," something it
apparently has forgotten since.

Nor have UCSD officials sought to suppress or even condemn
other inflammatory on-campus speech when it comes from other
protected minority groups. Amir-Abdel Malik-Ali, for instance,
the black former Nation of Islam member, convert to Islam, and
cheerleader for Hamas and Hezbollah, who has been a ubiquitous,
poisonous presence on the UC Irvine campus, has also appeared at
UC San Diego as a guest of the Muslim Student Association. Malik-Ali never hesitates to vilify and defame Israel, Zionists, Jewish
power, and Jews themselves as he weaves incoherent, hallucinatory conspiracies about the Middle East and the West. In a February
2004 speech Malik-Ali "implied that Zionism is a mixture of 'chosen people-ness [sic] and white supremacy'; that the Iraqi war is in
the process of 'Israelization'; that the Zionists had the 'Congress,
the media and the FBI in their back pocket.'"

Malik-Ali used a February 2005 event to proclaim that "Zionism is a mixture, a fusion of the concept of white supremacy and
the chosen people . . . You will have to hear more about the Holocaust when you accuse them of their Nazi behavior," he warned,
after railing against Zionist control of the press, media, and political decisions of the American government.

Speaking from a podium with a banner reading "Israel, the 4th
Reich" in May 2006, Malik-Ali referred to Jews as "new Nazis" and
"a bunch of straight-up punks." "The truth of the matter is your

days are numbered," he admonished Jews everywhere. At other of Malik-Ali's incendiary lectures, displays and posters regularly depict the Israeli flag splattered in blood and the Star of David shown to be equating a swastika, punctuated with numerous hysterical references to a "Holocaust in the Holy Land," "genocide," "ethnic cleansing," "Zionism = racism," and the oft-repeated blood libel against Jews that "Israelis murder children."

But tellingly, no officials in the UC system have tripped over themselves to denounce Malik-Ali's venomous speech and shut down those organizations which sponsored it and those publications that reported about it. They did not set up counseling sessions for Jewish students who might have been "intimidated," "harassed," or made to feel "unsafe" on campus as a result of hearing that they were the new Nazis, that the Jewish state was the chief impediment to world peace, that Jews control the media and Washington, and that Jews, who are committing genocide on the innocent, long-oppressed Palestinians, deserve to be murdered. Campus leaders did not reach out to civic leaders and other external stakeholders to help heal the wounds that this hate speech may have caused within the Jewish student body, nor did they bring in high-profile experts who could moderate between Muslim student groups and Jewish students made to bear these oppressive attacks on their religion and people. Mandatory "sensitivity" classes were not set up so that non-Jewish students could be forced to have positive attitudes towards Israel and Jews. And Jewish students did not submit a list of demands for on-campus Jewish art galleries, Israel studies programs, more Jewish faculty, special accommodations in recruiting and applications, or campus-apologies and repentance for spewing forth hateful, insulting, and odious speech.

None of this took place precisely because campuses today have a startling double standard when it comes to who may say what about whom. Either because they are feckless or want to coddle perceived protected student minority groups in the name of diversity, university administrations are morally inconsistent when taking a stand against what they consider "hate speech," believing, mistakenly, that only harsh expression against victim groups needs to be moderated. When other groups — whites, Christians, Republicans, heterosexuals, Jews, for example — are the object of offensive speech, no protection is deemed to be necessary.

So while campus free speech is enshrined as one of the university's chief principles, experience shows us that it rarely occurs as free speech for everyone, only for a few. But if we want speech to be truly free, to paraphrase Justice Oliver Wendell Holmes, Jr., then we have to embrace not only speech with which we agree, but also that speech with which we disagree, that speech that we hate.

20

Ignoring Anti-Semitism in the Name of Palestinian Solidarity at UC Davis

Since its founding in 2001, the radical campus group Students for Justice in Palestine has had as its mission to demonize Israel and promote a campaign to accuse the Jewish state of apartheid, racism, brutal occupation, and crimes against humanity, among other accusations. Its radical behavior has created a toxic atmosphere on campuses where its programs and events have regularly morphed into what has been categorized as being anti-Semitic in nature. Now, apparently in an effort to bring that same vituperative ideology to the faculty, a group on the University of California, Davis campus calling itself Faculty for Justice in Palestine recently decried a letter sent to the UC Davis administration by the Anti-Defamation League (ADL) which warned that "In the wake of the recent crisis, anti-Israel organizations are placing increasing pressure on academic institutions to engage in . . . 'Boycott, Divestment and Sanctions' (BDS) activities," and that school officials should be aware that groups were undertaking a campus campaign "all in an effort to isolate and demonize Israel and Jewish communal organizations. These efforts serve only to polarize students on campus, inflame existing tensions, and often isolate and intimidate Jewish students."

In an opinion piece that ran in *The California Aggie*, the UC Davis student newspaper, professor of English Joshua Clover and professor of Asian American studies Sunaina Maira preposterously claimed that the ADL, far from being a civil rights organization, "is an avowedly Zionist lobbying organization with a long history of attempting to silence criticism of the Israeli state," and claimed that the group's intention was actually to suppress Palestinian activism and obscure the predations of Israel, a view that professor Maira was bound to harbor, given that she is a member of the American Studies Association Council which voted for an academic boycott against Israeli scholars and an organizer in the U.S. Campaign for the Academic and Cultural Boycott of Israel.

The paranoid notion that the ADL's letter amounts to "unacceptable interference by off-campus interests" which is "baldly racist," and which somehow "chills" political advocacy on the UC Davis campus, is, of course, ridiculous. More troubling is that this statement reveals that the professors naively believed that pro-Palestinian activists can institute an ideological assault against Israel, call for Jewish academics to be shunned from the community of world scholars while simultaneously singling out and attacking the Jewish state as an illegal, colonial occupier on stolen Palestinian land, and libel and harass Jewish students and other supporters of Israel by making them complicit in, and responsible for, the actions of their government in perpetrating what activists define as an "illegal occupation" without anyone with opposing views answering back these slanders with counter-arguments and opposing views.

The faculty members' motivation was purportedly to "show support for Palestinian solidarity activism," but several working definitions of anti-Semitism, including those by the U.S. State Department and the European Union Agency for Fundamental Rights, suggest that such actions, in targeting Israel and holding it to a different standard of behavior than all other nations — something which the actions and speech of UC Davis's Students for Justice in Palestine and the organization American Muslims for

Palestine clearly do — is one criteria by which speech and actions can be considered anti-Semitic, which of course the professors here conveniently ignore or of which they are sadly ignorant.

Whether or not these Professors for Justice in Palestine believe the activism they support is anti-Semitic is not relevant; anti-Semites rarely admit to their behavior, or to the consequences of their actions and speech. And their accusation that the ADL sent its letter to then-Chancellor Linda Katehi, not on its own merits, but in an underhanded attempt to "silence criticism of the Israeli state" is also consistent with a pattern that David Hirsh of Engage in Britain has termed the "Livingstone Formulation," part of which is "the counteraccusation that the raisers of the issue of antisemitism do so with dishonest intent, in order to de-legitimize criticism of Israel. The allegation is that the accuser chooses to 'play the antisemitism card' rather than to relate seriously to, or to refute, the criticisms of Israel."

So not only did the professors reject some of the claims of underlying anti-Semitism in the ADL's letter itself, they also decided that those organizations and individuals who made efforts to expose that anti-Semitism were not authentic, but were merely attempting to promote their own, pro-Israel agenda.

Protestations and defenses aside, the issue is far more obvious than the UC Davis professors care to realize, and much less insidious. Those who speak back to ideologues do so not to suppress criticism of Israel; academic freedom grants the professors the right to spew forth any academic meanderings they wish, but it clearly does not make them free from being challenged for their thoughts.

The core issue is that just as the pro-Palestinian activists on the UC Davis campus and elsewhere have the right under the umbrella of academic free speech to express their views — no matter how factually inaccurate, vitriolic, or repellent they may be — those within and outside academia with opposing views also have the right, under the same precepts of free expression, to question the those views, and to call them anti-Semitic, or racist, or genocidal, or merely historically inaccurate or incorrect if, in fact, that is the case. Also, the radical Students for Justice in Palestine has repeatedly revealed that the true intention of the anti-Israel activists on campus is not, as it regularly claimed, dialogue and debate, but a strategy, not only of refusing to engage in conversation with any pro-Israel groups or individuals, but to actively, and corruptly, interfere with, shut down, and otherwise suppress any pro-Israel sentiment on campuses.

That type of behavior violates the concepts of academic freedom and academic free speech — rights that campus radicals prefer to exploit themselves while denying the same freedoms to others and deeming speech with which they disagree "hate speech." Spirited debate between people with opposing views is acceptable; shutting down or preventing the speech of one side of the argument, and not permitting those views to be aired in the marketplace of ideas, is not. Even though the professors claim that "the rhetoric of 'civility' has become the new discourse through which administrations seek to suppress political engagement," what thoughtful administrators are trying to achieve by calling for civility in scholarly debate is reasoned, thoughtful, and fact-based discourse — not riotous, offensive, and violent expressions, regardless of the supposed sanctity of the cause.

That may have been the motivation for the 2013 resolution passed by the ASUCD Senate, Senate Resolution 21, which sought to condemn and identify Islamophobic speech at the UC Davis. The resolution, which was passed after a controversial Ayn Rand Society event on radical Islam, "Islamists Rising," was held, defined Islamophobia as "the irrational fear of Islam, Muslims or anything related to the Islamic or Arab cultures and traditions." The authors of the resolution wished to use the resolution to suppress speech by critics of radical Islam, and were successful in categorizing any view about Islam with which they did not agree to be outside the bounds of acceptable speech; in fact, it was henceforth categorized as "hate speech" and unwelcomed on campus. Presumably, criticizing the genocidal charter is Islamic Hamas, or the group's unending attacks on Israeli civilians for the purpose of murdering Jews, could thereby be considered a type of hate speech, Islamophobic, or contrary to the accepted values of the UC Davis campus.

The suggestion that people be careful with their speech when assessing other people was apparently overlooked during a 2012 event at UC Davis at which two Israelis —a Jewish man and a Druze woman — were to speak and whose appearance was effectively shut down by members of Students for Justice in Palestine and others who had decided, in advance, that "Events like these are not welcome on our campus anymore." During the presentation, a protestor used the "heckler's veto" to silence the speakers, standing up and screaming to the podium that Israel has "turned the land of Palestine into a land of prostitutes and rapists and child molesters," and asking the speaker, "How many women have you raped? How many children have you raped? You are a child molester."

And pro-Palestinian activists on the Davis campus obviously were not concerned about civility when three Jewish students tried to speak on behalf of Israel at UC Davis at a November 2012 protest against Israel's Operation Pillar of Defense. The Jewish students were first shouted down with chants of "Leave our space!" "Shame on you!" "Fuck Israel," and "Long live the Intifada!" and then forced against a wall of windows while angry protesters threatened them with closed fists and physical aggression. The fact that this is what passes as intellectual debate about the Israeli/Palestinian conflict on campus is clear evidence that any hope of rational discourse or productive discussion has vanished. Civility has devolved into acrimony, and one can reasonably wonder, based on their language, what the true intentions are of those who defame, demean, and libel Israel in their effort to promote Palestinian self-affirmation.

Liberal-leaning academics at UC Davis and on other American campuses seemingly hold the notion that free speech is only good when it articulates politically correct, ideologically-acceptable views of protected victim or minority groups — and especially, as in the case, the perennially suffering Palestinians. But true intellectual diversity — the ideal that is often bandied about but rarely achieved — must be dedicated to the protection of unfettered speech, representing opposing viewpoints, where the best ideas become clear through the utterance of weaker ones.

For Justice Oliver Wendell Holmes, for instance, the protection of free expression for all views was essential, not only to allow discourse of popular topics, but, even more importantly, in instances where unpopular or currently-controversial speech is deemed offensive and unworthy of being heard. "If there is any principal of the Constitution," he observed, "that more imperatively calls for attachment than any other, it is the principal of free thought — not free thought for those who agree with us but freedom for the thought that we hate."

21

Defining, and Being Able to Condemn, Anti-Semitism on California Campuses

To anyone paying attention it is obvious that the California university system has the dubious distinction of being the epicenter of the campus war against Israel, an unwelcomed situation that has reached such intolerable levels that the UC Regents were forced to take some action. That effort, which resulted in a study entitled the "Final Report of the Regents Working Group on Principles Against Intolerance," attempts to establish guidelines by which any discrimination against any minority group on campus would be identified and censured, but the report specifically focused on the thorny issue of anti-Israelism and anti-Semitism as a prevalent and ugly reality throughout the California system.

The report examined a range of incidents occurring during the 2014-15 academic year, unfortunate transgressions that "included vandalism targeting property associated with Jewish people or Judaism; challenges to the candidacies of Jewish students seeking to assume representative positions within student government; political, intellectual and social dialogue that is anti-Semitic; and social exclusion and stereotyping."

In fact, the problem on California campuses, and on campuses across the country, is that pro-Palestinian activists, in their zeal to seek self-affirmation, statehood, and "social justice" for the ever-aggrieved Palestinians, have waged a very caustic cognitive war against Israel and Jews as their tactic in achieving those ends — part of a larger, more invidious intellectual jihad against Israel led by some Western elites and those in the Muslim world who also wish to weaken, and eventually destroy, the Jewish state.

It turns out that being pro-Palestinian on campuses today does not necessarily mean that one is committed to helping the Palestinians productively nation-build or create a civil society with transparent government, a free press, human rights, and a representative government. Being pro-Palestinian on campuses involves very little which actually benefits or makes more likely the birth of a new Palestinian state, living side by side in peace with Israel. What being pro-Palestinian unfortunately has come to mean is continually denigrating and attacking Israel with a false historical narrative and the misused language of human rights.

The moral uprightness that anti-Israel activists feel in denouncing what they perceive to be Israel's racist, apartheid character, combined with its role as what is defined as the illegal occupier of stolen Muslim land, has manifested itself in paroxysms of ideological assaults against Zionism, Israel, and, by extension, Jews in general. And of great concern to those who have observed the invidious byproduct of this radicalism, including the Regents Working Group, is the frequent appearance of anti-Israel sentiment that often rises to the level of raw anti-Semitism, when virulent criticism of Israel bleeds into a darker, more sinister level of hatred —enough to make Jewish students, whether or not they support or care about Israel at all, uncomfortable, unsafe, or hated on their own campuses.

In fact, a 2014 study commissioned by then-UC President Mark G. Yudof to measure the climate faced by Jewish students found that "Jewish students are confronting significant and difficult climate issues as a result of activities on campus which focus specifically on Israel, its right to exist and its treatment of Palestinians. The anti-Zionism and Boycott, Divestment and Sanctions (BDS) movements and other manifestations of anti-Israel sentiment and activity create significant issues through themes and language which portray Israel and, many times, Jews in ways which project hostility, engender a feeling of isolation, and undermine Jewish students' sense of belonging and engagement with outside communities."

If anything, things have gone from bad to worse since that study was written, and this latest report affirmed Yudov's earlier findings, and stated more specifically, although somewhat controversially, it turns out, that "Anti-Semitism, anti-Zionism and other forms of discrimination have no place at the University of California. Most members of the University community agree with this conclusion and would agree further that the University should strive to create an equal learning environment for all students."

That reference to anti-Zionism being henceforth prohibited as acceptable speech or behavior has received immediate and thunderous denunciation, unsurprisingly from those very groups and individuals who have been the worst perpetrators — groups like Students for Justice in Palestine, the Muslim Student Association, Jewish Voice for Peace, and other pro-Palestinian students and faculty. And they have been joined in their criticism of the adoption of this language about anti-Zionism by free speech advocates and others who feel that guidelines proscribing speech about a topic that many see as merely political is contrary to the notion of academic free speech, not to mention unconstitutional in seeking to censor people's speech at all.

But the guidelines crafted by the Regents were not hobbled together for the purpose of criminalizing or suppressing certain speech. In fact, one of the difficulties pro-Israel groups and activists have had in making the Regents see the necessity of a workable code for gauging what is and what is not anti-Semitism has been the difficulty university officials have themselves had in knowing when pro-Palestinian activism on their campuses has become something else, something more in keeping with the elements of classic anti-Semitism. For that very reason, pro-Israel groups had encouraged the Regents to incorporate in their report the working definition of anti-Semitism used by the U.S. Department of State, which defines anti-Semitism existing by "Using the symbols and images associated with classic anti-Semitism to characterize Israel or Israelis; drawing comparisons of contemporary Israeli policy to that of the Nazis; blaming Israel for all inter-religious or political tensions; applying double standards by requiring of it a behavior not expected or demanded of any other democratic nation; [and] denying the Jewish people their right to self-determination, and denying Israel the right to exist" — exactly the type of expressed attitudes and accusations regularly seen on California campuses.

If the UC system adopts the use of the State Department's working definition of anti-Semitism, and incorporates it into the Principles Against Intolerance, does that mean, as critics of the Principles have suggested, that the free speech of pro-Palestinian activists — supporters of Palestinian solidarity, as they like to call themselves — will be suppressed, censored, or punished? No, it does not. Pro-Palestinian student and faculty can continue to sponsor virulent Israel Apartheid Weeks, promote annual divestment and boycott resolutions against Israel, construct mock apartheid walls and hang blood-strewn Israeli flags, accuse Israel supporters of being racist and genocidal, give tacit support to murder of Jews by apologizing for Palestinian terror and chanting "Intifada, Intifada, long live Intifada," referencing the murderous Arab campaigns against Israeli civilians, and regularly also chant "Palestine will be free, from the River to the Sea," meaning that the creation of a new Palestinian state will ideally replace Israel, not exist in peace beside it. They will still enjoy their Constitutionally-protected right to speak freely and in whatever manner they choose, even if that speech is corrosive, factually defective, hate-filled, biased, historically-inaccurate, defamatory, even what we normally define as "hate speech."

The existence of the Principles and the working definition of anti-Semitism will not prevent anyone from spewing forth whatever intellectual garbage he or she chooses. But, importantly, administrators will finally have the ability to identify instances when pro-Palestinian activism crosses the line into anti-Semitism, and can publicly and immediately condemn that speech and behavior when it occurs, just as they regularly, and appropriately, do if a noose is found on campus, or slurs are made against gay students, or if students wear little sombreros at a tequila-fueled off-campus party, or when, in those rare instances, Muslim students are characterized as supporters of terror.

And because they have been unable to separate the political critiquing of Israel by pro-Palestinians from the latent and overt anti-Semitism that often reveals itself in this activism, university administrators have been reluctant to identify and condemn anti-Semitic behavior and speech when it occurs. Armed with the State Department's working definition and the other language in the Principles Against Intolerance, school officials will be able, without moral or ethical qualms, to stand up against intolerance when directed at Jewish students and other pro-Israel members of the campus community, which they have, in the past, been unwilling or unable to feasibly do.

Pro-Palestinian activists have successfully hijacked the narrative about the Israeli/Palestinian conflict on campuses, but in elevating the Palestinian cause by degrading Israel and its supporters they have unleashed an ideological tsunami replete with virulent language, slanders, blood libels, inversions of history and fact, and, often, as former Harvard president Lawrence Summers put it, have unleashed forms of expression that are "anti-Semitic in their effect, if not their intent." That is the issue here, and why it is necessary and important that, in the effort to promote the Palestinian cause and help them to achieve statehood, another group — Jewish students and other pro-Israel individuals on American campuses — do not become victims themselves in a struggle for another group's self-determination — something that leaders on California campuses, at least, can now help prevent from taking place.

22

Marching in Support of the Murder of Jews at Northeastern University

In 2012, Northeastern University's chapter of Students for Justice in Palestine (SJP), paralleling the moral incoherence of anti-Israel activists demonstrating elsewhere in American and European cities, sponsored a November 15th Boston rally in support of Gaza and, presumably, its genocidal thugocracy, Hamas.

The members of SJP who attended the demonstration, along with their fellow travelers of anti-Semites, Israel haters, and such psychologically mystifying groups as Jewish Voice for Peace, apparently were not sufficiently concerned when some 12,000 rockets and mortars were launched almost daily into southern Israeli towns from Gaza by Hamas over the past eleven years, aimed at civilian targets for no other reason than the intended victims were Jews.

Once Hamas began to deploy more sophisticated, and lethal, Iranian-supplied Fajr-5 rockets, able to reach Tel Aviv and Jerusalem, and Israel finally retaliated, as it had in 2008-09 during Operation Cast Lead, with targeted strikes against Hamas, the inevitable civilian casualties were immediately elevated by Israel's worldwide critics to "crimes against humanity," "genocide," and "disproportionate" responses to what they evidently believe to a mere inconvenience for Israelis upon whom rockets and mortars have incessantly rained down.

What was particularly revealing, and chilling, about the Boston rally was the virulence of the chants and messages on the placards, much of it seeming to suggest that more sinister hatreds and feelings — over and above concern for the current military operations — were simmering below the surface. Several of the morally self-righteous protesters, for instance, shrieked out, to the accompaniment of drumbeats, "Long live Intifada," a grotesque and murderous reference to the Second Intifada, during which Arab terrorists murdered some 1,000 Israelis and wounded more than 14,000 others.

That pro-Palestinian student activists, those who purport to be motivated by a desire to bring "justice" to the Middle East, could publicly call for the renewed slaughter of Jews in the name of Palestinian self-determination demonstrates quite clearly how ideologically debased the human rights movement has become. Students on U.S. campuses, who never have to face a physical threat more serious than getting jostled while waiting in line at Starbucks, are quick to downplay Israel's very real existential threats and the necessity of the Jewish state to take counter measures to thwart terrorism. And quick to label the killing of Hamas terrorists by the IDF as "genocide," these morally blind individuals see no contradiction in their calls for the renewed murder of Jews for their own sanctimonious cause.

Of course, the notion of murdering Jews to extirpate Israel is not a unique one, since words to that effect were regularly uttered by, among others, Iran's raving president Mahmoud Ahmadinejad, who dreamed of such apocalyptic final solutions. What is unique is the morally-defective logic that would enable otherwise sane people to justify a second Holocaust, the mass murder of Jews, on the basis of Israel having defended itself from years of rocket attacks and having killed murderous terrorists in the process.

Making the Middle East free of Jews is exactly what Hamas, the group of genocidal brutes cheered on by the Boston demonstrators, ardently longs for; in fact, Hamas's charter expresses as one of its core tenets that Israel should be eliminated and that Jews should be murdered.

Another deadly chorus emanated from protesters during the rally: "When people are occupied, resistance is justified." This is an oft repeated but disingenuous and false notion — that stateless terrorists have some recognized human right to murder civilians whose government has purportedly occupied their territory. That is clearly not any longer the case in Gaza, where every Jew was removed in 2005 and where there is a blockade in effect to prevent the influx of weapons, but clearly no occupation.

It may be comforting for Israel's ideological foes to rationalize the murder of Jews by claiming some international right to do it with impunity and a sense of righteousness. But as legal experts have pointed out, the rally participants and their terror-appeasing apologists elsewhere are completely wrong about the legitimacy of murder as part of "resistance" to an occupying force.

Article IV of the Third Geneva Convention, the statute that defines combatants and legitimate targets in warfare, is very specific about who may kill and who may be killed, and it does not allow for the murder of either Israeli civilians or soldiers by Palestinian suicide bombers who wear no identifying military uniforms and do not follow the accepted rules of wars. Nor, certainly, does it recognize the legitimacy of launching more than 12,000 random rocket and mortar attacks from Gaza aimed at Israeli neighborhoods, a violation of the Geneva conventions that require "distinction" in the targeting of opponents and clearly a more salient example of "collective punishment" than, say, the Gaza blockade itself.

The fact that so many demonstrators feel comfortable with openly supporting a terrorist group with the single purpose of murdering Jews indicates quite dramatically how prevalent, and acceptable, genocidal Jew-hatred has become, both in the streets of Boston and on campuses in America and Europe. This is clearly not, as it is regularly asserted, merely "criticism" of the Israeli government's policies; this is what many define as a "new" anti-Semitism — an irrational, seething animus against the Jew of nations, Israel.

23

Moral Dementia at Stanford and Berkeley

S tanford University students staged a public protest on October 19, 2015 to once again denounce Israel and, presumably, to honor the slain homicidal Palestinians who had so far claimed the lives of at least 11 Israelis in a recent spate of violence in Jerusalem and parts of Judea and Samaria.

The protest, organized by the vitriolic Students for Justice in Palestine (SJP), followed in style and substance an equally debased display of moral self-righteousness at Berkeley, where a similar gathering on October 13th saw protesters enthusiastically chanting "long live the Intifada" and "we support the Intifada" in other words, extolling the current homicidal rampage in Israel in which youthful terrorists have used knives, guns, stones, and vehicles to randomly murder Jewish civilians.

Students for Justice in Palestine was founded by Berkeley professor Hatem Bazian, who in 2004 called for an intifada in the United States, and has become a disruptive, corrosive presence on many campuses with its disruptive, mendacious anti-Israel activism. The Stanford chapter, like others, has as its stated mission to work "toward justice and the recognition of universal rights for all current and displaced residents of historic Palestine," meaning *only* the Palestinians at the expense of, and to the detriment of,

Israelis. This notion of "justice" has only one beneficiary in a zero sum game where justice is achieved, not by having two states living side by side in peace, but through the creation of a new Palestinian state in the place of Israel.

"We stand in solidarity with the Palestinian people's struggle for self-determination, justice, and equality," the mission statement continues, intentionally ignoring the current existence of a sovereign Jewish state and allowing that self-determination is only acceptable for Palestinian Arabs and not, it seems, for Jews.

In reality, the pro-Palestinian SJP seem to care very little about the actual self-determination and state building of the hapless Palestinians. As is frequently the case when speaking about the Israeli/Arab conflict, the discussion often glosses over the real problems of Palestinian culture, politics, and society (including its cult of death and martyrdom), and targets all criticism on the perceived defects of Israel, Zionism, and Jewish power. All of the blame for the conflict is placed on the so-called occupation, the "apartheid wall," the oppression and militarism of the Zionist regime, and the brutal humiliation and collective punishment Israel is said to mete out on a daily basis upon the wholly innocent Palestinians.

The chronic truculence of the Palestinians in having rejected opportunities for statehood on multiple occasions, of course, is never mentioned, and other causes that have supposedly contributed to Palestinian suffering are pointed to instead. One of the placards at the Stanford rally, for instance, read "Settler colonialism has killed 7 Israelis and 32 Palestinians this month," naively assigning blame for the recent carnage, not where it belongs — with the homicidal young teenagers and others who barbarically murdered or tried to murder Jewish parents in front of their children, or riding at buses, or standing on street corners — but with the disingenuous and factually defective charge of "settler colonialism."

At Berkeley, protesters were shouting out the oft-heard slogan, "From the river to the sea, Palestine will be free." That phrase suggests the same situation that a rekindled Intifada would help bring about, namely, that if the fictive nation of "Palestine" is "liberated," is free, there will, of course, be no Israel between the Jordan River and Mediterranean — and no Jews.

Those students who lend their moral support to terrorism, and who continually see the existence of "grievance-based violence" as a justifiable tool of the oppressed, have helped introduce a sick moral relativism into discussions about radical Islam and Palestinianism, not to mention Israel's right to protect its citizens from being slaughtered.

That those students purporting to care about attaining social justice for the downtrodden are willing to let another group of people be murdered as part of that well-meaning campaign demonstrates quite clearly that a moral dementia has enveloped the anti-Israel crowd in a way that is both frightening and tragic, and we should see it for what it really is.

24

Pseudo-Scholarship, Intersectionality, and Blood Libels Against Israel

Jews have been accused of harming and murdering non-Jews since the twelfth century in England, when Jewish convert to Catholicism, Theobald of Cambridge, mendaciously announced that European Jews ritually slaughtered Christian children each year and drank their blood during Passover season.

That medieval blood libel, largely abandoned in the contemporary West, does, however, still appear as part of Arab world's vilification of Jews — now transmogrified into a slander against Israel, the Jew of nations. But in the regular chorus of defamation against Israel by a world infected with Palestinianism, a new, more odious trend has shown itself: the blood libel has been revivified; however, to position Israel (and by extension Jews) as demonic agents in the community of nations, the primitive fantasies of the blood libel are now masked with a veneer of academic scholarship.

On February 3, 2016, for example, Jasbir K. Puar, Associate Professor of Women's and Gender Studies at Rutgers University delivered a lecture at Vassar College, "Inhumanist Biopolitics: How Palestine Matters," sponsored, shamefully, not by radical student groups but by the school's American Studies Department and departments of Political Science, Religion, and English, and the programs of Africana Studies, International Studies, Women's and Gender Studies, and Jewish Studies.

The lecture examined "the use of technologies of measure to manufacture a 'remote control' occupation, one that produces a different version of Israeli 'home invasions' through the maiming and stunting of population. If Gaza, for example, is indeed the world's largest 'open air prison' and an experimental lab for Israeli military apparatuses . . , what kinds of fantasies (about power, about bodies, about resistance, about politics) are driving this project?" In other words, Professor Puar's central thesis was that Israeli military tactics involve the deliberate the "stunting, "maiming," physical disabling, and scientific experimenting with Palestinian lives, an outrageous resurrection of the classic anti-Semitic trope that Jews purposely, and sadistically, harm and kill non-Jews.

Puar, who writes on "gay and lesbian tourism, queer theory, theories of intersectionality, affect, homonationalism, and pink-washing" (the perverse theory that Israel trumpets its broad support of LGBT rights to obscure its mistreatment of the Palestinians), is also, unsurprisingly, on the Advisory Board of the U.S. Campaign for the Academic and Cultural Boycott of Israel, a leading coordinator of Boycott, Divestment and Sanctions (BDS) movement on campuses.

More alarming than her open support of the BDS movement, and her vocal support for Vassar's own ongoing BDS campaign, was Puar's explicit support for terrorism against Israeli citizens as a corollary aspect of the BDS movement. BDS "is such a minor piece of how Palestine is going to be liberated, [and] we need BDS as part of *organized resistance and armed resistance* in Palestine as well," she said. "There is no other way the situation is going to change [emphasis added]."

When pro-Palestinian activists and critics of Israel, such as Professor Puar, repeat the claim that Palestinians somehow have an internationally-recognized legal "right" to resist so-called occupation through violent means, they are both legitimizing that terror and helping to insure that its lethal use by Israel's enemies will continue unabated. Those who lend their moral support to terrorism, and who continually see the existence of "grievance-based violence" as a justifiable tool of the oppressed, have made themselves apologists for radical Islam and terrorism, not to mention questioning Israel's right to protect its citizens from being slaughtered.

In her speech, Professor Puar also leveled a grotesque, never-proven charge against Israel, namely, that its soldiers harvest organs from Palestinians it has killed, charges that have been made by others, without any substantiation, including after the deadly 2010 earthquake in Haiti where Israeli experts assisted with search and rescue operations and were later accused of harvesting organs from Haitian victims of the natural disaster. "Protests, stabbings, flagrant refusals of IDF control, clashes and revived commitment to a peoples' rumble," Puar said, "have resulted in more than 120 deaths by field assassinations of young Palestinian men, largely between the ages of 12 to 16, by IDF soldiers. On January 1st, 2016, the Israeli government returns 17 bodies of these youth that purportedly lay in a morgue in West Jerusalem for two months. No explanation has ever been given for their detention." And without offering any proof or citing the source of her information, Puar then mendaciously claimed that "Some speculate that the bodies were mined for organs for scientific research."

Puar continued with spurious charges against the Israeli military, leaving out entirely any context in which Palestinian terrorism, including the reality that the "field assassinations" to which Puar so carelessly refers took place during current "knife Intifada," in which psychotic Arabs randomly sought to, and were often successful in, murdering Israeli civilians, a jihad that necessitated military intervention by the IDF.

She also accused Israel of randomly, and recklessly, targeting medical facilities and other infrastructure as a deadly way "to provide the bare minimum for survival, but minimal enough to attempt to defeat or strip resistance" where " . . . the target here is not just life itself but resistance itself." Puar's view that Israel's military operations are characterized by disproportionality and a disregard for human life — even of its mortal foes — was in fact totally contradicted by a report prepared by The High-Level International Military Group on the Gaza Conflict in 2014, which found that "during Operation Protective Edge . . . Israel not only met a reasonable international standard of observance of the laws of armed conflict, but in many cases significantly exceeded that standard."

In her speech the central, grotesque theme was that Israel is also intent on "Targeting youth, not for death but for stunting" as a "tactic that seeks to render impotent any future resistance." Even Israel's attempt to *not* kill Palestinians, but maim them, is given a perverse character by Puar, who contended that "Maiming masquerades as let live when in fact it acts as will not let die," and that this technique, as part of a sadistic, imperialistic militancy on the part of Israel, "is used to achieve . . . tactical aims of settler colonialism."

Professor Puar is a feminist and gender studies specialist, and one may wonder why she has invested so much of her academic energy in vilifying Israel. But her obsession with Israel and its various perceived modes of oppression and brutality toward a weak, innocent victim group is consistent with many academics in the humanities and social sciences who increasingly find a linkage as they seek to affirm the rights of the victimized and name the villains responsible for this oppression. The more that seemingly unrelated instances of oppression can be conflated, it is thought, the greater the ability to confront these oppressors and neutralize the negative effect they have on society. This trend has been called "intersectionality," and it has meant that someone who is a gender studies professor, or queer theorist, or American studies expert can, with no actual knowledge or expertise about the Middle East, readily pontificate on the many social pathologies of Israel, based on its perceived role as a racist, colonial oppressor of an innocent indigenous population of Arab victims. For Professor Puar and her fellow travelers, to know one victim group is to know *any* victim group — with Israel being a tempting and habitual target of their opprobrium.

Thus, for instance, supporters of the Black Lives Matter movement have often linked racism and police violence "from Ferguson to Palestine," as their placards have announced, making Israel somehow complicit in American racism and police brutality and creating a moral equivalency between Palestinian and black American victims of brutality. "Intersectionality holds that various forms of oppression," said David Bernstein, president and CEO of the Jewish Council for Public Affairs, "constitute an intersecting system of oppression . . , [and] the BDS movement has successfully injected the anti-Israel cause into these intersecting forms of oppression and itself into the interlocking communities of people who hold by them."

Supporters of the Palestinian cause have come to accept the fact that Israel will not be defeated through the use of traditional tools of warfare. Instead, the Jewish state's enemies, abetted by the academic and media elites in the West, have begun to use different, but equally dangerous, tactics to delegitimize and eventually destroy Israel in a cognitive war. By dressing up old hatreds against Jews, combined with a purported goal of seeking social justice for the oppressed, and repackaging ugly biases as seemingly pure scholarship, Israel's ideological foes have found an effective, but odious, way to insure that Israel is still accused of fostering social chaos and bringing harm to non-Jews — the ugly trope that Jews still exhibit murderous, sadistic militarism and racism against non-Jews, now with the Palestinian Arabs as victims.

25

Ideology Parading as Scholarship at Brandeis

Seeming to confirm the notion that hatred of Israel can infect even a school dedicated to educating Jewish college students, Brandeis University hosted a troubling series of events during the tellingly-named "Israeli Occupation Awareness Week," held in November 2010 and advertised on a Facebook page with a vile composite photograph of Louis D. Brandeis with a keffiyeh draped around his neck. Co-sponsored by the radical group Students for Justice in Palestine and the self-righteous Jewish Voice for Peace, the events once again demonstrated the moral incoherence seen on college campuses whenever there is debate about the Israeli/ Palestinian conflict.

Brandeis University, of course, was named for Justice Brandeis, who, though he was a secular Jew raised in the comfort of the social elite, still asserted that "Zionism finds in it, for the Jews, a reason to raise their heads, and, taking their stand upon the past, to gaze straightforwardly into the future," a notion that might well have informed the thinking on the University's campus for much of the 20th century.

But that was before campus ideology was hijacked by the left's obsessive reverence for something that came to be known as "social justice," a leftist way of thinking that informs the very educational mission of Brandeis today (or "social action," a term which Brandeis uses in its Diversity Statement). Students, and liberal faculty on campus, as well, are urged to advocate for social and economic goals described in decidedly liberal intellectual formulations such as 'social and economic justice,' 'distributive justice,' and 'the global interconnections of oppression,' this latter view ideal for conflating, at least in liberal imaginations, the shared complicity of America and Israel in their long-term oppression of the indigenous people of Palestine and the "occupation" of their land.

So it should come as no surprise that the list of guest speakers for the toxic "Israeli Occupation Awareness Week" included a galaxy of notorious anti-Israel Jew-haters whose contribution to the week's awareness-raising would not be an animated discussion of alternate views of the Israeli/Palestine conflict, but a one-sided, biased, inflammatory series of exhortations calling for the continued murder of Jews in the name of "resistance" and the eventual extirpation of the Jewish state.

Headlining at Brandeis was a speech entitled "Israel's Escalating Policies of Apartheid" by the intellectually notorious Noam Chomsky, who clearly lives in an academic netherworld of political fantasies, conspiracies, and intellectually-disingenuous distortions of history and fact. If Chomsky's vituperation against America has been a defining theme in his intellectual jihad, an obsessive, apoplectic hatred for Israel has more completely dominated his screeds and spurious scholarship. Like other anti-Zionists in the West and in the Arab world, Chomsky does not even recognize the legitimacy of Israel, believing that its very existence was, and is, a moral transgression against an indigenous people, and that the creation of Israel was "wrong and disastrous . . . There is not now and never will be democracy in Israel."

Chomsky denounces Israel's identity as a Jewish state as being essentially racist on its face, and decries the very notion of its Jewishness as necessarily violating the concept of social equity by being exclusionary and elitist. While he is happy to, and regularly does, ignore the murder of Jews by Arabs, Chomsky never hesitates to point to the perfidy of Israel, and its barbarous assault on its Arab neighbors who, in his socialist fantasies, wish for nothing more than to live in peace.

A second odious guest at the Brandeis event was Alice Rothchild, a physician, activist, and member of Jewish Voice for Peace, a far-left, pro-Palestinian group that seeks to weaken Israel for it alleged human-rights violations through targeted boycotts, divestment, and sanctions. Its stated goal in promoting a divestment campaign is to prevent companies from "[profiting] from the Israeli occupation of the Gaza Strip and the West Bank, including East Jerusalem," and while it regularly excuses the murderous behavior of Palestinians, it scolds the U.S. to "stop supporting repressive policies in Israel and elsewhere."

Rothchild not only believes that Israel has no moral right to exist as a Jewish state, she has written that Jews are not even a people, so of course are undeserving of a state of their own. "It is important to stress that the historic hatred of Jews was traditionally not part of the Arabic-speaking world until Jews began to claim Palestine for themselves," she wrote in a letter to the *Boston Globe*, "and that the 'return of land to Jewish people' involves a particular reading of history, obliterates the several thousand years of others' claims to this land, and ignores the academic questions regarding the probable multiple origins of the 'Jewish people.'"

Rounding off the one-sided dialogue about the faults inherent in Israel's so-called occupation of the West Bank was Diana Buttu, whose reason for being at the Brandeis event is her credentials as a former legal advisor to the Palestinian Liberation Organization, and whose stream of anti-Israel propaganda is characterized by misstatements, contortions of history, and lies. In 2009, for instance, after some 6000 rockets had rained into southern Israeli towns from Gaza, Buttu repeatedly claimed "that none of these rockets actually [had] an explosive head on them, unlike the Israeli weaponry." And the actual lethality of the "crude, homemade rockets" aside, "the reason that they have been launched," she asserted, is not because of any genocidal impulses on the part of Hamas, but "is because of the fact that Israel has maintained a siege and a blockade against the Gaza Strip for the past three years, in addition to military operations in the Gaza Strip" — in other words, the rocket attacks were Israel's fault. In a CNN interview with Rick Sanchez, Buttu also suggested that Israel's initiatives to protect its citizenry from being murdered by random terrorist attack were unjustified. "Israel has a right to protect itself," she admitted, but "it doesn't have a right to protect its occupation. And what it has done is, it's protecting its occupation."

Of course, if the organizers of Brandeis' Israeli Occupation Awareness Week actually wanted different views of the situation on the ground in Israel, the West Bank, and Gaza, they might have invited participants with opposing, alternate views. Such speakers might call into question the repeated, though mistaken, references to the West Bank and Gaza, as well as East Jerusalem, as "Arab" land, encumbered only by Israeli oppression, the dreaded occupation, and those pesky settlers.

That is a convenient fable, as is the fictive people that the Palestinians have been conjured up to be: an indigenous nation that had sovereignty, a coherent society, leadership, and some form of continuous government — none of which, obviously, have ever existed. More to the point, it is historically and legally incorrect to overlook the fact that not only all of the land that is current-day Israel, but also Gaza, the West Bank, and, in fact, the land east of the Jordan River that became Jordan, is part of the land granted to the Jews as part of the League of Nations Palestine Mandate, and that no "occupation" by Israel therefore exists. According to Eugene V. Rostow, the late legal scholar and one of the authors of UN Security Council Resolution 242 written after the 1967 war to outline peace negotiations, "the Jewish right of settlement in Palestine west of the Jordan River, that is, in Israel, the West Bank, Jerusalem, and the Gaza Strip, was made unassailable.

So if the Brandeis community wanted to make itself collectively feel better by seeking to bring "social justice" to the long-suffering Palestinians by demonizing, delegitimizing, and libeling Israel, they will have achieved that objective with the noxious, Israel-hating event. But the only awareness that such events create is the realization that much of what tries to pass as scholarly debate on campuses today is nothing more than propaganda and ideology dressed up as true intellectual inquiry.

26

'Speech for Me, Not for Thee' at UC Irvine

Of the many intellectual perversions currently taking root on college campuses, perhaps none is more contradictory to what should be one of higher education's core values than the suppression of free speech. With alarming regularity, speakers are shouted down, booed, jeered, and barrage with vitriol, all at the hands of groups who give lip service to the notion of academic free speech, and who demand it when their speech is at issue, but have no interest in listening to, or letting others listen to, ideas that contradict their own world view.

Coincidentally, in early 2010, Deputy Foreign Minister Daniel Ayalon and Ambassador to the United States Michael Oren had the unpleasant experience of confronting virulent anti-Israel, pro-Palestinian Muslim students whose ideology on academic debate seems to be "free speech for me, but not for thee."

Ayalon, who spoke at Oxford University, had his speech interrupted by several audience members, including one who yelled incessantly and called Ayalon a "racist" and "a war criminal" while waving a Palestinian flag. Another student who loudly read passages of the incendiary Goldstone Report. There were calls from one charming scholar to "slaughter the Jews," and the intrusion of a third student who remained standing for the entire balance of the lecture while she hurled anti-Israel invective. Still another radical brat threatened Ayalon with: "We will do to you what we did to Milosevic."

The genteel, soft-spoken Ambassador Oren did not fare much better during his visit to the University of California at Irvine, a notorious hotbed of radical anti-Israelism by Muslim students. During the aborted speech to some 500 people about U.S.-Israeli relations, which was loudly interrupted 10 times, boorish hecklers screamed over Oren's talk such profound observations as "Michael Oren, propagating murder is not an expression of free speech," "I accuse you of murder," "How many Palestinians have you killed?" and "Israel is a murderer."

Even after he took a 20-minute recess to let the crowd cool off and regain its collective composure, he returned to the podium with more volleys of invective, shouting, and speech-stopping bombast from the Muslim students, 11 of whom — eight from UC-Irvine (including the Muslim Student Union's president) and three from UC Riverside — were eventually escorted out of the hall and arrested.

The fact that UCI's habitually craven administrators, led by feckless Chancellor Michael Drake, were even motivated enough by the students' errant behavior to have them ejected from the event is a promising sign. While the university has always claimed to be dedicated to encouraging debate and scholarly inquiry by letting the Muslim Student Union mount annual hate-fests to demonize and vilify Israel and Jews, the MSU has effectively hijacked all discussion of the Middle East on campus, and their odious events are not platforms at which opposing views are aired and discussed. In fact, these so-called pro-Palestinians seem to care very little about the actual self-determination and state building of the hapless Palestinians. As is frequently the case when speaking about the Israeli/Arab conflict, the discussion often glosses over the real problems of Palestinian culture, politics, and society (including its cult of death), and targets all criticism on the perceived defects of Israel, Zionism, and Jewish power.

Ambassador Oren is hardly what even his staunchest critics could consider an Islamophobe or even a rabid Zionist, someone who is perfectly willing to trample the Palestinian's aspirations for their putative state. A Columbia and Princeton graduate, former Georgetown professor and fellow at Jerusalem's Shalem Center, the American-born Oren is also the author of two seminal books on the Middle East, *Six Days of War: June 1967 and the Making of the Modern Middle East* and *Power, Faith and Fantasy: America in the Middle East: 1776 to the Present*, all of which clearly make him at least as qualified to speak about the Israeli/Palestinian situation as the raucous, boorish students who had decided, in advance of his UCI appearance, that Oren was morally unfit to even appear on their campus.

This notion that pro-Israel speakers and scholars do not even deserve, on a moral or intellectual basis, an opportunity to participate in scholarly debate is a very dangerous one, even if it comes from tendentious students. It starts with the assumption that Israel, because of its perceived moral defects and its oppression of the hapless Palestinians and the theft of their lands, does not even have the right to participate in intellectual debate; that academic free speech in Israel's case can be modified and is not absolute. And while Muslim students and other campus radicals have, both at UCI and other college campuses, seen to it that speech that they do not approve of, spoken by people with whom they disagree, is shut down with the "heckler's veto," they have never missed an opportunity to invite their own stable of slimy anti-Israel, anti-American speakers. What is more, these speakers have never been shouted down, chased away, or jeered by those students and professors who might well have found their views to be noxious.

A closer look at the ideas tossed about by some of the MSU's invited guests suggests both the moral incoherence and intellectual debasement that characterizes the human output of these events. Amir-Abdel Malik-Ali, for instance, former Nation of Islam member, convert to Islam, and cheerleader for Hamas and Hezbollah, has been a ubiquitous, poisonous presence on the Irvine campus who never hesitates to castigate Israel, Zionists, Jewish power, and Jews themselves as he weaves incoherent, hallucinatory conspiracies about the Middle East and the West. Speaking from a podium with an execrable banner reading "Israel, the 4th Reich" in May 2006, Malik-Ali referred to Jews as "new Nazis" and "a bunch of straight-up punks." "The truth of the matter is your days are numbered," he admonished Jews everywhere. "We will fight you. We will fight you until we are either martyred or until we are victorious."

At a 2008 event, dubbed "Never Again? The Palestinian Holocaust," Malik-Ali was at his hateful best once again, standing behind a banner that read "Death to Apartheid" while he wildly contended that "The Islamic revival should only be feared by those who support imperialism, colonialism, racism, occupation . . . Groups like Hamas and Hezbollah" are not the real terrorists at all, he proclaimed. No, the actual "terrorists are the United States; the terrorists are Israel!"

Another odious guest speaker who regularly makes appearances on the hate-fest circuit is Muhammad al-Asi, an anti-Semitic, anti-American Muslim activist from Washington, D.C. who has written, among other notorious ideas, that "The Israeli Zionist are [sic] the true and legitimate object of liquidation." At a MSU-sponsored event in February 2008, "From Auschwitz to Gaza: The Politics of Genocide," which repulsively tried to draw parallels between the Holocaust and Hamas-controlled Gaza, al-Asi was a featured speaker. In his speech, he repeated the canard of Jewish control of world politics, suggesting that "Zionists or what some people call the Jewish lobby" had reduced the United States to playing "second fiddle to the Israeli government."

Just months after 9/11, al-Asi had similar invective to utter towards Jews, in the context of Israeli oppression of Palestinians. Using his favorite image of the ghetto when describing Jews, he observed that "We have a psychosis in the Jewish community that is unable to co-exist equally and brotherly [sic] with other human beings. You can take a Jew out of the ghetto, but you can't take the ghetto out of the Jew, and this has been demonstrated time and time again in Occupied Palestine."

If ever there were utterances which deserved to be shouted down and drowned out with reason and fact, al-Asi's hallucinatory ravings probably would qualify. But despite continual complaints from the Orange County Task Force on Anti-Semitism and other concerned UCI stakeholders, the tenor and frequency of speakers at the MSU's lurid hate-fests continue unabated, seemingly with the tacit approval of the university administration. The same Muslim students who could not abide even the presence of Israel's ambassador to the United States, listen rapturously to the loathsome bloviating of Malik Ali, al-Asi, Norman Finkelstein, Ward Churchill, and any other ideological thug who has come to UCI's campus with the purpose of vilifying Israel and defaming Jews.

It is, of course, the MSU's choice to hear whatever ideas they wish from whichever speakers to whom they choose to listen. What is not their choice, however, is to be able to prevent other views from being heard on campus, particularly the complex and thorny Israeli/Palestinian conversation, merely because pro-Palestinian students have decided that they will not recognize the very existence or legitimacy of a sovereign nation, Israel, nor hear the ideas of individuals who are able to defend it and explain the Israeli side of the argument. University officials must repeatedly make clear that campuses must allow many different views and perspectives, and should not try to exclude unpopular thought from being heard in the proverbial marketplace of ideas.

27

HR 35 and the Boundaries of Academic Free Speech

No sooner had the California State Assembly voted on and passed House Resolution 35 (HR 35) that calls upon California public universities to "increase their efforts to swiftly and unequivocally condemn acts of anti-Semitism" than the University of California Students Association (UCSA), a system-wide student organization with representatives from each campus, hastily passed a resolution denouncing the resolution, contending that it compels educational institutions "to directly suppress legitimate criticism of Israeli policy and Palestine solidarity activism, and stifles robust political debate on public university campuses."

Scheduled to be voted on the day before the Jewish holidays, and allowing no debate from pro-Israel students or those with opposing views, the UCSA resolution suggested that "While HR 35 purports to oppose anti-Semitism, much of HR 35 is written to unfairly and falsely smear as 'anti-Semites' those who do human rights advocacy focusing on Israel's illegal occupation, alleging that the UC faculty and staff involved in such work are motivated by anti-Semitism rather than by the political ideals of equality and respect for universal human rights they affirm, ideals UCSA and most California students share."

Campus radicals who promote the Palestinian cause may purport to be guided by "political ideals of equality and respect for universal human rights," but it will come as a surprise to no one that they are less than willing to extend those same rights and ideals of equality for Israelis or Jews, and for anyone on North American campuses — Jewish or not — who wishes to articulate his or her own support for the Middle East's only democracy.

In fact, the problem on campuses across the country is that pro-Palestinian activists, in their zeal to seek self-affirmation, statehood, and social justice for the ever-aggrieved Palestinians, have waged a very caustic cognitive war against Israel and Jews as their tactic in achieving those ends — part of a larger, more invidious intellectual jihad against Israel led by some Western elites and those in the Muslim world who also wish to weaken, and eventually destroy, the Jewish state.

A central part of that cognitive war involves the speech and behavior that HR 35 specific sought to address, namely, the demonization and venomous intellectual attacks on the character, moral standing, legality, and social behavior of Israel, and its role as colonial occupier, brutal oppressor, and racist state. Where that anti-Israel speech and behavior has seemingly crossed the line of civil discourse, and why the California lawmakers passed their resolution in the first place, is in those frequently, and ever increasing, instances when what is described by activists as criticism of Israel has devolved into speech, representations, and tropes that can be considered raw anti-Semitism, not the political discourse or academic inquiry it is said to be by those who perpetrate it.

HR 35 was very specific in relying on working definitions of anti-Semitism used by, among others, the U.S. Department of State, Britain's All-Party Parliamentary Group Against Antisemitism, and the European Union Agency for Fundamental Rights, which, as the Bill states, observe "that in context certain language or behavior demonizes and delegitimizes Israel or attacks Israel with classic anti-Semitic stereotypes, such as denying the Jewish people their right to self-determination, applying double standards by requiring of Israel a behavior not expected or demanded of any other democratic nation, drawing comparisons of contemporary Israeli police to that of the Nazis, and accusing the Jewish people, or Israel, of inventing or exaggerating the Holocaust" — exactly the type of expressed attitudes and accusations regularly seen in academia.

In fact, being pro-Palestinian on campuses today does not mean that one is committed to helping the Palestinians productively nation-build, or creating a civil society with transparent government, a free press, human rights, and a representative government. Being pro-Palestinian on campuses involves very little which actually benefits or makes more likely the birth of a new Palestinian state, living side by side in peace with Israel. What being pro-Palestinian unfortunately has come to mean is continually denigrating and attacking Israel with a false historical narrative and the misused language of human rights.

In fact, a study commissioned by then-UC President Mark G. Yudof to measure the climate faced by Jewish students found that anti-Israel activism and on-campus attacks on Israel and Zionism regularly "engender a feeling of isolation, and undermine Jewish students' sense of belonging and engagement with outside communities."

Those findings aside, critics of HR 35 were quick to denounce the resolution as an attempt to suppress academic free speech, that instead of a measure to protect Jewish students and others from having to endure a hostile campus climate the resolution was actually a way of "chilling" expression and, more specifically, of suppressing what some believe to be legitimate criticism of the Israeli government and its policies.

Universities continually give lip service to how much they embrace the notion of "academic free speech," using it as a license to permit both professors and outside speakers to hurl invectives at activists' favorite targets, while simultaneously sheltering designated victim groups from any kind of critique or examination.

In the Israel/Palestinian debate this has had the pernicious effect in which outrageous extremists and academic cranks are regularly invited to speak against Israel, Jews, and the United States, but when conservative or pro-Israel speakers are invited to defend Israel, their speeches are interrupted or cancelled entirely because the speakers are accused of being Islamophobes, racists, or purveyors of "hate speech." So while administrators and faculty have never had any difficulty in identifying so-called hate speech on campus when it is aimed at African Americans, Hispanics, LGBTs, Muslims, or other victim groups, when the discussion is about Israel and the Palestinians, and the target of the virulent speech and demonstrations is Zionism, the Jewish state, or Jews in general, both administrators and campus radicals conveniently inoculate themselves from responsibility for what they would otherwise deem hate speech by invoking the protection of academic free speech.

Pro-Palestinian activists have successfully hijacked the narrative about the Israeli/Palestinian conflict on campuses, but in elevating the Palestinian cause by degrading Israel they have unleashed an ideological tsunami replete with virulent language, slanders, blood libels, and inversions of history and fact.

That is the issue here, and why it is necessary and important that, in the effort to promote the Palestinian cause and help them to achieve statehood, another group — Jewish students on American campuses — do not become victims themselves in a struggle for another group's self-determination.

28

Students for Justice in Palestine Seeks Justice for All — Except Jews, Of Course

The virulent Students for Justice in Palestine (SJP) is a toxic campus group of anti-Israel activists who have helped lead, and intensify, a campaign of libel and delegitimization against the Jewish state, and, at times, ugly anti-Semitism disguised as being merely criticism of Israeli government policies.

SJP has a long history since its founding in 1993 of bringing vitriolic anti-Israel speakers to their respective campuses, and for sponsoring Israeli Apartheid Weeks, building mock "apartheid walls," and sending mock eviction notices to students in their dorms to help them empathize with Palestinians. And SJP members apparently wish to live in a world where only their predetermined virtues and world view prevail, and feel quite strongly that, in the case of the Israeli/Palestinian conflict, at least, the answers are black and white, there is a moral side and an immoral side, and that anyone who does not, or cannot, see things as clearly and unambiguously as these enlightened students do is a racist, an oppressor, or a supporter of an illegal, apartheid regime trampling the human rights of the blameless, hapless Palestinians.

Of course, this vituperative activism has not gone unnoticed by pro-Israel groups and individuals on campus, even resulting in SJP chapters being suspended for their errant behavior, as happened in 2014 at Northeastern University, as one example, after "a series of violations, which included vandalizing university property, disrupting another group's event, failure to write a civility statement, and distributing flyers without permission."

In general, however, SJP has been unimpeded in spreading its calumnies against Israel, fending off any criticism of their invective as attacks on the rights of free expression and academic freedom. The problem for SJP, unfortunately, is that while they are perfectly content to propel a mendacious campaign of anti-Israel libels, and base their analysis of the Israeli/Palestinian conflict on falsehoods, distortions, and a false reading of history and fact, so certain are they of their moral authority that they will never countenance any views — even facts as opposed to opinions — which contradict their hateful political agenda.

SJP communications are now frequently defined by the disingenuous behavior of these ideological bullies intent on having only *their* views aired while suppressing the contradictory views of others, meaning, of course, that the so-called intellectual debate that universities purport to promote in exactly this type of debate will never take place when SJP is involved.

And because they cannot win an honest, open ideological debate about the Israeli/Palestinian conflict because they deal solely in untruths, false history, and misrepresentations (Israeli apartheid, as the central example), SJP has characteristically tried to insure that no pro-Israel voices are heard, either by disrupting or shutting down pro-Israel events and speakers or urging administrators to disinvite speakers they deem to be Islamophobic, too pro-Israel, or critical of their own tactics and activism. Accomplishing that, the memo continues, should include "Political theater to protest the event, engaging in non-violent disruption of the event, or any other tactic deemed appropriate by the attending members not including violence."

They also react in feigned horror when pro-Israel groups use some of the same tactics that SJP has made their modus operandi. At the University of Chicago, for example, SJP distributed posters across campus on October 14, 2015 as part of the "International Day of Action on University Campuses for Palestine," the stated purpose being "to commemorate the lives of these latest victims of Israeli state violence," including, they mistakenly stated, a 13 year-old boy. They were, in other words, paying homage to the murderous young psychopathic Arab men and women who had spent the last weeks stabbing, shooting, stoning, and ramming cars into Jewish civilians for the purpose of murdering them. In SJP's morally defective view, though, the murders should be honored, not the innocent victims of the terroristic carnage.

In response, an unidentified group plastered posters of their own around the Chicago campus, these with the phrase "Stabbing Jews for Peace" under the three letters above, SJP, a clear reference to Students for Justice in Palestine. The SJP members were shocked, shocked that anyone with a moral compass at all would be offended by their offensive poster, writing that "Shockingly, some members of the University community have taken offense at our simple efforts to acknowledge the humanity of those Israel has summarily executed." And then, with no apparent sense of irony, given their history of suppressing the speech of those who disagree with their lethal ideology, SJP wrote that the attack posters not only showed "disrespect to the dead, [but] these reactions display a profound lack of concern for our freedom of expression, a core principle of any university community."

And morally blind as they are, they did not understand why some members of the University of Chicago community might wonder why only dead Arabs were being counted and honored by SJP, and none of the eight Jewish victims murdered over the past weeks. How did SJP analyze this issue? By seeing it as collective racism against Palestinians, and that it is "More worrisome . . . that [the posters] are also evidence that some members of our community seemingly suffer from an inability to see Palestinians as human beings." Perhaps it is because many normal people view a Palestinian who murders two parents in front of four small children in the back seat of their car, as one gruesome example, as a human being, but not one who deserves respect, adoration, or honor.

SJP's Boston University chapter exhibited some of the same moral obtuseness when members complained in a letter to the editor of BU's *Daily Free Press* about an October 2015 event, sponsored by BU's Students for Israel and Hillel, "Vigil for Victims of Terrorism," which, in SJP's view, "was an example of the one-sided, manipulative propaganda present on our campus." Why was that? First, said SJP, "The deliberate use of the word 'terrorism' to refer to the Palestinians is an attempt to dehumanize them." Always completely insensitive to the sensibilities of Jewish students, Israelis, or anyone supporting Israel in word and deed, SJP did, however, in this instance take great umbrage at the potential harm the vigil could do to the BU community. An event like the vigil "serves to divide our campus by triggering families and students at BU, who are deeply connected to Palestine and the experiences of living under the ongoing occupation. We are calling for a condemnation of this inexcusable political agenda that cannot coincide with the mission of inclusivity and cultural diversity at BU."

Apparently, BU's SJP chapter members could not understand why only the victims of terror would be mourned, not the murderers, who, propelled by raw Jew hatred, had chosen to martyr themselves in the name of jihad. And then, the group who will not even engage in dialogue with anyone with opposing views on the very thorny and difficult Israeli/Palestinian conflict, denounced the vigil as a political event. "We are calling for a condemnation of this inexcusable political agenda that cannot coincide with the mission of inclusivity and cultural diversity at BU," they wrote. "We urge BU students, professors, and administration to foster an inclusive environment and prevent outside organizations from propagating toxic rhetoric that destructs the common ground this community is built on" — this from an activist group which arguably has had the most corrosive, divisive effect on campuses nationwide.

While universities have always claimed to be dedicated to encouraging vigorous debate and dialogue by letting SJP and other radical groups to mount annual hate-fests to demonize and vilify Israel and Jews, SJP has effectively hijacked most discussion of the Middle East on campus, and their odious events, including resolutions for boycotts and divestment against Israel, are not platforms at which opposing views are generally aired and discussed.

Concern for the long-suffering Palestinians may be a commendable effort, but SJP's caustic activism and demonization of pro-Israel supporters as a tool for seeking social justice for that one group "represents a profound betrayal of the cardinal principle of intellectual endeavor," observed commentator Melanie Phillips, "which is freedom of speech and debate," something universities should never stop diligently defending.

29

The Agony of Moral Defeat

Perhaps when literary critic C.S. Lewis despaired of "omnipotent moral busybodies . . . who torment us for our own good," he was speaking about those well-meaning, but naïve college students who "torment us without end for they do so with the approval of their own conscience." Lewis's observation seemed to have been given credence in the past weeks by the very public, tendentious rants of two coeds, one at Harvard University and one at UCLA, as they railed against a world in which their dreams of social justice for the oppressed and weak was not being realized, despite their best efforts.

In the first instance, in a February 2014 op-ed in the *Harvard Crimson* entitled "The Doctrine of Academic Freedom," Sandra Y.L. Korn, majoring at Harvard, tellingly, in the history of science and studies of women, gender and sexuality, decided that academic freedom was undeserved by those who hold beliefs different than hers and her fellow "moral busybodies" — those who have decided what is moral and what is acceptable ideology on Harvard's campus and in the world beyond. "Why should we put up with research that counters our goals simply in the name of 'academic freedom?'," she asked, seemingly without embarrassment. Academic freedom, she contended, should be put in check so that unwelcomed viewpoints can be suppressed. As an alternative virtue, she suggested "a more rigorous standard: one of 'academic justice.'"

One example of how that justice might be applied, at the expense of academic freedom, was the recent academic boycott against Israeli academics called for by the American Studies Association (ASA). Though the boycott was subsequently denounced by over 200 university presidents and scores of academic organizations and scholars, Ms. Korn thinks that the loss of academic freedom by Israelis is of secondary importance to her notion of "academic justice;" that is, justice for the oppressed and the victimized. "The ASA, like three other academic associations," she wrote, "decided to boycott out of a sense of social justice, responding to a call by Palestinian civil society organizations for boycotts, divestment, and sanctions until Israel ends its occupation of Palestine." Despite universal protestations from many people far more insightful than Ms. Korn, in her mind, any critics of the boycott are, by definition, morally wrong, and, she asserted, "only those who care about justice can take the moral upper hand."

The UCLA incident revealed a similar leftist obsession with obtaining social justice for the Palestinians, even if it necessitates the weakening or destruction of the Jewish state. On February 26th, the UCLA undergraduate student government voted 7-5 against a Students for Justice in Palestine-proposed "Resolution to Divest from Companies that Violate Palestinian Human Rights." After the charged hearings, which included some 500 people in the audience and went on for ten hours, an identified UCLA undergraduate, who was serving as a note taker for the hearings, broke down and railed at the cameras with an expletive-laden rant about how disappointed she was that the resolution failed, how bad the people were who voted against divestment, and how Palestinians would now continue to be "hurt" because of their inaction. For two minutes the hysterical woman can be seen screaming "I've never been so fucking disappointed" and complaining that "we just fucking blew it" by not passing the corrosive divestment resolution.

This UCLA student, like the Harvard undergraduate who wishes to live in a world where only her predetermined virtues and world view prevail, feels quite strongly that, in the case of the

Israeli/Palestinian conflict, at least, the answers are black and white, there is a moral side and an immoral side, and that anyone who does not, or cannot, see things as clearly and unambiguously as these gifted undergraduates do is a racist, an oppressor, or a supporter of an illegal, apartheid regime trampling the human rights of the blameless Palestinians.

This cynical, and historically and factually inaccurate, view has meant that the left frequently denounces Western democracies as imperialistic, racist, militaristic oppressors, precisely because they wish them to evolve to a purer, newly-structured society and feel that they have the collective insight and moral strength to effect this change as they strive for the social justice, or its intellectually-flaccid offspring as articulated by Ms. Korn, "academic justice."

Thus, when such radical campus groups as Students for Justice in Palestine have as their core mission, as their name implies, bringing their own vision of justice to the Middle East, it is justice *only* for the oppressed, the Palestinians, and not for the perceived oppressor, Israel, whose position of power was made possible only because of military strength and imperialistic tendencies.

In their mission to protect the sensibilities and emotional well-being of identified campus victim groups, universities, often violating their own written guidelines and codes of behavior, have also instituted speech codes to prevent what is generally called "hate speech" now, but which has become a perverse tactic to marginalize, and exclude, the speech and ideology of those with whom liberals and leftists do not agree, those individuals who express ideas that offend the sensibility of Ms. Korn, for example.

The acting out and vitriolic language against Israel that so often defines campus anti-Israelism may make the activists feel good about themselves for striving for social justice, but, as journalist Khaled Abu Toameh has contended, these are hollow efforts, that "[i]nstead of investing money and efforts in organizing Israel Apartheid Week, for example, the self-described 'pro-Palestinians' could dispatch a delegation of teachers to Palestinian villages and refugee camps to teach young Palestinians English . . . ."

What was Abu Toameh's conclusion about this misdirected effort to support the Palestinian cause? "What is happening on the U.S. campuses," he wrote, "is not about supporting the Palestinians as much as it is about promoting hatred for the Jewish state. It is not really about ending the 'occupation' as much as it is about ending the existence of Israel . . ," and "we should not be surprised if the next generation of jihadists comes not from the Gaza Strip or the mountains and mosques of Pakistan and Afghanistan, but from university campuses across the U.S."

"The whole problem with the world," observed philosopher Bertrand Russell, "is that fools and fanatics are always so certain of themselves, but wiser people so full of doubts." That these two undergraduates display a certainty that is so stringent and so contrary to intellectual inquiry should give us all pause, and might make us question if we are teaching a whole generation of college students *what* to think instead of *how* to think.

30

The Eliminationist One-State Solution at the Kennedy School of Government

In March 2012, Harvard's Kennedy School of Government hosted a student-run conference called "Israel/Palestine and the One-State Solution," yet another example of how purported scholarship about the Middle East is frequently biased and diluted by ideology.

The one-state solution to the issue of what to do with the ever-suffering Palestinians is not so much an authentic, or even rational, plan for effecting statehood for Palestinian Arabs; instead, it proposes to do with votes and demography the same thing that hostile Arab armies and Palestinian leadership have themselves tried to do to Israel for the past 68 years; namely, extirpate the Jewish state — not by driving it into the sea with arms and military might, but by subsuming its Jewish identity in a sea of returning Palestinian refugees coming into to Israel to form a bi-national state.

While most in the sentient world have recognized that the only workable solution to the Israel/Palestinian issue is what has been called the "two-state solution," that is, Israel and a new Palestinian state "living side by side in peace," nineteen speakers at the Kennedy School conference proposed that appropriate social justice would be achieved only by deconstructing sovereign Israel and transforming it into a new state with millions of radicalized

Palestinian Arabs as new citizens with equal civil and human rights, and the ability, of course, to vote on what form the future Israel will take.

Three quarters of Israelis and nearly that same percentage of Palestinians favor a two-state solution, precisely because it would result in what people of good faith have always said that they wanted: a new, autonomous state for the Palestinians, living peaceably beside, and not jeopardizing the safety of, Israel. The notion of one state, a bi-national state where millions of Palestinian Arabs instantly become citizens of a new Israel, and thereby force Israel to commit demographic suicide, is, of course, the long-held wish of much of the Arab world — and, evidently, of many in the West — who are very content to let Israel as it exists today merely disappear. That is, they imagine, as did Ahmadinejad at his Holocaust denial conference in Iran, a world without Israel.

The premise for effecting a one-state solution is, on its face, obscene, a thinly-disguised ploy to offer a diplomatic solution to an intractable problem, which its proponents know full well would be implemented only for the benefit of Palestinian self-affirmation and to the detriment, and destruction, of Israel. That is exactly why the participants of the Harvard conference comprised a retinue of the usual suspects in the hate-Israel crowd, a traveling road-show of politicized scholars, propagandists, and non-academic activists with only a thinly-veiled animus towards Israel and Jews. What this conference clearly was not is a true academic or scholarly exercise designed to reveal some rational and reasonable solutions in the Middle East; instead, it was yet another opportunity for ideologues with an anti-Israel, anti-Western agenda to trumpet their perverse views under a cloak of academic respectability, and here even with Harvard's imprimatur.

As one example, the notorious Israeli historian Ilan Pappé spoke at the Harvard conference. Already exposed for having invented history and contorting facts to suit his personal enmity toward Zionism, Pappé has nevertheless become the dream Jew of anti-Semites, someone who offers apologetics for terrorism against Israelis and justifies it as an understandable, and inevitable, response to "occupation." "Terrorism is not the essential question," Pappé has said, oblivious to the murder of Jews riding on buses or sitting at cafes. "Israel expelled the Palestinians and colonized the area," and this behavior is "far worse than suicide bombing and armed struggle."

Pappé, and many on the left, condone resistance by the oppressed Palestinians but despise self-defense by Israel in trying to prevent its citizens from being murdered. Another speaker at the Harvard conference, Diana Buttu, a former legal adviser to the Palestinian Liberation Organization, has repeatedly claimed, for instance, after some 8,000 rockets had rained into southern Israeli towns from Gaza, "that none of these rockets actually [had] an explosive head on them, unlike the Israeli weaponry," and, in reality, "the reason that they have been launched" is not because of any genocidal impulses on the part of Hamas, but due to "the fact that Israel has maintained a siege and a blockade against the Gaza Strip for the past three years in addition to military operations in the Gaza Strip" — in other words, the rocket attacks were Israel's fault.

Nadim N. Rouhana, a professor at Tufts University's Fletcher School of Law and Diplomacy and another panelist, has announced her belief that "it would be politically and morally wrong for the United States to support recognition of Israel as a Jewish state."

Another speaker, Boston College's Eve Spangler, who takes students to Israel to teach them to embrace the pro-Palestinian narrative and loathe Israel, has in one of her course syllabi the telling language in one assignment that asks students to analyze the "three images of the Israeli occupation of Palestine: genocide, apartheid, and sociocide," as if those characteristics were facts as opposed to politicized scholarship. These views are hardly surprising, after all, from a professor who contends that "there is no 'real' history, only competing narratives, in which power, not truth, determines the outcome." In other words, facts do not matter when purported scholarship is politicized.

Another participant was Ali Abunimah, whose online newsletter, the *Electronic Intifada*, is the veritable *Der Stürmer* of the pro-Palestinian cause and the one-state solution, a formula that if introduced, Abunimah has admitted, might mean that "we couldn't rule out some disastrous situation" for Jews.

And as if to lend some intellectual weight to the conference, the sponsors had invited the Kennedy School's own Stephen Walt, who, with co-author John Mearsheimer, wrote the incendiary book, *The Israel Lobby*. In that work, Walt and Mearsheimer accused the Israel lobby, what they described as a powerful, manipulative cabal of pro-Israel Jewish individuals and organizations, of having gained a "stranglehold" on US policymakers, an influence that they said explained America's longstanding support of Israel, even when it harms our security interests and global standing. Apparently, in his zeal to help US policymakers rid themselves of the annoyance of having to moderate their loyalty to Israel, Walt has now moved to an even more radical position than simply exposing the perfidy of the Israel Lobby — namely, eliminating the Jewish state altogether, a viewpoint that has made him the darling of anti-Israel hate-fests around the globe.

The one-state solution is the legacy of the ideology of the left, which manifests itself in a reverence for Third-World victims and an obsession with redressing the wrongs of history by seeking social justice and a radical social change to overturn the status quo. But the notion that the perceived rights to statehood and self-affirmation of the Palestinians are so legitimate and compelling, and that they should be granted at the expense and to the detriment of the sovereign state of Israel, is one that certainly has no precedent, from a legal, moral, or politically realistic standpoint. It also exposes an inexplicable fixation with Israel, and only Israel, on the part of its detractors who purport to support human rights everywhere. Given some of the civil deformities that have emerged from the "Arab Spring," there is certainly no guarantee that a new bi-national Israel that emerged from this scheme would be free from protracted internecine strife and the eradication of the

Jewish identity of Israel, let alone the type of functioning state Israeli citizens now enjoy with its open, democratic society.

Having a conference with the primary intention to demonize and delegitimize Israel is not an academic enterprise of any merit; it is propaganda parading as scholarship, and violates not only one of the basic precepts of scholarship but also the spirit of the Kennedy School, which was conceived as a place where future leaders could debate, with academic integrity, reason, and insight, the important global issues facing decision makers.

31

The Paranoid View of History
Infects Oberlin

"Anti-Semitism," wrote Stephen Eric Bronner, author of the engaging book *A Rumor About The Jews,* "is the stupid answer to a serious question: How does history operate behind our backs?" For a wide range of ideological extremists, anti-Semitism is still the stupid answer for why what goes wrong with the world does go wrong. It is a philosophical world view and interpretation of history that creates conspiracies as a way of explaining the unfolding of historical events; it is a pessimistic and frantic outlook, characterized in 1964 by historian Richard Hofstadter as "the paranoid style" of politics, which shifts responsibility from the self to sinister, omnipotent others — typically and historically the Jews.

Long the thought product of cranks and fringe groups, Hofstadter's paranoid style of politics has lately entered the mainstream of what would be considered serious, and respectable academic enterprise. Witness, for instance, the Facebook posts of Joy Karega, an assistant professor of Rhetoric and Composition at Oberlin College, who wildly claimed that Jewish bankers control the world economy and have financed every war since Napoleon, that Israelis and Zionists were not only behind the 9/11 attacks in New York but also orchestrated the *Charlie Hebdo* attacks in Paris, and that Israeli fingerprints could be found in the downing over Ukraine of Malaysian Air Flight 17 and also in the rise of ISIS.

What troubles observers of this type of intellectual incoherence emanating from academia, is that, unlike its intellectually flabby predecessors from right-wing hate groups or left-wing cranks, this political analysis comes complete with academic respectability of Oberlin, a trend that Professor Hofstadter had himself originally found noteworthy. "In fact," he wrote, "the idea of the paranoid style as a force in politics would have little contemporary relevance or historical value if it were applied only to men with profoundly disturbed minds. It is the use of paranoid modes of expression by more or less normal people that makes the phenomenon significant."

For Karega, the archetypal malevolent Jew is found in the person of Jacob Rothschild, whose photograph she posted in December 2014, along with text, allegedly from him, stating that, "We own nearly every central bank in the world. We financed both sides of every war since Napoleon. We own your news, the media, your oil and your government" — oft-repeated tropes about Jewish domination of media and banking which suggest, to Karega and like-minded conspiracists, that Jewish wealth and influence enable Jews — and by extension Zionists and Israelis — to get away with various predations and political manipulations. She raises the specter of the Jewish banker in a later Facebook post when she blames Israel, "the same people behind the massacre in Gaza," of shooting down the Malaysian airliner over Ukraine. "With this false flag," Karega rants, "the Rothschild-led banksters [sic], exposed and hated and out of economic options to stave off the coming global deflationary depression, are implementing the World War III option."

Karega's assertions that Jews and agents of the Jewish state and high-placed government officials are manipulating current events, fomenting war, profiting from global unrest — secretive, underhanded actions whose end result would not otherwise honestly, fairly, or reasonably be achieved — this language has drawn such immediate and thunderous denunciation of Karega's various Facebook posts, as first made public with captured Facebook screenshots in the *The Tower*. And it is a particularly incendiary bit of language when discussing Israel, a Jewish state, for it parallels so invidiously the classic anti-Semitic canards, such as the *Protocols of the Elders of Zion*, which purport to reveal the intention of Jews to furtively rule and dominate the globe. Karega not only attempts to expose the hidden wealth and power of Rothschild, but she further suggests that this wealth is put to nefarious purposes, shooting down a Malaysian civilian aircraft to draw attention away from Israel's incursion into Gaza, as well as a more deadly agenda based on "the Rothschild's propensity for whacking scientists who dare interfere with their depopulation agenda" Karega mused, "of which AIDS is a key component," the oft-cited, but never substantiated, libel, repeated here by Karega, that Jewish scientists introduced AIDS into the black community as an act of genocidal racism.

"The central image," said Hofstadter, of this defective way of looking at how history works, "is that of a vast and sinister conspiracy, a gigantic and yet subtle machinery of influence set in motion to undermine and destroy a way of life . . . [The] enemy is clearly delineated," Hofstadter observed, much in the way the Jew is depicted in the vicious forgery gaining renewed interest of late, *The Protocols of the Elders of Zion*: "He is a perfect model of malice, a kind of amoral superman: sinister, ubiquitous, powerful, cruel, sensual, luxury-loving."

As Hofstadter described it, the paranoid scholar sees the manipulator, here Jewish bankers, the Mossad, Prime Minister Netanyahu, as an enemy, one with disproportionate and unreasonable influence. "Unlike the rest of us," however, he wrote, "the enemy is not caught in the toils of the vast mechanism of history . . . Very often the enemy is held to possess some especially effective source of power: he controls the press; he directs the public mind through 'managed news'; he has unlimited funds . . . he is gaining a stranglehold," in this case on world politics. Israel, and the Rothschilds, in Karega's hallucinatory universe, symbolize Jewish power in the way that classic anti-Semitic depictions of the Jew have always depicted them: they comprise a shady cabal of omnipotent, money-hungry, unscrupulous moneymen, loyal to no single nation, willing to profit from wars and contagion, the enemies of morality, law, and virtue. Jews are at once a separate race who keep to themselves and never assimilate and adopt the host culture and manipulative insiders who penetrate host societies from within and undermine mores and economies for their own gain.

In a March 2015 Facebook post, Karega provided what she apparently thought was a helpful link to a crazed speech by Minister Louis Farrakhan of the Nation of Islam, "Muslims for 9/11 Truth: Farrakhan on 9-11: What You Need to Know #False Flag," in which, to no one's great surprise, the enlightened minister ascribed the blame for the 9/11 attacks, not to the homicidal Muslim terrorists who clearly perpetrated them, but to Israel and greedy Jews who realized financial and political gains from the felling of the Twin Towers. "Farrakhan is truth-telling in this video," Karega wrote in her post, and "we need more of us willing to venture into these areas."

Minister Farrakhan, it will be remembered, characterized Judaism as a "gutter religion," deemed Hitler "a great man," and, lest there be any doubt where his sympathizes lie regarding Israel, decided that the "plight" of American blacks puts them "in the same position" as the Palestinians. So his view that Israel's fingerprints are all over the 9/11 attacks, and that Jews in fact benefited from the terrorism, is not in variance from his twisted beliefs, nor, apparently, those of Karega.

"Now you know I'm going to be lambasted and called anti-Semitic," he said in a 2012 Chicago speech. "They'll say Farrakhan was up to his old canards; he said Jews control Hollywood. Well, they said it themselves! Jews control the media. They said it themselves! Jews and some gentiles control the banking industry, international banks. They do! In Washington right next to the

Holocaust Museum is the Federal Reserve where they print the money. Is that an accident?"

Once professor Karega's demented posts were made public, Oberlin's president, already reeling from a spate of other anti-Semitic, anti-Jewish incidents on his campus, reacted fecklessly, giving the disingenuous response that the college "respects the right of its faculty, students, staff and alumni to express their personal views," and that "the statements posted on social media by Dr. Joy Karega . . . are hers alone and do not represent the views of Oberlin College." That may well be true, and universities do not necessarily have to take responsibility for the outrageous views expressed publicly by its faculty; but neither do academic leaders have to refrain from denouncing the same speech that a faculty member is perfectly able to utter under the protection of academic free speech, just as they regularly do in those rare instances when slurs are made by faculty aimed at blacks, gays, Muslims, Hispanics, or other perceived victim groups for who such speech is deemed "hurtful," "oppressive," or "hateful."

The university campus is *not* the public square, where any idea — no matter how deranged, improbable, inaccurate, libelous, historically unfounded, or damaging — can be spoken and heard, unchallenged, without government interference. But while universities should, and do, protect the notion of unbridled expression and the ability to express any opinion as part of "scholarly inquiry," it has never been the intention of academic free speech to protect, or promote, irresponsible, inaccurate, or outrageous speech that is clearly outside the parameters of responsible scholarship, research, and factuality.

A professor has every right to contend that the earth is flat, or that the United States is a greater terrorist threat than ISIS, or that the Holocaust never took place, or, as professor Karega has contended, that Jewish bankers rule the world and enabled Israel to orchestrate 9/11 and the Paris shootings, but the right to express such madness does not insulate an individual from the responsibility of taking ownership of his or her opinions. Nor should university leaders, while granting faculty the right to express such intellectual perversities, hesitate from denouncing them for what they are: in this case, classic anti-Semitic tropes about Jewish power and perfidy dressed up, as is often normally and sadly the case, as mere "criticism" of Israel.

All the concern and intrigue engendered in Karega's Facebook posts show that the obvious, and easy, answers are not the ones the paranoid is likely to accept on face value. She is condemned by her nature to suffer in the labyrinthine schemes she uncovers. "We are all sufferers from history," Hofstadter concluded, "but the paranoid is a double sufferer, since he is afflicted not only by the real world, with the rest of us, but by his fantasies as well."

32

The Wesleyan Controversy and a Double Standard for Campus Free Speech

In what is yet more evidence that universities have become, at least where campus free speech is concerned, "islands of repression in a sea of freedom," the Wesleyan University community underwent collective apoplexy over an opinion submission in the school's student newspaper, *The Argus*, which critically examined the Black Lives Matter movement. The thoughtful, relatively-benign 2015 op-ed, written by sophomore Bryan Stascavage, a 30 year-old Iraq veteran and self-described "moderate conservative," questioned if the behavior of some BLM supporters "cheering after [a police] officer is killed, chanting that they want more pigs to fry like bacon" showed a moral and ideological flaw in the movement, leading him to wonder, "is the movement itself actually achieving anything positive? Does it have the potential for positive change?"

That opinion was apparently more than many of the sensitive fellow Wesleyan students could bear, and the newspaper's staff was inundated with denunciations of the implicit racism of the offending op-ed and the "white privilege" demonstrated by its author, demands that apologies be issued by the paper's editors, the widespread theft of *The Argus* around campus, calls for sensitivity/social justice training for staffers, and even a vote to halve the *Argus's* annual funding to instead subsidize alternate publications, presumably for marginalized students.

The shell-shocked editors even published a front-page apology for having run the piece in the first place, cravenly caving to the sensibilities of the campus crybabies and saying they understood "the frustration, anger, pain, and fear that members of the student body felt in response to the op-ed 'Why Black Lives Matter Isn't What You Think.'" More tellingly, they wrote, "in light of the Black Lives Matter op-ed, students of color *may not feel comfortable* [emphasis added] or welcome writing for *The Argus*. Of course, feeling "comfortable," feeling "safe," not being offended is now expected as a right on university campuses, where administrators, faculty, and students widely give lip service to the notion that academic free speech should have no limits, but continue to demonstrate that, in practice, free speech on campus relates only to accepted views by self-identified victim groups and not politically heterodox ideas such as the thesis of Stascavage's op-ed.

When political correctness first began to engulf our campuses, of course, the legacy of Marxist philosopher Herbert Marcuse and his notion of "repressive tolerance" meant that racist or "hateful" speech was attacked as just that: speech which was unacceptable to those "victim" groups who were perceived as needing protection from freely-expressed opinions — generally members of racial, ethnic, or sexual minorities. College students have therefore taken a new, misguided approach in their attempt to suppress speech whose content they do not approve of, as they seem to have done at Wesleyan. On college campuses, to paraphrase George Orwell, all views are equal, but some are more equal than others.

To illustrate how a double standard exists in the academy as it relates to academic free speech one only has to look at other opinion pieces that have appeared in the self-same *Argus*, such as a March 2015 column written by members of Students for Justice in Palestine (SJP), a corrosive, anti-Israel group, who published an op-ed with the mendacious title, "Israel's Apartheid State."

In the op-ed, written as the annual anti-Israel hate fest known as Israeli Apartheid Week was about to get underway at Wesleyan and campuses around the country, Israelis, and those Jewish students and other pro-Israel individuals on campus who support Israel, are described by the writers as racists, oppressors, ethnic cleansers, thieves and appropriators of Palestinian land, participants in "state terror," colonial settlers, and aggressive militants who randomly and barbarically initiate "wars against Gaza" while slaughtering innocent Arabs in violation of international law, seemingly without motivation or justification.

While *The Argus* editors, in their extensive apology for the BLM op-ed, claimed that the writer had "twisted the truth" and misrepresented facts in making his argument, and that they felt editorial responsibility for not fact-checking the piece, in fact the op-ed did not wildly distort facts or misrepresent the recent history of the Black Lives Matter movement, at all. Readers who denounced the piece did not like the motives of a victim group being critiqued and deconstructed by someone who questioned the morality of the movement itself, particularly a white writer. But one could just as easily, and perhaps more relevantly, ask why the editors had not employed that same editorial scrutiny when they agreed to publish the libelous piece by the SJP members in March, an opinion piece whose main message was built upon an analysis that was fraught with untruths, distortions of history and fact, libelous assertions about political behavior and military operations, and a view of the Israeli/Palestinian conflict that disingenuously assigns all of the blame on Israel and ignores Arab rejectionism and truculence, not to mention terrorism, in the decades-long assault on the Jewish state.

Specifically, there is no institutionalized apartheid in Israel, as any sentient observer knows, yet both the title and the main thrust of the piece repeatedly assert that Israel is practicing apartheid against the hapless Palestinians, and that, in the writers' view, "apartheid is a useful and accurate term to describe the myriad mechanisms of oppression and separation employed by the

Israeli state." As part of that apartheid system, they wrote, "Israel has . . . erected a 30-foot high concrete wall that snakes through the West Bank, annexing more Palestinian land, cutting farmers off from their farmland, and effectively separating the populations based on race," a liberal fantasy that the barrier was constructed to keep "brown" Arabs out of "white" Israeli neighborhoods that attempts to frame this conflict as a conflict between races, and ignores the reality that the barrier was built, not as a way of segregating neighborhoods, but to keep Israeli civilians from being murdered by terrorists.

In the analysis by the SJP members, of course, there was never any blame on the Palestinian side, characteristic of those who exonerate Third-world victims of imperialism of any blame for the terror and aggression that animates the Palestinian cause. Israel, they write, "continues its inhumane blockade on the Gaza strip [which] has prevented everyday necessities from entering and Palestinians from leaving," completing ignoring the fact that every Israeli left Gaza in 2005 so the Palestinians could start their state building, and that, instead, Hamas turned Gaza into a launching pad for rockets and mortars, some 12,000 of which have rained down on southern Israeli towns from terrorists wishing to kill Jews in homes, schools, and cafes. There is no mention in the op-ed of these deadly attacks on Israel by Hamas, nor the fact that each rocket launched against Israel amounts to a war crime; and the writers' statement that "from time to time, guised as counter-terrorism, the Israeli government launches wars against the population of Gaza" describes with absolutely no context the reason why Israel's incursions into Gaza were necessary in the first place — not, as the writers would have you believe, because Israel capriciously "launches wars," but as part of a defensive campaign to suppress deadly rocket from Gaza aimed at murdering Israeli citizens.

Another equally disingenuous SJP October 19th op-ed in *The Argus*, "Occupation Breeds Violence, Free Palestine," written as Palestinian murderers were stabbing, shooting, and driving over

Israeli citizens in a month-long wave of terror, remarkably assigned the blame for the recent carnage, not on the psychopaths who are perpetrating it, but on its victims, asserting that "SJP not only condemns terror, we go further by condemning the primary engine of the 'recent surge in violence': Israel's illegal military occupation of the West Bank." More ridiculously, they claim, not the terrorists who slaughter civilians but the so-called occupation is the cause of the current violence, and "'the occupation is the ultimate terrorist infrastructure,'" establishing a false moral equivalence between terrorists and Israeli forces trying to protect its citizenry from being killed. Even more Orwellian is their assertion in the piece that even if Israel seeks a negotiated peace, that effort is disingenuous and is aimed at neutralizing the Palestinian's right to conduct an Intifada. "Peace . . . is a concept," they ridiculously asserted, "often invoked by the powerful and wielded against the powerless to suppress resistance," suggesting that Israel would rather oppress Palestinians than live with them, side by side in peace.

The late Senator Daniel Patrick Moynihan once quipped that "everyone is entitled to his opinion, but not to his own facts," and the lesson here is that if *The Argus* editors are serious about excluding opinion pieces that "twist the facts" or distort truth in an effort to make a point, then these pieces by the SJP members would fail that editorial test as surely as the Stascavage op-ed was accused of doing when discussing Black Lives Matter. The SJP pieces were replete with distortions, libels, untruths, and a misreading of history and politics, yet no Jewish students came forward to denounce the editors for having published such an egregiously biased, erroneous piece, no Israel supporters called for defunding the paper for running blatantly propagandistic articles, and no champions of free speech demanded sensitivity training for newspapers staffers so that they could better understand how vilification of the Jewish state and holding it to a standard not demanded on any other nation on earth can rise to the level of anti-Semitism.

None of those actions were launched against *The Argus* precisely because it would be inappropriate to suppress the opinions of the SJP writers — no matter how virulent, incorrect, and misguided — both because it is the legitimate and intended function of the opinion section of a newspaper to run varied, even controversial, ideas, and because it violates the idea of free expression to have one group of self-identified victims dictate what can, and should, be said about matters relevant to them.

So while campus free speech is enshrined as one of the university's chief principles, the current *Argus* controversy shows us that it rarely occurs as free speech for everyone, only for a certain few.

33

Trying to Give Academic Respectability to the Right of Return Fantasy

S eeming to give credence to Orwell's observation that "some ideas are so stupid that only an intellectual could believe them," in April of 2013, Boston University hosted a Students for Justice in Palestine-run "Right of Return Conference," yet another example of how purported scholarship about the Middle East is frequently biased and diluted by ideology.

Most sentient observers of the Palestinian issue know that the "right of return" issue is a core tactic in rendering real peace, any viable Arab/Israeli solution, effectively impossible, that the prospect of some 5-7 million Palestinian refugees flooding into what is now Israel would, as University of Haifa professor Steven Plaut put it, "derail Israel demographically and turn it into the Rwanda of the Levant."

That is exactly why every one of the participants of the BU conference was part of a retinue of the hate-Israel crowd, a traveling road-show of politicized scholars, propagandists, and pseudo- and non-academic activists with only a thinly-veiled animus towards Israel, Zionism, and Jews in general. What this conference clearly was not was a true academic or scholarly exercise designed to reveal some rational and reasonable solutions in the Middle East; instead, it was yet another opportunity for ideologues with an anti-Israel, anti-Western agenda to trumpet their perverse views under a cloak of academic respectability, and here even with Boston University's imprimatur.

The demand for a right of return, a notion referred to by Palestinians and their supporters as "sacred" and an "enshrined" universal human right granted by UN resolutions and international law, in fact, has no legal or diplomatic standing at all, and is part of the propaganda campaign that is based on the thinking that if Israel cannot be eradicated by the Arabs through a military war, it can be effectively destroyed by forcing it to accept demographic subversion.

In the first place, it uses the fraud as its core notion that the Palestinians were "victimized" by the creation of Israel, and that they were expelled from a land of "Palestine" where they were the indigenous people "from time immemorial," as the late historian Joan Peters put it in her book of the same name.

More importantly, far from being either a "sacred" or, for that matter, legal right, the right of return is a one-sided concoction that deliberately misreads United Nations resolutions for political advantage, and conveniently embraces only those portions that fit the intent of Arabs to make good on their intent to "drive Israel into the sea." In continually repeating the lie that they are victims of the "Zionist regime" and that they were expelled from a country of their own and condemned to unending refugee status, the Palestinians — and their Arab enablers — have prolonged the myth of victimhood.

There is some irony in the fact that the Palestinians have repeatedly violated both the spirit and intent of 194, that particular UN resolution containing a reference to the concept of 'return' to one's country, although two key points are characteristically ignored by those pointing to this source as justification for their legal claim. First, Resolution 194 was the product of the UN General Assembly and "is an expression of sentiment and carries no binding force whatsoever," meaning that it is meant to make recommendations but not enforceable law.

Moreover, that permission is subject to two conditions — that "the refugee wishes to return, and that he wishes to live at peace with his neighbors," something the Arab world, even now, has clearly never seen fit to do. Legal scholars also point out that international law grants the right to leave or return to one's country only to individuals, not as a collective right as the Palestinians claim. More importantly, no population of refugees has ever presumed that the right of return — if such a right even exists — could be claimed, not only by the original refugees, but also by all of their descendants.

So it should come as no surprise that the list of guest speakers for the repugnant Right of Return Conference included a galaxy of notorious anti-Israel Jew-haters whose contribution to the event's awareness-raising was not likely an animated discussion of approaches to the Israeli-Palestine conflict, but a one-sided, biased, inflammatory series of exhortations calling for continued assault against the very existence of Israel and the eventual extirpation of the Jewish state.

One of the conference's keynote speakers, for example, was Columbia University's Joseph Massad, an associate professor of modern Arab politics who regularly espouses his loathing of Israel in fringe, anti-Semitic publications like *Counterpunch* and the *Electronic Intifada*, or in the Arab press, and never misses an opportunity to denigrate the Jewish state as a racist, colonial enterprise, a moral stain on the world without any semblance of legitimacy. He assigns blame for all of the turmoil in the Palestinian territories to the brutal Israeli regime, claims that the "Jewish state is a racist state that does not have the right to exist," and ignores completely any role the Arabs states may have had in inciting violence and murdering Jews in the name of what he, and his like-minded apologists for jihadist terror, categorizes as legitimate "resistance" to occupation.

In fact, in his perfervid imagination, Israelis have become the new Nazis and the Palestinians the Jews. "As Palestinians are murdered and injured in the thousands," he wrote after Operation Cast Lead in January of 2009 when Israel was defending itself against some 6,000 rocket attacks from Gaza, "world powers are cheering on . . , and it even happened during World War II as the Nazi genocide was proceeding." Perversely likening the barbaric aggression of Hamas from within Gaza to the efforts of Warsaw Jews to repel imminent extermination by the Nazis, Massad obscenely suggested that "The Gaza Ghetto Uprising will mark both the latest chapter in Palestinian resistance to colonialism and the latest Israeli colonial brutality in a region whose peoples will never accept the legitimacy of a racist European colonial settlement in their midst."

Professor Massad is also quite willing to invoke stereotypes and overlook history and fact when describing the malevolence of Israel and the victimization of Palestinians. In a 2009 article in the *Electronic Intifada*, ironically entitled "Israel's Right to Defend Itself," Massad concluded that Israel, due to its fundamental racist nature and oppression of the Palestinians, has no moral, or legal, right to self-defense, suggesting that "What the Palestinians ultimately insist on is that Israel must be taught that it does not have the right to defend its racial supremacy, and that the Palestinians have the right to defend their universal humanity against Israel's racist oppression."

A second keynote speaker was Salman Abu Sitta, co-founder of Al-Awda, The Palestine Right to Return Coalition, a grassroots organization that uses as its core tagline, "Palestine will be free, from the River to the Sea," meaning a new Palestinian state replacing, not co-existing with, Israel. He has referred to the "Nakba," the Palestinian's name for the tragedy they suffered upon the creation of Israel, as the "largest, longest operation of planned ethnic cleansing in history." In grotesque thinking similar to Massad's, Abu Sitta also tried to make analogous Israel's interaction with Palestinians with the Nazi's treatment of Jews by referring to Gaza as "the new Auschwitz."

Representing yet another virulently anti-Israel position is human rights activist and lawyer Noura Erakat, a fellow at Temple University's law school and the U.S.-based Legal Advocacy

Consultant for the Badil Resource Center for Palestinian Refugee and Residency Rights. In 2006, when recruiting legal volunteers on behalf of The Middle East Subcommittee of the National Lawyers Guild to work as activists for the Palestinian cause, Erakat invited prospects to do "human rights work" in what she termed "Occupied Palestine," "all lands occupied in 1967 and 1948" — meaning that she believes that all of present-day Israel is occupied Arab land.

The Conference's opening panel was entitled "Discourses of Return and Resistance Among Palestinian Refugees," which might be taken as a planning session for terror, given that the term "resistance" is pro-Palestinian activist's oft-used euphemism for suicide attacks. In fact, one of that panel's participants, Charlotte Kates, former Rutgers law student and leader of the New Jersey Solidarity Movement, long a champion of the Palestinian right of "resistance," has regularly supported "Palestinians' right to resist occupation and oppression . . . Why is there something particularly horrible about 'suicide bombing,' except for the extreme dedication conveyed in the resistance fighter's willingness to use his or her own body to fight?" In addition to calling on her own university, Rutgers, to divest from companies doing business with Israel, her ultimate ambitions were even more odious: "Israel is an apartheid, colonial settler state," she said. "I do not believe apartheid, colonial settler states have a right to exist."

And if this on-campus hostility towards Israel and Jews intimidated Jewish students, so be it, Kates said at Rutgers. "We have no desire to create an environment where racists may feel comfortable and secure in their racism; we very much want . . . to create an environment where it is, indeed, uncomfortable to declare oneself an unequivocal supporter of an oppressive, racist state. It should be uncomfortable . . . May the tension continue to escalate."

The motivation for this BU conference was very clear: prolong the myth of Palestinian victimization and grant them, as part of that mythology, exclusive international recognition and supposed legal rights. Why? "Unlike all those many millions of other people considered refugees in the late 1940s," answers professor Plaut, "the 'Palestinians' were the only ones for whom the 'right of return' to their previous homes was considered an entitlement. The reason was not a selective affection for Palestinians, but a selective hostility towards Israel and Jews."

Having a conference with the primary intention to demonize and delegitimize Israel, while promoting a legally- and morally-defective approach to achieving Palestinian self-affirmation, is not an academic exercise of any merit; it is propaganda parading as scholarship, and violates not only one of the basic precepts of scholarship but also the spirit of any university, which were conceived as places where faculty and students could debate — with academic integrity, reason, and an absence of bias — the important issues of the marketplace of ideas.

34

Victimology 101 at UC San Diego

Adding to the evidence that California campuses have become the epicenter for anti-Israel, anti-Semitic, and anti-American activism, student groups at the University of California, San Diego, led by Students for Justice in Palestine, introduced — for the third time — a 2012 initiative aimed at divesting university funds from "U.S. companies that profit from violent conflict and occupation."

This time, the divestment call was aimed specifically at General Electric and Northrop Grumman — firms that "produce parts of Apache helicopters used by the Israeli Defense Forces against Palestinians" — with the empty ambition that "by removing investments from companies who assist in perpetuating the violence in the area [supporters would be instrumental in] setting up a forum where peace is achievable."

As had happened on two earlier occasions on the UCSD campus when a similar divestment initiative was presented, the proposal was roundly defeated in a 20-13 vote, stunning its supporters.

The rejection of calls for divestment from companies doing business with Israel mirrors what has happened elsewhere on campuses, where such campaigns represent the continuing effort by some activist members of the academic left — joined happily by Islamists and other ideological enemies of the Jewish state — to prolong and enhance the demonization of Israel for the purpose of delegitimizing, weakening, and, it is hoped by these advocates, eventually extirpating Israel altogether. Positioned as a morally upright effort to assert and protect the rights of the long-suffering Palestinians, these efforts at demonizing Israel are not, in fact, benign gestures of peace activists and well-meaning academics in pursuit of social justice for the Palestinians.

But a telling, if not unexpected, thing happened once the student groups who had sponsored this odious divestment resolution actually lost their bid to implement it: supporters of the divestment initiative immediately proclaimed that the initiative had failed because opponents of the resolution were "racists" and bigots. They claimed opponents pressured the student government representatives to vote down the campaign in a manner that created a "hostile campus climate . . . for students of color and students from underserved and underrepresented communities," suffering victims who are now "hurt, [and] feel disrespected, silenced, ignored and erased by this University."

These victimized students and faculty also self-righteously and fatuously proclaimed in a letter to the UCSD administration that the pro-Israel faculty and staff who spoke against the resolution at the meeting should not even have had a voice in the proceedings: "The fact that they can state whatever they like at public meetings because of academic freedom but while also using their positions of authority as professors or staff for power and intimidation is not acceptable."

The language of the whining memo to the UCSD administration, like the language of the divestment resolution itself, is revealing. Both are laced with the tired Marxist, post-colonial vocabulary depicting a Manichean view of the world in which Israel is the brutal oppressor and the Palestinians are the innocent Third-World oppressed, and that the absence of peace in the region is only the fault of the militaristically mighty Jewish state. "The reality is," the memo clarified for those on the administration who might not know, "that [the Israeli/Palestinian conflict] is a human rights issue where the oppressed are fighting against the oppressor."

The language of human rights has, of course, been exploited to promote the Palestinian cause by many in the West and in the Arab world who wish the struggle to be seen not for what it actually is — a decades-old campaign to extirpate the Jewish state and "drive the Jews into the sea" — but instead as merely a process by which the Palestinian Arabs throw off the yoke of colonial oppression by Israel and achieve self-determination and statehood. But that formula requires that the Palestinians always remain victims, for it is in that way that they are able to acquire support in furtherance of their cause.

That same designation of victimhood had obviously become a tool for Students for Justice in Palestine and other student groups and faculty members who wrote the scolding entreaty to UCSD administrators. Nowhere in their accusatory memo did they address the central point of the resolution; that is, whether it had any merit at all and whether the vote to defeat it was handled transparently and fairly (which it obviously was). Instead, their reaction to losing the vote was not to look at the vacuity of their campaign but rather to make themselves into victims who now "feel uncomfortable" on campus because of the rejection of their ideas. In other words, on campuses today, feelings trump ideas.

"In the society of victims," Charles Sykes observed in his engaging book *A Nation of Victims: The Decay of American Character*, "individuals compete not only for rights or economic advantage but also for points on the 'sensitivity' index, where 'feelings' rather than reason are what count."

As victim groups become aware of their supposed classification as "authentic" victims, they are prone to contradict the stated goal of diversity by limiting real dialogue and interchange between opposing points of view such as those expressed by some pro-Israel, anti-divestment faculty and students at the February meeting. Thus, while "social justice" proponents, who claim a high moral ground because they fight for the rights of the oppressed, adamantly defend free speech for themselves in order to define their own ideology, they are clearly uncomfortable with the speech of others and exempt themselves from having to live by the suppressive rules of expression they craft for others.

In fact, the UCSD student crybabies claimed, the mere presence at the meeting of those with alternate views of the divestment resolution resulted in a "hostile campus climate being created for students of color and students from underserved and underrepresented communities," something that served to "erase the existence of many individuals in the room," presumably only those who hoisted the hateful resolution on this campus in the first place.

This technique is effective for those who make themselves victims on campus because it helps to insulate them from criticism and punishment for their often radical ideologies and behavior. As the signatories of the memo — members of the Muslim Student Association, Students for Justice in Palestine, MEChA, Student Affirmative Action Committee, and the Black Student Union, among them — had already made clear, the failure of the divestment resolution was the fault of others, not them, due to the racism and bigotry of pro-Israel faculty and students who obviously lack concern for social justice, Palestinians, and "students of color" like them. In his insightful book, *Illiberal Education: The Politics of Race and Sex on Campus*, Dinesh D'Souza noted that campus groups regularly "seek the moral capital of victimhood" as the UCSD students were doing. Why? Because, D'Souza said, "by converting victimhood into a certificate of virtue, minorities acquire a powerful moral claim that renders their opponents defensive and apologetic, and immunizes themselves from criticism and sanction."

Of course, proponents of boycotts, divestments, and sanctions against Israel are never apologetic about their efforts to hobble the Jewish state; in fact, they profess high moral purpose for their efforts to confront the racism, apartheid, and other vagaries of the Zionist regime. What they fail to admit, or what they clearly do not care about, of course, is that divestment resolutions like this one, which if successful would strip Israel of its ability to defend itself, are clearly not efforts that will bring peace at all, only help insure that Israel's jihadist foes can attack it more successfully and that its destruction can thereby be facilitated.

There is, of course, no mention in the divestment resolution of Palestinian terrorism and the random slaughter of Jewish civilians by Arabs on buses and at cafes, or the 12,000 rockets and mortars fired from Gaza into southern Israeli towns over the past decade or more (and that continues even today). No acknowledgement was forthcoming as to the reasons why "the use of force against the civilian Palestinian population" exists in the first place; specifically, that Israel's so-called "brutal occupation" and its military incursions were necessitated by Arab aggression and terrorism, and the use of force had not been a random occurrence based on the whims of a sadistic Israeli military.

In fact, by targeting firms which supply arms to Israel, the UCSD divestment effort was not more morally sound than other divestment calls that have included non-military firms, as well; the participants were actually helping to achieve what Israel's Arab foes have long-wanted — a militarily-weak Israel whose defenseless citizens could be massacred and the Jewish state weakened so it can be replaced by a new, Islamist state. More disingenuously, the UCSD divestment proponents fell into the morally convenient trap which ascribed the root cause of terrorism not where it belongs — with the homicidal madmen who perpetrate it in the name of jihad — but once again to Israel, due to its very presence in the Levant as an oppressor of the ever-suffering, always innocent Palestinians.

If the tendentious student and faculty activists at UCSD who purport to seek peace in the Middle East actually wanted to take steps to effect that noble goal, instead of seeking to deprive a sovereign nation from its ability to defend itself, they might consider some alternate tactics. Perhaps, for example, rather than obsessing about the defects of Israel and *only* Israel, they could focus on the pathologies of Palestinian society, crystallized and made more malevolent by the rule of Hamas itself.

They might speak to Palestinian parents, who glorify death and martyrdom and seek the death of their children if they distinguish themselves by murdering Jewish civilians. Perhaps they could also advise Palestinian leadership not to incite violence against Jews, and name summer camps and town squares after homicidal "martyrs" who slaughtered Jewish civilians. They could suggest that Hamas not broadcast children's TV shows with animal characters who repeat hateful propaganda about Israel and who encourage children to attack and kill Jews, and encourage them to recognize that it is morally perverse to produce Palestinian elementary textbooks that depict Jews as apes and pigs, that erase Israel from history and geography, and that demonize Israelis in particular and Jews in general as subhuman monsters who are subhuman thieves, and murderers.

"If you cannot answer a man's argument," Oscar Wilde once quipped, "do not panic. You can always call him names."

That advice has clearly been followed by the UCSD divestment proponents who, once they were defeated in their attempt to promote their odious divestment campaign, took to accusing their opponents of being racist victimizers of underrepresented students of color, as if that argument had anything to do with the core sentiment of the divestment initiative in the first place. The tactic of trying to demonize the thought of your ideological opponents and accusing them of having immoral motives for supporting their own views is obviously antithetical to the free and open debate that universities have traditionally sought.

Concern for the Palestinians may be a commendable effort, but the exclusion and demonization of support for the viability and continued existence of the Jewish state as a tool for seeking social justice for that one group interferes with and serves to eliminate actual debate and scholarly inquiry, something universities should never stop diligently defending. And neither UCSD nor any other university should certainly ever abandon that pursuit due to the baleful whining of ideological bullies intent on suppressing the views of others while simultaneously cloaking their enmity and loathing of Israel with their own victimhood.

35

Who May Say What About Whom on American Campuses?

oes it matter if a tenured professor expresses personal opinions, no matter how odious and controversial, but that may be acceptable under the umbrella of academic free speech? With great regularity, fraudulent scholarship has been substituted for reasoned inquiry on our campuses, and, as Michael Rubin, resident scholar at the American Enterprise Institute, observed, "academic freedom is meant to protect scholarship, not replace it." Nor, as he pointed out, does "free speech ... absolve anyone from professional incompetence."

This is the heart of the matter concerning Professor Kaukab Siddique, a Pakistani-born, tenured associate professor of English and journalism at Lincoln University in Pennsylvania, who seemingly puts great faith in conspiratorial dramas in which a crafty and all-powerful enemy — in this case, Jews — promotes, among other offenses, an oft-repeated claim that six million of their people were exterminated just to elicit the world's sympathy and promote Zionism and the creation of Israel.

Siddique, no stranger to controversy based on his incoherent and wild libels, was at it again, this time against not only Jews, but women, gays, and others. In May 2015 he posted items on his Facebook page decrying "dirty Jewish Zionist white supremacist thugs," the "homo lobby," "American women" being "slaves of rich men," and "many women" being "sluts."

While Siddique's odd posts included the notion that "no American Muslim is a terrorist," he lauded the terrorist group Hamas in a post that commented that "today Hamas fought very well against the zionist [sic] monster. Israel admitted that 13 of its best troops were killed today. One military Jew was captured . . . Civilian casualties of palestinians [sic] were extremely heavy because the rabid dogs of the Jews were doing their worst."

If you scratch a Holocaust denier long enough, you may reveal an anti-Semite, but not always. You will, however, probably find someone like Siddique, who has been embroiled in an intellectual firestorm, largely of his own making, since his bursts of hatred toward Israel were exposed in a video taken during his appearance at a 2010 Labor Day rally in Washington, D.C., posted by The Investigative Project, and reported on at the time by the Christian Broadcasting Network.

In vitriol-laced language that unfortunately is not at all uncommon these days from the professoriate and many of their impressionable students, Siddique was filmed crying out to the crowd at the September 3rd event: "I say to the Muslims, 'Dear brothers and sisters, unite and rise up against this hydra-headed monster which calls itself Zionism.'"

More troublesome than this example of creeping anti-Zionism was Siddique's exhortation to his receptive audience that Zionism itself was an aggressive, dangerous ideology that must be extirpated: "Each one of us is [its] target and we must stand united to defeat, to destroy, to dismantle Israel," he said, "if possible by peaceful means."

Tenure comes with some clear responsibilities, not the least of which is to be an intellectual and moral partner with the academic community with which one has made a professional contract. Saying that it is acceptable for a professor to harbor delusional, primitive attitudes about the Holocaust and Jews as long as he only utters his calumnies off campus, and not as part of his teaching in the classroom, is disingenuous at best, and a craven way that university officials try to excuse the inexcusable in the behavior of some of their tenured ideologues.

A Lincoln administrator, for example, in addressing the recent vile posts by Siddique, asserted that "His latest activities, like his earlier writings, statements and activities, are an insult to women and other groups singled out." However, the school's spokesperson added, "Dr. Siddique's statements and assertions are his own, and they in no way represent the views of Lincoln University, its administration, faculty or students . . . Like all faculty members, he is entitled to express his personal views in conversation or in public forums, as long as he does not present such opinions as views of the University."

Siddique's rabid anti-Israelism, of course, frequently animates the thinking of broad swathes of the West's professoriate, who, obsessed with Third-world victimism and a virtual cult of Palestinianism, think nothing of calling for the destruction — by boycott, divestment, delegitimization, as well as armed resistance — of Israel, a sovereign nation, an American ally, and the single democracy in the Middle East.

But Siddique, it was revealed several years ago, has another intellectual defect that calls into question not only his academic credibility, but his very qualifications to hold tenure at a university at all.

Linked to his attitudes about Zionism, Israel, and Jews, Siddique also plays a leadership role in Jamaat al-Muslimeen (JAM), a "radical separatist Islamist" group, according to a briefing paper prepared by the American Islamic Forum for Democracy, which focuses its limited intellectual resources on disseminating anti-Jewish conspiracy theories and engaging in Holocaust denial. At a meeting of this group, for instance, Siddique touched on the same theme of his that was revealed in the D.C. rally: the treachery of Jews and the boundlessness of their power. "We're under the grip of a Jewish Zionist power structure in this country," he told the audience, and further suggested that one reason Jews were able to obscure the sins of Israel and exploit the Holocaust for material and emotional gain was due to the existence of the dreaded "Zionist-controlled media."

In a now widely-circulated email thread on the crackpot conspiracy-theory web site Rense.com, for example, Siddique revealed that his perverse perspective creates conspiracies as a way of explaining the unfolding of historical events.

Thus, in his incoherent postings on the site, he suggested that the Nazis were not actually that harmful to European Jewry, a point he attempted to prove by cruelly suggesting that "The German behavior was so good that Elie Wiesel (the arch holocaust propagandist) left Auschwitz WITH the retreating Germans when the Russians advanced towards the camp."

Siddique concluded that the "Holocaust is a hoax," so those who still dwell on it should "Get over it!" as there "is not even ONE document proving the holocaust [sic]" — an assertion that might come as a surprise to the archivists at the U.S. Holocaust Museum and Memorial, as just one example, which has in its archives some 51 million pages of documents and 121 million images cataloguing the exact Nazi atrocities Siddique denies ever occurred.

If the victim status of Israel — and by extension, all Jews — can be diminished by exposing the lie of the Holocaust, which is what deniers dedicate themselves to achieving, Palestinians become the more aggrieved victim, a people victimized by former Jewish victims who deserve to be victimized and who now spread the lie of their own suffering for material ends.

More seriously, Siddique's chronic Holocaust denial, his calls for the destruction of Israel, and his demonization of Zionism, Israel, and world Jewry should be of enormous concern to Lincoln University officials. Far from being "a concerted act by the extreme right wing aligned with Israel to destroy someone who spoke out against them," as Siddique himself characterized the reaction to his opinions, his ideas have to be understood as blatantly anti-Semitic, and expressive of raw Jew-hatred, regardless of his own attempt to excuse it as mere criticism of Israel.

Putting aside the fact that Lincoln's own code of conduct forbids "any conduct or behavior that is disrespectful, absurd and rude," and despite the fact that the university has now distanced itself from comments and beliefs Siddique expressed publicly but outside of the campus walls, there should be universal denunciation of the professor's whole belief system, riddled as it seems to be with pathological and visceral hatred toward Israel and Jews.

This case also exposes a startling double standard that is currently prevalent in academia when it comes to who may say what about whom. Either because they are feckless or want to coddle perceived protected student minority groups in the name of diversity, university administrations are morally inconsistent when taking a stand against what they consider "hate speech," believing, mistakenly, that only harsh expression against victim groups needs to be moderated. When other groups — whites, Christians, Republicans, heterosexual males, Jews, for example — are the object of offensive speech, apparently no protection is deemed necessary.

More relevant is Lincoln's own reaction, or lack thereof, to Siddique's anti-Zionist invective at the rally, and the subsequent revelations about his Holocaust-denying hobby. Were it not for the waves of criticism coming from Pennsylvania officials, Jewish groups, and others, Siddique's behavior would have continued without comment, and it is likely that no introspection from the university community would have occurred at all.

Imagine for a moment that it was discovered that a tenured professor at Lincoln was "outed" as being a white supremacist, and his postings were sprinkled on the pages of a hate site such as Stormfront.org, in which he railed, as visitors to that site regularly do, against the threat of non-whites to a refined white culture, the harm that non-whites do to society through criminality, high birthrates, and questionable morality, and the overall superiority of the white race to other, "lower" forms of human existence. Would any member of the Lincoln community, a historically black university, care whether or not that professor brought those attitudes into his classroom or merely expressed them off campus?

Would they say that even if he had a right to express this type of attitude safely under the umbrella of academic free speech, he could do so without suffering universal opprobrium for his views? Could any sentient observer contend that a tenured professor who delved into the netherworld of neo-Nazism and white supremacism could somehow return to the cocoon of a campus and separate his other life from the person he is when he stands in front of students, helping young minds thoughtfully to explore human thought and achievement?

The answer obviously should be, no; that anyone who expressed such feelings in the academic community would be immediately and thoroughly shunned; that his or her actions and speech would be labeled for what they clearly were — repugnant hate speech that has no place on a campus.

When an offense is made to members of one of academia's favored victim-groups, the response is immediate, widespread, and thunderous in its self-righteousness. Consider, for example, what happened in March of 2015 when members of the University of Oklahoma's Sigma Alpha Epsilon fraternity were videotaped singing a racist chant in which the word "nigger" was repeatedly included in the refrain, as well as sentiments to the effect that there would never be an African American member of that fraternity. The University went into paroxysms of self-righteous denunciation of the behavior and speech in the secretly taped episode once it went viral on social media, and the university's president immediately suspended the fraternity chapter from campus and expelled, without due process and ignoring any First Amendments rights that protected even the odious speech of the frat brothers, two of the offending students.

While it is apparently a matter of academic free speech when a professor denigrates and libels Jews and Israel and denies the Holocaust off campus, at Oklahoma no such consideration was given, since the issue was racism and the supposed victims were black. "I have emphasized that there is zero tolerance for this kind of threatening racist behavior at the University of Oklahoma," OU's president, David Boren, wrote in a strongly-worded press release that forcefully condemned what he, and others, recognized was hateful speech, a moral stand seemingly absent in the Lincoln University incident since the victims were only Jews. "I hope that the entire nation will join us in having zero tolerance of such racism when it raises its ugly head in other situations across our country . . . I hope that students involved in this incident will learn from this experience and realize that it is wrong to use words to hurt, threaten and exclude other people . . . ."

Even more relevant to the discussion of Professor Siddique and his school's response to it is the ongoing case of Connecticut College professor Andrew Pessin, who has found himself vilified on campus, not only by a cadre of ethnic hustlers and activists, but by fellow faculty and an administration that has been slow to defend Pessin's right to express himself — even when, as in this case, his ideas were certainly within the realm of reasonable conversation about a difficult topic: the conflict between Israel and Hamas.

In August of 2014, during Israel's incursions into Gaza to suppress deadly rocket fire aimed at Jewish citizens, Pessin, a teacher of religion and philosophy, wrote on his Facebook page a description of how he perceived Hamas, the ruling political entity in Gaza: "One image which essentializes the current situation in Gaza might be this. You've got a rabid pit bull chained in a cage, regularly making mass efforts to escape."

That image of a pit bull did not sit well with at least one Connecticut College student, Lamiya Khandaker, who, not coincidentally, had founded a chapter of Students for Justice in Palestine, the virulently anti-Israel, sometimes anti-Semitic student activist group operating on more than 115 campuses across America.

Khandaker complained publicly about Pessin's old Facebook post, asserting that it was dehumanizing and racist, and claiming that Pessin was characterizing all Palestinians, not just Hamas, as pit bulls. Though it was clear from his previous posts and the context of the post in question that Pessin was referencing only Hamas, a U.S. State Department-designated terrorist organization, as a rabid dog, he deleted the offending Facebook entry, and even proffered an apology, writing that "I am truly sorry for the hurt and offense that I have caused," and offering his "deepest apology for causing such wounds."

Pessin's apology was insufficient for the ever-suffering moral narcissists on his campus. Editors of Connecticut College's student newspaper, *College Voice*, insisted that Pessin's thoughts were "dehumanizing" to Palestinians and had "caused widespread alarm in the campus community." The paper's editor, Ayla Zuraw-Friedland, initiated a campaign of lies against Dr. Pessin, contending that his post "caused widespread alarm in the campus community," that the college community could and should "identify racism when we see it," and that the very students viciously attacking Pessin for his thoughts were themselves "victims of racism."

The College's History Department joined the fray in vilifying Pessin and expressing their self-righteousness, announcing that "we condemn speech filled with bigotry and hate particularly when that speech uses dehumanizing language and incites or celebrates violence and brutality," an odd accusation to make against an individual who had critiqued the behavior of a terrorist group. More than that, Pessin, according to the enlightened history faculty, was complicit in a wide range of oppression, subjugation, and racism, pointing to "the particularly salient tactic of dehumanizing language as a means to justify brutality and lull otherwise 'well intentioned' people into silence and, effectively, complicity in racism, sexism, discrimination, colonialism and the numerous genocides throughout human history." The fact that the Hamas Charter is itself essentially a call to genocide — specifically of Jews — apparently was lost on these historians.

Even Connecticut College's President, Katherine Bergeron, publicly castigated Pessin. While she observed, appropriately, that "All our rights are better protected when free speech is the order of the day," and "This means that, just as everyone has a right to speak, everyone has the right to speak against, to confront speech that they consider destructive or inappropriate," she did not hesitate to evaluate — and condemn — the content of Pessin's original benign Facebook post. "I was taken aback as much by its central image as by its vehemence . . ," she said. "It was not in keeping with the level of discourse I have come to expect from the Connecticut College community and, in particular, from its faculty."

How administrators, faculty, and students at Lincoln University reacted (or, more to the point, did not react) when Professor Siddique was exposed for the bigoted, Holocaust-denying anti-Semite that he clearly is, compared to the reaction at other schools to perceived, or real, racism against identified victim groups, is instructive in taking the ideological pulse of academia today. The university officials and student groups who now try to expel all thought that "they hate;" who proclaim their desire for campuses where there will be vigorous discourse, on contentious issues, from many points of view, but end up allowing the expression of only acceptable opinions; who label speech with which they do not agree as hateful, and demonize or shun the speakers who utter those alternate views; who vilify Israel, Jews, Zionism, and U.S. support for the Jewish state with every sort of invective, but claim that criticism of Israel is suppressed by a cabal-like "Israel lobby;" and who shout down, heckle, and bully their ideological opponents during on-campus events — all of these individuals have sacrificed one of the core values for which the university exists.

In their zeal to be inclusive, and to recognize the needs and aspirations of perceived victim groups, they have pretended to foster inquiry — a core purpose of the university — but they have stifled and retarded it. And, as this otherwise noble purpose for the university has devolved, the first victim in the corruption of academic free speech has, unfortunately, been the truth.

36

Academic Progressivism Descends into Moral Madness

In the campus war against Israel, the all too familiar refrain from anti-Israel activists, many of whom form the loose coalition of groups and individuals spearheading the Boycott, Divestment, and Sanctions (BDS) campaign, is that their quarrel is only with Israelis and their government's policies, not with Jews themselves. But that specious defense has fallen away of late, revealing some caustic and base anti-Semitism, representing a seismic shift in the way that Jews now are being indicted not just for supporting Israel, but merely for being Jewish.

It was not without some historical irony, then, when student council leaders at Durban University of Technology (DUT) in South Africa in early February, 2015 floated a proposal that suggested, apparently without shame, that Jewish students should be expelled from the institution, that, as the student body's secretary, Mqondisi Duma, put it, "We took the decision that Jewish students, especially those who do not support the Palestinian struggle, should deregister." This is, one would think, a rather shocking sentiment from students who themselves benefited from a worldwide campaign in the 1970s and 1980s to end South Africa's racist apartheid system.

Also in February at UCLA, several council members on the USAC Judicial Board, UCLA student government's highest judicial body, grilled Rachel Beyda, a second-year economics student, when she sought a seat on the board. The focus on her candidacy was not her qualifications for the position (which no one seemed to doubt), but the fact that she was Jewish and how her "affiliation with Jewish organizations at UCLA . . . might affect her ability to rule fairly on cases in which the Jewish community has a vested interest in the outcome, such as cases related to the Israeli-Palestinian conflict," as the student newspaper described it. "Ruling fairly" in this case, of course, meant that she was likely *not* to support the increasingly virulent anti-Israel campaign on the UCLA campus, so she failed to pass the political litmus test that so-called progressive students see as their default position: namely, being pro-Palestinian. It was the same thinking that inspired a similarly discriminatory proposal last May by two members of UCLA's chapter of Students for Justice in Palestine which attempted to bar Jewish candidates for filling council positions if they had taken trips to Israel subsidized by the Anti-Defamation League, American Jewish Committee, or other organizations, which, according to the brazen SJP students, "have openly campaigned against divestment from corporations that profit from Israeli violations of Palestinian human rights."

Of course, there was no mention in this debate of trips paid for to send students to Israel or the territories on propaganda excursions designed to malign Israel and teach visitors an alternate, anti-Israel narrative. Once again, in addition to trying to stack the deck against the pro-Israel argument, this grotesque and inequitable proposal took as a given that anyone not committed to the anti-Israel Palestinian cause was by default not to be trusted, morally compromised, and unworthy of even having pro-Israel opinions.

Self-identified progressive students on campus are also enthralled by pursing "social justice" on the part of the Palestinians precisely because Third-world victimism parallels the identity politics of the same student groups who fuel the promiscuous BDS resolutions being proposed on campuses around the country. Thus, African-American student groups frequently rally in support of divestment when they are attracted to the narrative in which Israel is positioned as a racist, apartheid regime that suppresses an indigenous colored people and deprives them of human rights. And it is similarly manifested in such Orwellian-named groups as the anti-Israel "Queers for Palestine," whose very name is so ironic — given the treatment that homosexuals receive in the Middle East anywhere except Israel — that it is difficult to believe the group's own members can keep a straight face while parading with signs in support of the Palestinian cause.

In January, a student group at DePaul University, Feminist Front, produced a short video in which they proclaimed their support for a petition being circulated by DePaul Divests that asked the university to "uphold its Vincentian values by divesting from [companies that profit from] the Israeli occupation of Palestine." Members of the Feminist Front, who, if they were living in Hamas-controlled Gaza would be subjugated into silence and persecuted for their alternative sexual orientation, have also decided that divestment is "a feminist issue" and "a queer issue." Why? Because, they contend, "Israeli forces target queer folks with blackmail . . ," and because Israeli "methods of occupation historically target women, through violence, kidnapping, and rape."

These assertions are not only grotesque, counter-factual libels, but a precise inversion of the truth. In fact, Israel is so gay-friendly that its detractors have had to undertake mental contortions in order to put a negative spin on what normally would be seen as a cultural virtue: tolerating alternative sexual lifestyles. Instead, Israel's academic defamers, such as Sarah Schulman, Distinguished Professor of the Humanities at College of Staten Island, who normally would applaud a tolerant state, accuse Israel of what Schulman termed "pinkwashing," as she put it in a notorious 2011 *New York Times* op-ed, "a deliberate strategy to conceal the continuing violations of Palestinians' human rights behind an image of modernity signified by Israeli gay life." Nor is the Feminist Front's assertion that the Israeli occupation is linked to targeting women through rape accurate, either. In fact, the complete opposite is true: among militaries of the world the IDF is noteworthy for the extremely low incidence in its ranks of rape of Arab women.

That finding was brought to light, oddly enough, in a master's thesis written by a Hebrew University graduate student who actually wished to use these findings to indict the Israeli military, not applaud it. The student, Tal Nitzan, who received a prize from the University's Shaine Center for the "scholarly" study she wrote, and which the Center eventually published, came to the breathtaking and intellectually perverse conclusion that Israeli soldiers were racist because of the fact that they did *not* rape Arab women. The "lack of IDF rapes of Palestinian women is designed to serve a political purpose," Nitzan wrote. "In the Israeli-Palestinian conflict, it can be seen that the lack of military rape merely strengthens the ethnic boundaries and clarifies the inter-ethnic differences — just as organized military rape would have done."

Progressive students have decided, in their own moral self-righteousness, that the Palestinians and their campaign for self-determination is such a sacred cause that anyone who questions it or speaks for the Israeli point of view is a moral retrograde. To even support Israel's narrative is to risk being deemed a racist, an imperialist, a tacit supporter of apartheid. And more than that: now, if you are Jewish and even a student in South Africa — nowhere near or involved in the affairs of Palestinian Arabs and Israelis — if you have not publicly proclaimed your allegiance to the Palestinian cause and denounced the Israeli one, you can be deemed morally unworthy of attending a particular university.

The moral arrogance of the South African student's proposal is breathtaking, not only because of its grotesque version of the anti-Semitic practice of making any and all Jews responsible for the political actions of Israel; more serious than that, it reveals that the pro-Palestinian movement is so enthralled with the righteousness of its cause that anyone who harbors or expresses other views is considered a pariah, unworthy to even express his or her ideas in the marketplace of ideas.

Supporters of boycotts contend that they have answered the call of solidarity from "Palestinian civil society," a call issued in July of 2005 to wage a cognitive war against Israel "until Israel meets its obligation to recognize the Palestinian people's inalienable right to self-determination and fully complies with the precepts of international law."

Students and faculty who support BDS campaigns regularly admit, with pride, that they have responded to this call merely because they were asked, as if it is perfectly normal to respond affirmatively to support a cause which has a blighted history of terror, corruption, social fragmentation, and internecine conflict.

Any movement can make a world-wide call for support, but that obviously does not mean that individuals, or groups, have to heed that call without examining the motives and aspirations of the cause. None of these self-righteous moral narcissists who give unqualified support to the Palestinian cause on campus would answer similar calls from the Aryan Brotherhood, Minuteman Project, Ku Klux Klan, or Westboro Baptist Church for support of their various nefarious causes, and would, and do, breathlessly and indignantly denounce these groups for what they are — organizations animated with homophobia, xenophobia, racism, and violence against targeted, maligned groups. But when the cause is Palestinianism, and the enemy is Israel, no moral compass or rational thought seem to apply.

There is no other explanation for why educated, well-intentioned and humane individuals, experiencing paroxysms of moral self-righteousness in which they are compelled to speak out for the perennial victim, can loudly and publicly advocate for a movement that promotes and condones the murder of Jews — who already have created and live in a viable sovereign state — on behalf a group of genocidal enemies of Israel whose tragic condition may well be their own doing, and, at any rate, is the not the sole fault of Israel's. That these campus activists are willing, and ready, to sacrifice the Jewish state, and Jewish lives, in the name of social justice and a specious campaign of self-determination by Palestinian Arabs, shows how morally corrupt and deadly the conversation about human rights has become.

Notes

CHAPTER 1

1. The European Forum on Antisemitism, "Working Definition of Antisemitism," 2008, http://www.european-forum-on-antisemitism.org/working-definitionof-antisemitism/english/?fontsize=0.
2. Ibid.
3. Jamie Glasov, *United in Hate: The Left's Romance with Tyranny and Terror* (Los Angeles: WND Books, 2009).
4. Juan Cole, "Have Arabs or Muslims Always Hated Jews?" *Informed Comment*, December 14, 2004, http://www.juancole.com/2004/12/have-arabs-ormuslims-always-hated.html.
5. Joseph Massad, "Israel's Right To Defend Itself," *The Electronic Intifada*, January 20, 2009, http://electronicintifada.net/v2/article10221.shtml.
6. Ruth Wisse, *If I Am Not for Myself: The Liberal Betrayal of the Jews* (New York: The Free Press, 1992).
7. Julian Perez, "Divest Now from a Racist Government," *Yale Daily News*, November 15, 2002, http://www.yaledailynews.com/news/2002/nov/15/divest-now-from-a-racist-government.
8. Jennifer Lowenstein, "If Hamas Did Not Exist," *Counterpunch*, January 1, 2009, http://www.counterpunch.org/2009/01/01/if-hamas-did-not-exist.

9. Tony Judt, "Israel: The Alternative," *The New York Review of Books,* October 23, 2003.

10. Richard Falk, "Slouching Toward a Palestinian Holocaust," *Middle East,* June 29, 2007.

11. Edward W. Said, *Orientalism,* (New York: Vintage Books, 1979).

12. Martin Kramer, *Ivory Towers on Sand: The Failure of Middle Eastern Studies in America* (Washington, DC: The Washington Institute for Near East Policy, 2001).

13. M. Shahid Alam, "How to Be a Good Victim," *Counterpunch,* August 27-28, 2005, http://www.counterpunch.org/2005/08/27/how-to-be-a-good-victim.

14. Hamid Dabashi, "For a Fistful of Dust: A Passage to Palestine,"*Al-Ahram Weekly,* September 23-29, 2004, http://weekly.ahram.org.eg/2004/709/cu12.htm.

CHAPTER 9

1. Irwin Cotler, "Making the world 'Judenstaatrein,'" *Jerusalem Post,* February 22, 2009. http://www.jpost.com/servlet/Satellite?cid=1233304849224&pagename=JPArticle%2FShowFull

2. Gil Troy, "Center Field: Delegitimizing the delegitimizers," *The Jerusalem Post,* November 12, 2009.

3. Ariella Charny, "UC Berkeley and the Israel divestment bill," *Tufts Daily,* May 3, 2010. http://www.tuftsdaily.com/uc-berkeley-and-the-israel-divestment-bill-1.2257399)

4. Nobel Peace Prize, Discover The Networks, http://www.discoverthenetowkrs.org/groupProfile.asp?grpid=6979

5. Solidarity, New Jersey, and Rutgers University Campaign for Divestment from Israeli Apartheid, "Divestment from Israeli Apartheid: Acting for Human Rights, Taking a Stand for Justice," 2003.

6. Francis A. Boyle, "The Al-Aqsa Intifada and International Law." http://www.mediamonitors.net/francis4.html. November 30, 2000.

7. Ibid. (Emphasis added.)

8. Ibid.

9. Alana Goodman, "Academic Front for PLO," Academia.org, August 19, 2009. http://www.acadmia.org/academic-front-for-plo/(accessed November 20, 2009).

10. Fayyad Sbaihat, "Fighting the New Apartheid: A Guide to Campus Divestment From Israel," June 9, 2008, http://alawda.rso.wisc.edu/docs/divestguide.pdf.

11. Ibid.

12. Ruth Wisse, *If I Am Not For Myself: The Liberal Betrayal of the Jews*, (New York: The Free Press, 1992).

Index

A

Abbas, Mahmoud, 131
Abdulhadi, Rabab, 100
Abunimah, Ali, 195
Adventures of Huckleberry Finn, 49
Afghanistan, 191
Ahmadinejad, Mahmoud, 159
Al-Agha, Haifa, 101
Al-Ahram Weekly, 13, 20
Alam, M. Shahid, 12
Al Aqsa Brigades, 35
Al-Aqsa Intifada, 132
al-Asi, Muhammad, 177
Al-Awda, The Palestine Right to
    Return Coalition, 212
Al-Azhar University, 79
Aleppo University, 79
Alexander, Edward, 60, 91, 111
Al-Ghneimi, Zainab, 102
Al-Hayat Al-Jadida, 102, 131
All-Party Parliamentary Group
    Against Antisemitism, 180
Al-Najah University, 128, 129
Al-Saeh Library, 80
al Shabaab, 104
American Anthropological
    Association, 98
American Association of University
    Professors (AAUP), 83
American Enterprise Institute, 221
American Islamic Forum for
    Democracy, 223
American Jewish Committee, 231
American Muslims for Palestine, 149
American Studies Association (ASA),
    76, 77, 82–101, 106, 108, 113, 189
American Studies Association
    Council, 148
A Nation of Victims:
    The Decay of American Character, 217
ANSWER, 32
Anti-Defamation League (ADL),
    147, 231
Anti-Semitism on the Campus:
    Past and Present, 57
apartheid wall, 47, 70, 72, 84, 162
Arab and Muslim Ethnicities and
    Diasporas Initiative (AMED), 100
Arab Spring, 195
Arafat, Yasser, 73, 131
Areikat, Maen Rashid, 128
Arizona State University, 117
Article IV of the Third Geneva
    Convention, 160

A Rumor About The Jews, 197
Aryan Brotherhood, 234
Asian Studies Association, 98
Assad, Bashar, 119
ASUCD Senate, Senate Resolution
    21, 150
Auerbach, Jerold S., 59
Auschwitz, 29, 212
Avery, Evelyn, 61
Ayalon, Daniel, 174
Ayers, Bill, 51
Ayn Rand Society, 150

B
Badil Resource Center for Palestinian
    Refugee and Residency Rights, 213
Baker, Mona, 29
Barak, Ehud, 110
Barghouti, Omar, 77, 107
Bazian, Hatem, 161
Beinart, Peter, 39
Beinin, Joel, 39, 109
Ben-Dor, Oren, 136
Bengal, 139
Bergeron, Katherine, 228
Berkeley, UC, 39, 70, 80, 142,
    161–162
Bernstein, David, 47, 168
Beyda, Rachel, 231
Binghamton University, 41
Bir Zeit University, 129
Bisharat, George, 136
Black History Month, 141
Black Lives Matter, 46, 47, 51, 168,
    203, 204, 205, 207
Black Student Union, 141, 142, 218
blood libel, 6, 16, 145, 164
Boren, David, 227
Boston College, 194
Boston Globe, 171
Boston University, 24, 112, 186, 209
Boycott, Divestment, and Sanctions
    (BDS), 26, 39, 44, 46, 47, 52, 55,
    67, 68, 69, 71, 73, 74, 75, 78, 87,
        92, 101, 117, 119, 147, 154, 165,
        168, 230, 232, 234
Boyle, Francis A., 26, 72
Brandeis Center for Human Rights
    Under the Law, 40, 61
Brandeis, Louis D., 169
Brandeis University, 169
Breaking the Silence, 41
British Medical Journal, 20
Bronner, Stephen Eric, 197
Burnham, James, 89
Butler, Judith, 80
Buttu, Diana, 171, 194

C
Cairo University, 79
California Aggie, The, 148
California State Fresno, 83
Chalmers, Iain, 20
Charlie Hebdo, 197
Chesler, Phyllis, 18
Cheyfitz, Eric, 85, 95
Chomsky, Noam, 22, 110, 111, 170
Christian Broadcasting
    Network, 222
Christian Science Monitor, 112
Churchill, Ward, 85, 178
Churchill, Winston, 23, 38
City University of New York, 39
Clinton, Hillary, 132
Clover, Joshua, 148
CNN, 172
Code Pink, 32
Cole, Juan, 7, 111
College of Staten Island, 232
College Voice, 228
Columbia University, 8, 11, 13, 28,
    29, 54, 105, 108, 118, 176, 211
Compton Cookout, 141
Connecticut College, 227, 228
Cornell University, 85
Corrie, Rachel, 100
Cotler, Irwin, 25, 31, 67
Counterpunch, 12, 28, 211

D

Dabashi, Hamid, 13, 29
Daily Free Press, 186
Darfur, 119
Deek, George, 53
De Genova, Nicholas, 105
Deir Yassin, 29
Department of Defense, 108, 109, 110, 112
Department of Middle Eastern and Asian Languages and Culture (MEALAC), 28
DePaul University, 27, 232
Dershowitz, Alan, 110
Der Stürmer, 195
Drake, Michael, 175
D'Souza, Dinesh, 218
Duma, Mqondisi, 230
Durban University of Technology (DUT), 230
Durham College, 44

E

Edley, Christopher, 143
Eid, Bassam, 53
Electronic Intifada, 195, 211, 212
Engage, 94
Erakat, Noura, 212
Erdoğan, Tayyip, 24
EUMC, 5, 8
European Union Agency for Fundamental Rights, 94, 148, 180
European Union Monitoring Centre on Racism and Xenophobia, 5
Exeter University, 136

F

Falk, Richard, 10, 26, 95, 136
Farrakhan, Louis, 200
Fatah, 35, 129, 131
Feminist Front, 232
Feminists for Justice in Palestine, 99
Ferguson, Roger W., 117
Final Report of the Regents Working

Group on Principles Against Intolerance, 153
Finkelstein, Norman, 27, 178
Fish, Rachel, 61
Fletcher School of Law and Diplomacy, 194
Foundation for Individual Rights in Education (FIRE), 143
Frattini, Franco, 127

G

Gaskill, Jay B., 46
Gaza, 4, 8, 9, 16, 17, 19, 20, 21, 27, 28, 29, 30, 32, 34, 39, 54, 69, 70, 75, 76, 79, 80, 81, 84, 86, 87, 94, 96, 98, 99, 101, 107, 112, 120, 121, 123, 128, 132, 137, 158, 165, 167, 171, 172, 177, 191, 194, 198, 199, 205, 206, 212, 219, 227, 232
General Assembly Resolution 3379, 69
General Electric, 215
Georgetown University, 176
Ginsberg, Benjamin, 58
Glasov, Jamie, 6
Goldberg, Jonah, 44
Goldberg, Whoopi, 89
Goldstone Report on the Gaza War, 9, 174
Goldstone, Richard, 9

H

Habash, George, 131
Haifa University, 136
Haiti, 166
Halbertal, Moshe, 54, 123
Hamas, 6, 17, 27, 32, 33, 34, 35, 39, 53, 54, 79, 80, 83, 84, 87, 99, 100, 112, 120, 121, 128, 129, 132, 133, 144, 150, 158, 171, 176, 177, 194, 206, 212, 219, 220, 222, 227, 228
Harvard Center for Middle East Studies (CMES), 112
Harvard Crimson, 188

Harvard University, 36, 43, 57, 60, 74, 93, 110, 112, 141, 157, 182, 188, 189, 192, 193, 194
Hasbara Fellowships Canada, 44
Hastings College of the Law, 136
Hebrew University, 54, 123, 233
Hezbollah, 6, 35, 39, 80, 120, 144, 176, 177
Hillel, 38–43, 186
Hirsh, David, 94, 149
Hizbul Islam, 104
Hofstadter, Richard, 197
Holmes, Oliver Wendell, 146, 152
Holocaust, 3, 15, 20, 24, 26, 27, 28, 29, 32, 57, 60, 70, 72, 136, 144, 145, 159, 177, 181, 193, 201, 222, 223, 224, 225, 226, 229
House Resolution 35 (HR 35), 179

I

IDF, 33, 54, 100, 123, 132, 159, 166
If I Am Not For Myself
    The Liberal Betrayal of the Jews, 8, 43, 74
Illiberal Education:
    The Politics of Race and Sex on Campus, 218
Informed Comment, 7, 111
Institute for Israeli Studies, 54, 123
International Court of Justice, 69
International Day of Action on University Campuses for Palestine, 185
International Solidarity Movement (ISM), 99
intersectionality, 47, 165, 167
Islamophobia, 42, 51, 52, 55, 150, 151, 184
Israel Defense Forces, 118, 120
Israeli Apartheid Week, 41, 54, 183, 205
Israeli Occupation Awareness Week, 170, 172
Israel's Dead Soul, 30

Ivory Towers in the Sand:
    The Failure of Middle Eastern Studies in America, 12

J

Jamaat al-Muslimeen (JAM), 223
Jankélévitch, Vladimir, 24
Jerusalem Post, 69
Jewish Council for Public Affairs, 47, 168
Jewish Voice for Peace, 32, 41, 155, 158, 169, 171
Johns Hopkins University, 58
Joseph Massad, 211
Judt, Tony, 10

K

Karega, Joy, 197–202
Katehi, Linda, 149
Kates, Charlotte, 213
Kennedy School of Government, 192–196
Kent State University, 30
Khaled, Leila, 100
Khandaker, Lamiya, 227
Kimball, Roger, 76
Koala, 141–43
Korn, Sandra Y.L., 188
Kramer, Martin, 12
Ku Klux Klan, 234

L

Lancet, 16, 18, 20, 21
Lancet-Palestinian Health Alliance (LPHA), 20
Landes, Richard, 24
League of Nations Palestine Mandate, 172
LeVine, Mark, 39
Levin, Richard, 128
Levitt, Matthew, 128
Lincoln University, 221, 229
Liu, David Palumbo, 89
Livingstone Formulation, 94, 149
Lloyd, David, 78, 109

Lowell, A. Lawrence, 57
Lowenstein, Jennifer, 10, 29

M
Maira, Sunaina, 148
Malik-Ali, Amir-Abdel, 144, 176
M. Ali, Samer, 76
Manduca, Paola, 19
Marcuse, Herbert, 90, 204
Marcus, Itamar, 129
Marcus, Kenneth L., 61, 130
Marez, Curtis, 82, 100
Martin, Tony, 59
Massachusetts Institute of
    Technology, 110
Massad, Joseph, 8, 28, 212
McGill University, 69
Mearsheimer, John, 195
MEChA, 143, 218
Medical Aid for Palestinians, 20
Million Student March, 124
Mill, John Stuart, 126
Minnesota Anti-War Committee,
    54, 123
Minuteman Project, 234
MLA's Radical Caucus, 81
Modern Language Association
    (MLA), 71–81, 106
Moynihan, Daniel Patrick, 207
Mughrabi, Dalal, 131
Mullen, Bill, 87
multiculturalism, 36
Muslim Student Association, 40, 42,
    144, 155, 218
Muslim Student Union, 175

N
Nakba, 98, 99, 212
Nasrallah, Hassan, 120
National Association of Women's
    Studies, 47, 49
National Lawyers Guild, 213
National Women's Studies
    Association, 101
National Women's Studies

Association (NWSA), 98–104
Netanyahu, Benjamin, 30, 199
New Criterion, 76
New Jersey Solidarity
    Movement, 213
New Weapons Research Group, 19
New York City Students for Justice in
    Palestine, 48
New York University, 10, 117
Nitzan, Tal, 233
Northeastern University, 12, 158, 184
Northrop Grumman, 215
Norton, Augustus Richard, 112
Nusseibeh, Sari, 129

O
Oberlin College, 197, 201
Occupy Movement, 46
On Liberty, 126
Open Hillel, 38–43
Operation Cast Lead, 9, 20, 28,
    158, 211
Operation Pillar of Defense, 151
Operation Protective Edge, 18,
    24, 32, 167
Orange County Task Force on
    Anti-Semitism, 178
Oren, Michael, 174
Orientalism, 11, 13
Orwell, George, 204
Oxford University, 174

P
Pakistan, 139, 140, 191
Palestine Solidarity Committee, 54
Palestinian Authority, 53, 101
Palestinian Authority (PA) Minister
    of Women's Affairs, 101
Palestinian Campaign for the
    Academic and Cultural Boycott of
    Israel (PACBI), 77, 78, 106
Palestinian Human Rights
    Monitoring Group, 53
Palestinian Liberation
    Organization, 194

Palestinian Liberation Organization
(PLO), 73
Palestinian Media Watch, 129
Pappé, Ilan, 136, 193
Perez, Julian, 9
Pessin, Andrew, 227–229
Pew Research Center, 130
Phillips, Melanie, 50, 187
pinkwashing, 165, 232
Pino, Julio, 30
Plaut, Steven, 209
Polanski, Roman, 89
Pollack, Eunice G., 57
Popular Front for the Liberation of
Palestine, 100
_Power, Faith and Fantasy:
America in the Middle East:
1776 to the Present_, 176
Princeton University, 10, 26, 95,
136, 176
Principles Against Intolerance,
156–157
Professors for Justice in Palestine, 149
proportionality, 35
Protocols of the Elders of Zion, 199
Puar, Jasbir K., 164–167
Purdue University, 87

Q
Queers for Palestine, 232

R
Radosh, Ron, 96
Resolution 194, 210
Resolution to Divest from Companies
that Violate Palestinian Human
Rights, 189
right of return, 137, 139–140,
209–211, 214
Right of Return Conference, 209
Robinson, William I., 27
Rosenfeld, Alvin, 61
Rossman-Benjamin, Tammi, 61, 62
Rostow, Eugene V., 172
Rothchild, Alice, 171

Rouhana, Nadim N., 194
Roy, Sara, 112
Rubin, Michael, 221
Rutgers University, 71, 164, 213

S
Said, Edward W., 11, 77
Salah, Sheikh Raed, 100
Salaita, Steven, 30
Sanchez, Rick, 172
San Francisco State University, 100
Saudi Arabia, 88, 103
Scholars for Peace in the Middle
East, 22
Schueller, Malini Johar, 84
Schulman, Sarah, 232
Sderot, 80
Second Intifada, 33, 129, 159
Shaine Center, 233
Shalem Center, 176
Sharon, Ariel, 7, 110, 111
Sharoni, Simona, 99
Shlesinger, Miriam, 29
Siddique, Kaukab, 221–225,
227, 229
Sigma Alpha Epsilon, 226
Sitta, Salman Abu, 212
_Six Days of War:
June 1967 and the Making of the Mod-
ern Middle East_, 176
social justice, 3–4, 14, 32, 35, 37, 44–
51, 55, 62, 69, 74–75, 82, 86–87,
89, 117, 125, 134, 137–138, 153,
163, 168–169, 172, 180, 187–190,
192, 195, 203, 216–218, 220, 231,
235
Solway, David, 35
Somalia, 105
South Africa, 230
Spangler, Eve, 194
Stanford University, 39, 54, 89,
109–110, 123, 161, 162
Stascavage, Bryan, 203
State University of New York at
Plattsburgh, 99

Stephen Roth Institute for the Study of Contemporary Anti-Semitism and Racism, 127
Stormfront.org, 225
Students for Israel, 186
Students for Justice in Palestine, 32, 40–42, 46–47, 52–55, 90, 117, 123–124, 147–148, 150–151, 155, 158, 161–162, 169, 183–187, 189–190, 204–209, 215, 217–218, 227, 231
Sudan, 88, 104, 118–119
Suicide of the West:
  An Essay on the Meaning and Destiny of Liberalism, 89
Summerfield, Derek, 20
Summers, Lawrence, 93, 157
Sweeney, Tara, 143
Sykes, Charles, 217
Syria, 79, 103, 119, 138
Syrian Network for Human Rights, 103

T
Tel Aviv University, 77, 127
Temple University, 212
The Argus, 203–208
The Electronic Intifada, 28
The High-Level International Military Group on the Gaza Conflict, 167
The Investigative Project, 222
The Israel Lobby, 195
The Jewish Onslaught, 59
The New York Times, 9, 232
Theobald of Cambridge, 16, 164
Thernstrom, Abigail, 141
The Sbarro Cafe Exhibition, 129
The Secret Relationship between Blacks and Jews, 59
The Telegraph, 29
The Tower, 199
The Tyranny of Clichés:
  How Liberals Cheat in the War of Ideas, 44

The Washington Institute, 128
Thornton, Bruce, 83
Tibi, Bassam, 130
Toameh, Khaled Abu, 190
Toury, Gideon, 29
Troy, Gil, 69
Trump, Donald, 51
Tufts University, 194
Tutu, Desmond, 70

U
UC Regents, 153
U.N. Human Rights Commission, 26, 72
UN Human Rights Council, 67
United in Hate:
  The Left's Romance With Tyranny and Terror, 6
University of California, Davis, 53, 147–148, 151
University of California, Irvine, 39, 91, 144, 175
University of California, Los Angeles, 188–189, 231
University of California, Riverside, 109, 175
University of California, San Diego, 82, 101, 141–144, 215
University of California, Santa Barbara, 27
University of California, Santa Cruz, 61
University of California Students Association (UCSA), 179
University of Chicago, 51, 184
University of Florida, 84
University of Goettingen, 130
University of Haifa, 209
University of Illinois, 26, 30, 72
University of Manchester Institute of Science and Technology (UMIST), 29
University of Massachusetts, Boston, 117
University of Michigan, 7

University of Minnesota Law School, 54, 123
University of North Texas, 57
University of Oklahoma, 226
University of Ontario Institute of Technology (UOIT), 44
University of Southampton, 135
University of Texas at Austin, 54, 123
University of Washington, 91
University of Wisconsin, 10, 24, 29, 123, 128, 129
UN Security Council Resolution 242, 172
UN Security Council Resolution 1701.1, 120
U.S. Campaign for the Academic and Cultural Boycott of Israel, 148, 165
U.S. Department of State, 156
U.S. Holocaust Museum and Memorial, 224
U.S. State Department, 27, 76, 79, 94, 107, 120, 148, 227

V
Vardi, Gil-Li, 54
Vassar College, 164
Veblen, Thorsten, 45
Voz Fronteriza, 143–144

W
Walt, Stephen, 195
Watson, Joseph W., 144
Wellesley College, 59
Wesleyan University, 203
West Bank, 4, 22, 39, 70, 75–76, 79–81, 84, 87, 94, 96, 98, 101, 107, 131, 171–172, 206–207
Westboro Baptist Church, 234
Wiesel, Elie, 224
Wilde, Oscar, 220
Winston, Andrew S., 58
Wisse, Ruth, 8, 36, 43, 60, 74
Women's Legal Counseling Center, 102

Y
Yale Daily News, 9, 130
Yale Initiative for the Interdisciplinary Study of Antisemitism (YIISA), 127
Yale University, 9, 127–130, 134
Yassin, Sheikh Ahmed, 131
Yudof, Mark G., 154, 181

Z
Zuraw-Friedland, Ayla, 228

40605215R00144

Made in the USA
San Bernardino, CA
24 October 2016